To
Serve

A History of
Group Health Cooperative
of Puget Sound

the
Greatest
Number

To
Serve

A History of
Group Health Cooperative
of Puget Sound

the
Greatest
Number

Walt Crowley

Group Health Cooperative
of Puget Sound

in association with

University of Washington Press
Seattle & London

Dedication

*To the few hundred pioneering members and employees
who launched Group Health Cooperative of Puget
Sound on January 1, 1947, and the hundreds of
thousands who followed in their footsteps, this book is
dedicated on the occasion of the fiftieth anniversary of
the founding of Group Health Cooperative.*

Table of Contents

Preamble to the Bylaws of Group Health Cooperative of Puget Sound

The Cooperative shall endeavor:

a. To develop some of the most outstanding hospitals and medical centers to be found anywhere, with special attention devoted to preventive medicine.

b. To serve the greatest possible number of people under consumer cooperative principles without discrimination.

c. To promote individual health by making available comprehensive personal healthcare services to meet the needs and desires of the persons being served and to reduce cost as a barrier to healthcare.

d. To place matters of medical practice under direction of physicians on the staff employed by the Cooperative and to afford strong incentive for the best possible performance on their part.

e. To recognize other employees of the Cooperative for purposes of collective bargaining, and to provide incentive, adequate compensation and fair working conditions for them.

f. To educate the public as to the value of the cooperative method of health protection, and to promote other projects in the interest of public health.

Prologue

*F*rom a tiny band of founders in 1946, Group Health Cooperative has grown in size and stature to become the largest consumer-governed healthcare organization in the United States. In 1996, it serves more than 650,000 people in the Pacific Northwest, and is nationally recognized for its quality, cost effectiveness, and attention to its members' needs.

This book is the story of how it happened, and commemorates the Cooperative's first 50 years of delivering healthcare. It shows that "to serve the greatest number" means social responsibility and community service, as well as healthcare itself. It means speaking up to influence the public debate on healthcare reform. And it means being a national model for prevention, consumer oversight of quality, and effective medical practices within a system that integrates delivery of care and financing.

Through its balanced partnership of consumers, medical staff and management, the Co-op has made numerous contributions to healthcare. Some of them are: the refinement of the self-managed medical group practice; coordination of care among family doctors, specialists, and other care team members; prepayment for care; consumer governance; use of evidence-based medical practices; commitment to patient self-education; incorporation of scientifically proven, effective new technologies; and management of the continuum of care from home to medical center to hospital, to home again.

Group Health Cooperative was and continues to be a healthcare pioneer. Its record has an important place in the medical and social history of America.

History Committee
Group Health Cooperative

Preface

Democracy, Medicine, and Group Health

*T*he title of this book is drawn from the preamble to Group Health Cooperative's bylaws, which is reprinted ahead of the prologue. The declaration of purposes has changed little since it was first written in 1946, and it spells out Group Health's genetic code. This book essentially traces how these founding principles have been translated into practice — and mutated by social and economic realities — over the past 50 years.

As a result, the narrative that follows is in large part a political chronicle, or better, a political biography. This fact might strike the reader as odd since the book's subject is an organization devoted to medicine and health. In truth, healthcare has become a highly politicized field of social endeavor over the past century, and Group Health is itself a most political animal.

Group Health was established in the optimistic years immediately following World War II, before the grey overcast of the Cold War rolled in to smother dreams of major social reform. Group Health's founding members represented a sturdy coalition of farmers, workers, and political activists, many of whom had worked arm-in-arm since the Great Depression. They believed that consumer-owned cooperative enterprises could steer an economic "middle way" between the excesses of laissez-faire capitalism and Soviet-style state socialism.

As idealistic as their prescription of a democratic style of medicine was, these pioneers were also impatient. They wanted affordable hospitals and clinics now, not at some distant point in a utopian future. They were not content to wait for the medical profession or government to deliver them into the promised land, so they set out to build a prepaid healthcare system of their own.

It was an absurd ambition, and it would probably have failed but for a happy accident on March 14, 1946, when Cooperative attorney Jack Cluck met Dr. Sandy MacColl at a healthcare forum. A young pediatrician just back from the war, MacColl worked at Seattle's struggling Medical Security Clinic, one of the area's few prepaid group practices. He and his 15 colleagues held their own brief against conventional, fee-for-service medicine, which struck them as chiefly dedicated to enriching its practitioners at the expense of sick and desperate people. They were also ardent advocates of a new and controversial idea, preventive medicine, and concerned themselves as much with promoting wellness as with treating illness.

This meeting was the political-economic equivalent of love at first sight, but the in-laws took some convincing. The proposed marriage of Group Health and the Medical Security Clinic sparked a furious debate within the Cooperative, and Group Health's original trustees prevailed only narrowly at a special membership meeting in October 1946.

Group Health officially began delivering healthcare on January 1, 1947, when the Cooperative took formal control of Medical Security's downtown clinic and St. Luke's Hospital, a tiny, aging facility on Seattle's Capitol Hill. On that day, Group Health began serving about 400 consumer members and another 8,000 or so worker-enrollees inherited from Medical Security's previous industrial healthcare contracts.

The medical establishment did not pass out cigars to mark Group Health's birth, and we forget how radical Group Health's healthcare philosophies were at the time. Group practice was still a novelty distrusted by many physicians in the 1940s and 1950s, despite the international fame of the Mayo Clinic (and local example of the Virginia Mason Clinic). Preventive medicine was held in even lower repute by the medical profession, and even its advocates were uncertain what the term meant in real practice.

The prepayment of medical services was also rare 50 years ago, along with health insurance. Such plans inspired near-hysterical opposition from solo, fee-for-service physicians, and the American Medical Association and local medical societies denounced prepaid programs as stalking horses for socialized medicine. Group Health's left-wing roots and vocal advocacy of national healthcare reform made it all the more menacing in the eyes of traditionalists.

Private physicians slandered Group Health as "Group Death," and the King County Medical Society blacklisted the Cooperative's doctors as "unethical" simply because they charged patients uniform monthly dues for care. This campaign of harassment culminated in 1951 with a landmark Washington State Supreme Court ruling that found the Medical Society guilty of a monopolistic conspiracy against Group Health.

Beyond such external threats, Group Health was torn from the beginning by two fundamentally contradictory drives: an expansionist imperative to attract and serve ever more members, and an isolationist imperative to safeguard its cultural integrity by remaining small. This bipolar quality of competing impulses still sets the rhythm of Group Health's periodic identity crises.

But these forces are not in balance. While Group Health's founders honored cooperative values of mutual aid, shared sacrifice, common ownership, member equality, and democratic decision-making, they also recognized that the price of utopian purity was usually sterility. They had seen too many cooperatives wither and die because their leaders feared that growth would dilute their memberships or contaminate their internal cultures with antithetical business values.

In contrast, Group Health's 1946 bylaws dedicated it "to develop the most outstanding hospitals and medical centers" and "to serve the greatest possible number of people." This was the birth cry of a healthcare colossus-to-be, not some cozy little co-operative clinic dispensing aspirins and advice to a few hundred loyal members. Whenever members, trustees, physicians, and managers debated whether or not to add members or services, they always chose growth over stasis.

Similarly, Group Health was animated from its first days by an evangelistic zeal to promote broader social and medical reforms. While Group Health's costs and philosophy of healthcare have chiefly attracted a membership of skilled workers and middle-class professionals, its leaders have campaigned tirelessly for more far-reaching political and economic change to serve the poor. Group Health has proselytized every president from Harry Truman to Bill Clinton, and every Washington governor from Arthur Langley to Mike Lowry, in the cause of universal access to affordable healthcare — even at the risk of stimulating the creation of competing organizations.

Group Health has never retreated from proving itself in the marketplace, thanks to an unshakable democratic faith in the ability of consumers and medical professionals to organize, finance, and deliver high-quality healthcare at relatively low cost in the real world. Just because Group Health's leaders disdained profit as the exclusive measure of quality or effectiveness did not mean that they ignored the balance sheet. Group Health has been led from the beginning by creative and skillful fiscal managers who knew, in the words of one longtime trustee, that "Group Health must survive as a business in order to survive as a cooperative, not the other way around."

It should not, therefore, surprise the reader to learn that Group Health is not a true cooperative in which members legally own equal shares. Instead, it was incorporated in 1945 as a non-profit charitable association, constituted by a membership that elects trustees who, in turn, manage the business and contract with an autonomous medical staff for healthcare delivery.

Thus, Group Health's culture reflects a unique hybrid of economic realism and social idealism, and its internal structure is far from monolithic. Group Health began operation in 1947 as an alliance among four distinct and self-aware "estates": an active voting membership of consumers, an elected Board of Trustees, a self-governing staff of physicians and medical professionals, and a largely unionized corps of nurses and other support staff. Over time, a fifth estate emerged within Group Health in the form of a cadre of professional business administrators. Although not enfranchised in Group Health's constitution, hundreds of thousands of non-voting group enrollees have also played a crucial economic role in the Cooperative's affairs by choosing — or not choosing — to sign up for its services.

In this sense, Group Health might be likened to a "consumers' republic" with an electorate of members, a legislature of trustees, an executive of business administrators, and a civil service of physicians and other healthcare professionals. The fusion of these constituencies, their interests, and their cultures has not always been stable. Only an overarching sense of common purpose, and the fortuitous intervention of some remarkable personalities at critical moments, averted more than one civil war within Group Health.

These struggles and the evolving institution they shaped are the main focus of this book.

The record of Group Health's internal debates and dynamics has been largely preserved in detailed minutes of the Board of Trustees, annual membership meetings, and Group Health's myriad committees, subcommittees, and task forces. I am grateful to recorders such as longtime Board secretary Isabelle Stanley for writing such readable and candid accounts. An equal debt is owed Group Health's founding archivist, Alma Howard, and the current archives manager, Willie Foster, for organizing and preserving these records in such good and accessible order.

Group Health's official record is enriched by an array of publications devoted to member information and health education. Periodicals such as *View* magazine earned major awards for journalism and design, and featured the work of such talented editors and contributors as Paul Temple, Nick Gallo, Regina Hackett, Teri Nakamura, Kim Zumwalt, and Joan DeClaire, among others.

The task of personalizing Group Health's story was aided immeasurably by oral history interviews of founders and charter members conducted in the early 1980s by volunteers under the direction of Nan Fawthrop. Byron Fish, a popular *Seattle Times* columnist for many decades, also captured the memories of several key individuals in preparing an unpublished historical essay in the early 1970s.

This book relies heavily on the work of several scholars, beginning with John Phillip Holden, who analyzed Group Health's early history in a 1951 thesis on its institutional structure. Jonathan Rae Tompkins followed up 30 years later with a thesis focusing on the role of consumer participation in shaping Group Health's services and organization.

I am especially indebted to Nancy Rockafeller, Ph.D., a medical historian who was retained to research Group Health's development in 1992. She conducted scores of revealing interviews and completed a draft narrative of Group Health's history though 1955. Other professional demands prevented her from completing her work, which is how I came on the scene in June 1995.

While I necessarily carried out my own independent review of all primary Group Health records and accounts, these earlier investigators helped me to avoid blind alleys in tracing essential events and personalities. Without them, this project could not have been completed in the mere 14 months allotted, a schedule which still leaves me a little breathless.

The real credit for any success which this book may enjoy rests with Group Health's History Committee, comprising Aubrey Davis, Dr. Charles Strother, Dr. Howard Kirz, George Corcoran, Lyn Sauter, and Don Glickstein. Several of its members were themselves major participants in Group Health's development, and all made countless helpful suggestions to guide my research and sharpen my narrative.

At the same time, they made no effort whatsoever to censor my account, to cover up or gloss over pivotal conflicts or insititutional failings. The result is, I believe, an honest, if sympathetic, portrait that depicts Group Health's flaws along with its virtues, and I take full responsibility for any errors of omission or commission.

I am most grateful of all to project coordinator Linda Andrews and to her predecessor, Jeanne Semura, who headed me in the right direction. A skilled writer and editor, Linda's tireless, always cheerful approach to reviewing and polishing some very ragged early drafts kept me going through the rough spots. I also want to thank copy editor Charles Smyth, proofreader Kim McKaig, and production assistant Pam Heath for fine-tuning the text. Finally, deep appreciation goes to my wife Marie McCaffrey for the design of a beautiful book and dust jacket — and for putting up with my yearlong obsession with this story.

A writer always ends a project like this one with some regrets. I wish time had allowed me to conduct more interviews, and to construct fuller accounts of Group Health's innovations in medical practice and healthcare administration, which deserve a book of their own. I also wish space had permitted the acknowledgment of the hundreds, perhaps thousands, of Group Health members and employees not mentioned in this narrative who made their own special contributions to the Cooperative.

They are true pioneers who blazed the trail for a more humane, accessible, scientific, and efficient system of healthcare to serve the greatest possible number of people.

Walt Crowley
GHC Member #15330
August 1996

To
Serve

A History of
Group Health Cooperative
of Puget Sound

the
Greatest
Number

Chapter 1

Crusading Consumers

1844 ~ 1945

*A Doctor for the People ~ Roots of the
Cooperative Movement ~ Farmers, Workers and
Reformers Join Forces ~ Addison Shoudy and
Bob Mitchell Have an Idea ~ Founding Group
Health Cooperative*

*F*our dozen people gathered in the Gold Room of downtown Seattle's Roosevelt Hotel on August 14, 1945. They came to hear a talk by Dr. Michael Shadid, who had founded America's first cooperatively owned and managed hospital in Elk City, Oklahoma, some 16 years earlier.

Billed as "small in stature, dynamic in nature," Dr. Shadid had come to Seattle to expose "dark and unwholesome medical practices and to guide the common people of the United States into a safer and more economical system of medical care and hospitalization." His crusade was to overthrow the traditional practice of fee-for-service medicine dominated by solo general practitioners, expensive specialists, and private hospitals and clinics. He wanted to usher in a new system that would give patients affordable, prepaid healthcare through the cooperative ownership of hospitals staffed by physicians who practiced as a group and promoted something called "preventive medicine."

To the medical establishment, Shadid's message was heresy, even apostasy. But that day in Seattle, Shadid's evangelism fell on more receptive ears. His audience was made up of dedicated members of farmer granges, consumer cooperatives, and labor unions, and kindred political and social idealists who were fed up with the scant supply and high cost of healthcare for working people.

They had postponed their dreams of reform through four long, bitter years of war, and they were impatient to return to the work of building a better, more just society. The assembly eagerly embraced Shadid's message and approved follow-up meetings by a committee comprising two representatives each from local granges, unions, and cooperatives.

That evening, radio bulletins and two-inch-high headlines shouted the news: Emperor Hirohito had accepted the Allied terms of surrender. The Second World War was finally over. It was a new, atomic age, full of unimagined possibilities and unfinished business.[1]

Michael Shadid was born in 1882 in a village on the eastern slope of Mount Lebanon in what was then part of the enfeebled Ottoman Empire. He was the last of 12 children borne by his mother, and only 1 of 3 to survive beyond infancy. Impelled by the misery of his neighbors and the example of a missionary physician at Beirut's American University, Shadid resolved to become a doctor when he left Beirut at age 16 to join relatives in the United States.

The young Lebanese sold jewelry door-to-door to earn his tuition to Washington University's medical school in St. Louis, where he graduated in 1906. His first practice was making rounds on horseback in rural Missouri as an assistant to the local general practitioner. He married his childhood betrothed and relocated to Oklahoma two years later.

By then, Shadid had been thoroughly appalled by the burden of medical costs on farmers who barely eked a subsistence out of the dry soil. While taking specialty courses in Chicago, he joined Eugene Debs' Socialist Party. His comrades in Oklahoma, who had delivered as much as a third of the state's vote to leftist candidates in recent elections, advised him to set up practice in the little town of Carter, "where every other man is a Socialist." His new clinic indeed prospered and he relocated to the larger town of Elk City. There he earned enough to finance a visit to his homeland in 1929.

Shadid was horrified by the poverty and primitive medical

services that still prevailed in Lebanon, and he realized that the conditions for poor farmers and workers in Oklahoma were not much better. Upon his return, he decided to change things. Perhaps naively, Shadid tried to rally fellow physicians to his cause, explaining that "scientific medical care is a costly business and none but the well-to-do can avail themselves of its benefits." He also chided conventional medical practitioners for failing to make "a frontal assault on the prevention of disease," because it "busies itself with treating the 2 percent of the population who are sick and neglects the 98 percent who appear well."

Shadid saved his harshest words for the concept of fee-for-service, particularly when charged by overeager specialists. The appendix, he observed, is an "evolutionary hangover with no known physical function. There is nothing in the books, however, to indicate that nature left the appendix behind to be a perennial source of income for the operation-minded surgeon."

Shadid's prescription for curing such ills was a "community hospital" owned by a cooperative made up of its patients. Some of his colleagues laughed, and the rest sneered, but Shadid's poor, sod-buster patients already knew from experience that "cooperatism" worked well to establish cotton gins, to buy supplies for their farms, and to market their produce. Why couldn't it work to deliver healthcare?

Despite such popular support, it took Shadid two years to organize his prepaid, cooperative hospital plan, and only financing from Oklahoma's Farmers' Union made it possible. The virulent opposition of his medical colleagues convinced him that "private ownership of hospitals is wrong and detrimental to the best interests of mankind, physically, morally, and financially." The nation's first cooperative hospital opened in the spring of 1931, and the Farmers' Union took control of it in 1935 (Shadid remained its director and leading booster until shortly before his death in 1966).[2]

Shadid's achievement in Elk City was only the latest in a long line of cooperative enterprises. History is full of examples of self-help associations of varying sizes and degrees of organization. In America, such cooperation was vital to early settlers, and Ben Franklin was an ardent advocate of community enterprises such as volunteer fire brigades and lending libraries.

The notion of economic cooperation among allied producers and consumers is less an ideology than a tradition of practice. In the 19th century, the cooperative movement became a discrete, self-conscious body of thought, experiment, and application, thanks in large part to the eloquent advocacy of Robert Owen, a Welshman who had made millions, paradoxically, as a savvy capitalist. Unlike most industrial magnates of his time, Owen did not forget his own struggles growing up poor. He used much of his wealth to promote worker-owned and -managed "cooperative villages" and mills in England, as well as utopian communities in the United States.

Modern cooperatism traces its birth to Toad Lane, a grubby industrial street of the Dickensian milltown of Rochdale, in the heart of the central English district that had already spawned the myth of Robin Hood and the anti-industrial Luddites of the early 1800s. There, four days before Christmas 1844, the doors of the world's first "cooperative store" opened to welcome a crowd of curious millworkers and suspicious merchants. The venture had been chartered only two months earlier, on October 24, by a group of 27 men and 1 woman, Ann Tweedale. They were flannel weavers, shoemakers, printers, carpenters. Most proudly proclaimed themselves socialists, believers in the social ownership of wealth, land, and industry, and they banded together to break the stranglehold of company stores and rapacious middlemen who controlled clothing, housing, and other necessities in Lancashire.

The Rochdale cooperators saluted "the benevolent Mr. Owen" in establishing their new enterprise, but the idea of a cooperative owned and directed by *consumers* rather than producers was not his. And they surpassed Owen by articulating a set of concise precepts for all such collective undertakings.

These Rochdale Principles, adapted and simplified over time, mandate equality of membership shares, one vote per member in guiding decisions, no discrimination on any basis among members, active political education of members and the public, provision of work or services for unemployed members, and the

dedication of any net revenue either to capitalize new cooperative ventures or to refund membership purchases.

The Rochdale ideal is a self-contained community dedicated
to mutual aid, economic self-sufficiency, and social progress without bankers, without bosses, and, as was a common cry of reformers of the time, without booze. From this experiment in utopian marketing sprang what became the largest retail enterprise
in Great Britain, with 30,000 members and nearly 1 million
pounds in annual sales a century after its founding.[3]

The spores scattered by the Rochdale Principles reached fer-
tile soil in the rural United States following the Civil War. American farmers, particularly in the Mid- and Far West, found themselves held hostage by banks, brokerage agents, railroads, and a
tight money supply based on gold. In 1867, they banded together
as "Patrons of Husbandry" and called their initially secret lodges
"granges," after the communal granaries of antiquity. Granges
did more than agitate against high railroad rates and for "free
silver." They established producer cooperatives to help grow and
market their crops and consumer cooperatives to reduce the cost
of farm supplies and machinery by pooling purchases and eliminating middlemen.

In the last decades of the 19th century, rural granges made
common cause with the struggling trade and industrial unions
of the big cities. The enemies of farmers and workers were the
same: giant corporations, financial trusts, and industrial monopolies. Their goals were also largely the same: "restoring" an
America where honest men and women could enjoy the fruit of
their labor without fear and exploitation. Their People's Parties,
Farmers' Alliances, and Farm-Labor Parties swept reformers into
power in many states and created a new national movement,
Populism.

Farmers and workers expected the brand-new state of Washington to embrace populism in 1889, and campaigned in its first
constitutional convention to establish a commission to regulate
the hated railroads and set their rates. When they lost, bitter farmers gathered in late summer of that year to establish the Washington State Grange—which admitted women as equals and

championed universal suffrage—and they joined with organized labor to found a state People's Party three years later. In an 1896 "fusion" with reformers of other parties, Populists carried Washington State for the Democrat William Jennings Bryan and elected a Populist governor, John R. Rogers.[4]

The philosophy of grange populism took firm root in the small farms and dairy pastures around Puget Sound, just as labor radicalism found many recruits among the lumberjacks, coal miners, longshoremen, millworkers, and skilled mechanics who manned local industries. The political solidarity of these local farmers and workers was cemented by deeper ancestral and ideological kinships. Most were unabashed socialists and many were newly arrived from Scandinavia (or sons and daughters of immigrants), a region with a strong tradition of cooperative enterprise.

Some joined together in utopian communities such as the Puget Sound Cooperative Colony, founded by Seattle labor leader George Venable Smith in 1897, while others worked to reform local governments and elect sympathetic officials. The King County Grange and Seattle's Central Labor Council formed a cooperative Seattle Market in 1918, and farmers supplied workers with milk and food during the city's weeklong General Strike the following year. Between 1916 and 1920, farmers and consumers established 99 cooperative associations across the state. Among these was the antecedent of today's Western Farmers, which became one of the region's largest agricultural producer co-ops.[5]

This explosion of cooperative organizing was just an episode in a national phenomenon. Cooperatism offered immediate rewards for those who, by dint of economic necessity or impatient idealism, could not wait for either reform or revolution to improve their lot in life. It was also good business—too good in the eyes of many conventional businesses, which used every legal and political trick to hobble such unwelcome competition. It took passage of the federal Capper-Volstead Act in 1922 to finally shield co-ops from antitrust prosecutions and other forms of state interference.[6]

For a distinguished New York surgeon named James P. Warbasse, cooperatism was something more, a "middle way" between capitalism and socialism that avoided the sins of both. On March 18, 1919, Dr. Warbasse invited a handful of fellow believers to his home and founded the Cooperative League, U.S.A. Although Warbasse was the first to admit, "I am by nature a non-cooperative person," he abandoned his practice and dedicated the next quarter century to guiding the Co-op League as its president and proselytizing for cooperative solutions to virtually every social and economic problem.[7]

Warbasse summed up his philosophy by describing the meaning of the Cooperative League's emblem, a pair of arrow-like pine trees in a circle:

> The pine tree is the ancient symbol of endurance, fecundity and immortality—qualities of the Cooperative movement. Twin pines mark the mutual cooperation necessary to the movement—people helping people. Their trunks and roots form the endless circle which symbolizes not only eternal existence, but the world, the all-embracing cosmos.[8]

Notwithstanding such nearly mystical faith in the cooperative ideal, economic hardship was the movement's best salesman. The stock market crash of 1929 and ensuing Great Depression convinced millions of Americans that capitalism was a dead end, and many groped for a formula for a better social order. There were many contenders: technocracy, a new, briefly popular movement based on the scientific management of energy and natural resources; the democratic socialism of Norman Thomas; and the dream of a Soviet-style proletarian revolution led by the Communist Party, U.S.A.

Among these competing ideologies, cooperatism offered something unique: immediate economic relief through the creation of associations to produce needed goods and share scarce resources. Cooperatism played a major role in one of the state's seminal rebukes of corporate power: passage of the Grange's Public Utility District initiative in 1930 to spur "rural electrification" and encourage publicly owned utilities. Among Initiative

1's advocates was Jack Cluck, a young attorney from Bothell, who would go on to play an expanding role in events to come.

In 1931, the Unemployed Citizens League (UCL) was established in Seattle to promote "self-help cooperatives and a modified barter economy." The UCL quickly added 12,000 members to its ranks, and joined with similar groups in other cities to form United Producers of Washington in 1932. Many UCL members rallied to Franklin Roosevelt's call for a "New Deal," although most stood far to his left on the political spectrum. Their radicalism was noted in the apocryphal toast, "To the 47 States of the Union and the Soviet of Washington," attributed to U.S. Postmaster "Big Jim" Farley.

Upton Sinclair made cooperative enterprises the core of his 1934 bid for the governorship of a "California Commonwealth." Although Sinclair was ultimately defeated by a business-financed media campaign of unprecedented scope and viciousness, he inspired radicals and reformers in Washington State. State UCLs, granges, unions, activists, and sympathizers such as Seattle attorney Rolla Houghton met on August 18, 1934, to charter Washington's Commonwealth Builders, Incorporated (CBI). The following year, Jack Cluck joined with the Rev. Fred Shorter to establish a "Cooperative Commission" to raise funds for CBI's campaigns. Ironically, local Teamsters listed the Commission's new co-op bakery as "unfair to labor."[9]

Shorter was a radical pastor who founded his own Church of the People in Seattle's University District after being ousted from the prestigious pulpit of Pilgrim Presbyterian Church. He was later converted to cooperatism by a forum on the subject conducted one Sunday in 1934 at his church at the suggestion of Charles Rollit Coe. Other Church of the People members who took up the cooperative cause were Sidney Gerber, a successful businessman and tireless social advocate, and Mandel Nieder, described by his friend Hilde Birnbaum as a "professional liberal," who served as president of the state Public Power Association. When he was disabled by a heart condition, Birnbaum says, he devoted himself to co-op medicine and other good works "with religious zeal."[10]

The state's champion cooperative organizer had to be

Addison Shoudy. Born in Cle Elum in 1900 and raised in Ellensburg, "Ad" Shoudy organized his first cooperative, a rural telephone system, at the age of 16. He later took his degree in economics, but lost his shirt in real estate during the Depression, and turned full-time to serving the cooperative movement. By the time he was named manager of the Puget Sound Cooperative, a consumer-owned grocery store in West Seattle, Shoudy had helped to launch 78 co-ops around the state.[11]

He and other activists seeded a flowering of cooperatives in Seattle during the late 1930s: the People's Memorial Association, which helped to break the national mortuary monopoly by offering hundreds of thousands of members low-cost, prepaid cremations and funeral services; the Student Cooperative Association, which established communal housing for University of Washington students in 1935; the Rainier Cooperative and the North End Cooperative, which ran grocery stores in Seattle's Rainier Valley and Wallingford neighborhoods; the Evergreen Cooperative, which delivered milk and dairy products throughout King County; and Recreational Equipment, Incorporated (REI), a co-op organized by Lloyd and Mary Anderson and other mountaineers to help reduce the cost of camping and alpine goods. (Addison Shoudy gave REI its first retail space, a shelf in the PSC's satellite store near the Pike Place Market.) The Grange had also established a number of thriving cooperatives in Seattle by this time, including Grange Press and a Mutual Insurance agency.[12]

Amid this ferment, Commonwealth Builders reorganized and allied with other left-wing groups to create the Washington Commonwealth Federation (WCF) on October 5, 1935. A central tenet of the WCF was the creation of state-financed cooperative industries to hire the unemployed and to supply cheap goods to cash-starved citizens. It never achieved this goal, but under the leadership of radio commentator and activist Howard Costigan, the WCF would dominate Democratic state politics by promoting social reforms and the political careers of Marion Zioncheck, Homer T. Bone, Lewis Schwellenbach, Hugh Mitchell, and Warren G. Magnuson, among many others, until its dissolution in 1945.

The internal and external politics of the WCF also set the stage for bitter battles to come. Many members were uneasy with the covert participation of Communist Party members such as William Pennock, who led the state Pension Union and won election as a Democrat to the state legislature in 1938 (and would later become the center of a wrenching controversy at Group Health). At the same time, the Communist Party's overt manipulation of WCF as a "popular front" before and during World War II was no secret. These ties irked liberals who were more interested in genuine reform than in scoring rhetorical points against capitalism, and they supplied ammunition to WCF's conservative opponents. For example, a doctor-led Public Health League used Warren Magnuson's WCF links to brand his proposals for New Deal healthcare reform as "Red Medicine" during his congressional campaign of 1938.[13]

That same year, Addison Shoudy learned the hard way that the real color of American healthcare was green—lots of green.

In 1938, one of his meat cutters became sick. Although the man had insurance with the doctor-owned King County Medical Bureau (a "Blue Shield" plan), he was billed more than $1,000 for his treatment because his illness was deemed a "pre-existing condition." Not long after, one of Shoudy's clerks had to be treated for a week, with the same result: no coverage for a pre-existing condition.[14]

Outraged, Shoudy resolved to organize a "prepaid health co-op." He was not alone. On November 4, 1939, Lily Taylor led a "discussion and report on cooperative medicine" at the Newcastle Grange, in southern King County. "Sister Taylor" had recently read Dr. Shadid's book, *A Doctor for the People*, and she pursued the issue with her fellow grangers until they forwarded a supportive resolution to the higher King County Pomona Grange the following spring. There, Taylor won the active support of Ella Williams, a teacher and farmer in Maple Valley, and on May 18, 1940, the county Grange in turn encouraged the state Grange convention to explore the formation of medical cooperatives.[15]

In the summer of 1941, Shoudy traveled to Portland, Oregon,

to attend a conference on cooperatives. He roomed with his old friend, R. M. "Bob" Mitchell, education director of the giant Pacific Supply co-op, founded in Walla Walla in 1933 to provision farmers with low-cost fuel and fertilizer. Despite his title, Mitchell was really an organizer who crisscrossed the Northwest promoting the creation of co-ops. During a break in the proceedings, Shoudy and Mitchell came across a copy of Dr. Warbasse's new pamphlet, *Cooperative Medicine*, a virtual cookbook for health co-ops. It was a revelation, and the two men agreed to learn more.[16]

Shoudy consulted Dr. Warbasse, who told him that a minimum of 72 families was required to fund a contract with a physician for cooperative care. Shoudy also corresponded with Dr. Shadid, who outlined what he would need by way of staff and facilities to serve memberships of 500 and 1,000.[17]

The only discouragement Shoudy encountered was from local physicians. "They all believed offering full coverage was not possible," he later recalled. Shoudy thought them overly pessimistic given the successes of the Kaiser Permanente program, which covered many defense industry workers in the Northwest, and the Ross-Loos Clinic, which contracted with municipal workers in Los Angeles. Several healthcare cooperatives were also up and running, including the Milwaukee Medical Center, Little Rock's Trinity Hospital, the new Group Health Association, established by federal employees in Washington, D.C., and, of course, Shadid's Community Hospital. There were enough employee-based or cooperative health programs by 1937 to justify the Co-op League's creation of a special Bureau of Cooperative Medicine.[18]

Even Bob Mitchell was surprised by the appetite for cooperative hospitals that he encountered during his travels around the region. By 1942, nearly a dozen communities from rural Idaho to Bremerton had expressed interest in forming a Northwest Cooperative Hospital Federation, but the mounting war effort forced Shoudy and Mitchell to shelve their efforts for the duration.[19]

With the war's end in sight by May 1945, the two men met in Seattle to resume serious discussions. Mitchell was particularly eager to get something organized; at age 58, he was weary of spending most of his days on the road, and Shoudy's health co-op sounded like the ticket to a more sedate lifestyle. They divided up the list of potential supporters, with Mitchell taking the Granges, while Shoudy contacted Seattle-area co-ops and labor unions. In a lucky break, Mitchell encountered Dr. Shadid at a co-op conference in Berkeley, California, in late July. He called Shoudy with the news, and Shoudy phoned Shadid to see if he might delay his return to Elk City to fit in some speaking appearances in the Northwest during August. Shadid agreed, and with that call the first serious step toward organizing Group Health Cooperative was taken.[20]

Dr. Shadid's presentation at the Roosevelt Hotel was part of a tour that can only be described as triumphal.

Pacific Supply picked up his expenses and assigned its Seattle area representative, Bill Jordan, to chauffeur him on an intinerary that included Bremerton and cities in eastern Washington, Oregon, and Idaho. In all, Shadid met with more than 2,000 activists and citizens, and encountered one of his most enthusiastic audiences at the Renton Grange Hall.[21]

At each stop, Shadid told his listeners that they could establish cooperative hospitals with a mere 1,000 members paying a $75 initiation and as little as $5 per month. Shadid was accompanied by Stanley D. Belden, an attorney who had worked with Shadid for many years in Oklahoma before moving to Oregon. Belden offered to help the State Grange organize cooperative hospitals for a fee plus a commission for each member recruited on Shadid's formula. It does not appear that the Grange formally retained Belden, but he remained in the area long enough to help launch a short-lived health co-op in Deer Park, near Spokane, and to advise the new Kitsap County Cooperative Hospital Association, which sought to acquire a federal hospital in Bremerton. He also assisted the organizing commitee that led to Group Health.[22]

A Seattle Hospital Committee was promptly formed after Shadid's departure. The group was modeled on Shoudy's plan to form a small steering committee composed of two represen-

tatives each from the local co-op community, Grange, and organized labor, but its actual membership varied from meeting to
meeting. Early participants included John L. King, State Grange
education director (and later chair of the University of Washington Board of Regents); Ella Williams, secretary of the King County
Pomona Grange; Stanley Erickson, a veteran co-op organizer
from Minnesota then employed by the federal government; Robert Scott, Ernie Conrad, and Nettie Jean Ross Cawley, respectively former president, former manager, and current manager
of the Student Co-op Association at the University of Washington; Fred Nelson, Orilla dairy farmer, former State Grange Master and leader in the King County Pomona Grange; Robert Wells,
a businessman and leader in the Rainier Co-op; Harry Stockinger,
aeromechanic union member and North End co-op member; Sid
Shaudies, a sympathetic businessman and property owner in
Renton; Chester Kingsbury, a Seattle printer and co-op activist;
and Bernard Pearce, a labor and community organizer and editor. State Grange Master Henry Carstensen and Grange lecturer
Ira Shae as leaders of 50,000 farmers across the state also lent
their prestige to the fledgling committee.[23]

Shoudy and Mitchell had already decided who should head
up the effort: Thomas G. Bevan, president of Lodge 751 of the
International Association of Machinists (now Machinists and
Aerospace Workers; commonly abbreviated IAM and called
"Aeromechanics"). This powerful local represented most of
Boeing's huge wartime work force, and its leaders were known
as some of the most progressive within the Seattle labor movement. Tom Bevan himself was a dedicated cooperator who would
later leave IAM to establish Co-op Builders, the area's first cooperative housing developers.[24]

It didn't hurt that Lodge 751 had also raised $50,000 in 1945
to fund healthcare coverage for its members, which was not then
a standard fringe benefit. Here, too, Shadid struck a chord: during a Grange-sponsored meeting with the King County Medical
Bureau, an IAM representative declared, "We want the bestest
and the mostest for the leastest. If Dr. Shadid can give us the
best deal, we'll go for that. If you can do better, we'll go along

with you." (In truth, solidarity on the picket line, not the financial bottom line, would ultimately cement IAM's commitment to a cooperative health plan.)[25]

Shoudy also knew that he wanted Jack Cluck to handle the legal work of setting up the co-op. Edward Henry, one of Cluck's partners in Rolla Houghton's law firm, later called Cluck "the brains of the thing, the brains of the whole movement." Houghton and his partners let Cluck do most of the co-op's work for free.[26]

By the second meeting, Shoudy had everything in place except a name. Stan Erickson suggested "Group Health Cooperative of Puget Sound." Erickson was likely inspired by the Group Health Association of Washington, D.C., which had been founded by employees of the federal Home Owners Loan Corporation in 1937. Shoudy thought the moniker "was too big to handle," but he was outvoted, "so we got a name."[27]

Over the next several meetings, the steering committee set its sights on Renton, where the federal government had finished a $750,000, 80-bed hospital just in time for the end of the war. Now it was surplus property, to be disposed of by the Federal Works Administration's Bureau of Community Facilities. With Renton's high concentration of aeromechanic workers, co-op members, and grangers, it seemed like a natural fit.[28]

Shoudy and Bevan were not convinced, however. As Shoudy told Bob Mitchell, "Sure, consumers always want hospitals, but when they find out the hospital is run by the medical staff, why they're left out in the cold." He added prophetically, "They'd better organize cooperative *health plans*" (emphasis added).[29]

Whatever doubts some had, the decision to pursue Renton became official at Group Health's first recorded meeting on Monday, October 29, 1945. The steering committee assembled in the IAM Lodge 751 hall near Boeing Field "for the purpose of planning the organization of a cooperative hospital." Bevan chaired the meeting, which included Shoudy, Ella Williams, Stan Erickson, Harry Stockinger, Stanley Belden, and new recruits Victor G. Vieg and Robert LaDue. They voted to hire a former state planner, John Nordmark, to coordinate their bid for the Renton

Hospital. The committee was also advised that Dr. Shadid could return to the Seattle area after December 1 to conduct a series of lectures to aid Group Health's fundraising.[30]

State records indicate that Group Health filed its original articles of incorporation on October 29. Significantly, the corporation was established as a not-for-profit association, not as a legal cooperative in which members held actual equity shares. This approach gave the new organization the greatest flexibility under Washington's liberal laws for nonprofit corporations. It also invested all real authority for the management of the corporation, with the exception of amending bylaws, in a Board of Trustees elected by the members.

On November 2, the several members of the steering committee reconvened to "subscribe" officially as the association's founding board. Bevan signed as president, Williams signed as secretary, and Shoudy, Erickson, and Vieg signed as trustees. Jack Cluck notarized the document, which declared that Renton would be Group Health's "official place of business." The actual articles were not voted on until November 20, when Shoudy was elected treasurer, and the corporation was officially registered by the secretary of state on December 22, 1945.[31]

Group Health was in business, but only on paper.

Chapter 2

Medical Mavericks

1900 ~ 1946

*Roadblock in Renton ~ The Medical Security
Clinic ~ Prepaid Group Practice and Its
Enemies ~ Enter Dr. William MacColl ~ A
Fateful Forum in Kirkland*

B y the date of Group Health's founding, Dr. Michael
Shadid had already arrived and begun his second lecture tour. He consulted with the acting board on December 11, 1945, at the Hungerford Hotel, as they adopted their first
annual dues structure. This presumed that most members would
join as families, not individuals, and set yearly rates at $30 for
the "first person," $20 for the second, $15 for the third, and $7
for the fourth, regardless of age or gender—or medical condition.[1]

At about this same time, the Board established a "life" (later
"charter") family membership of $100. Of this sum, $10 was applied to operating costs, and $90 was set aside as a capital re-
serve to be refunded "if for any reason this hospital is not established within a reasonable time" (after Group Health began operating in 1947, the full $100 became refundable if a member left
the Seattle area; this refund was reduced to $75 in 1948). Bill
Jordan picked up the membership cards from the printer and
gave himself number 1. Addison Shoudy, remembering Dr.
Warbasse's advice about the minimum memberships needed to
launch a clinic, took number 72 for luck.[2]

The Board hoped to finance "establishment of a hospital and

clinic facilities in or near Seattle as soon as practicable" through the sale of these life memberships. Not everyone shared this promise's implied optimism. Stan Erickson, like many at the time, feared that demobilization and defense industry layoffs would trigger a deep postwar depression. Listening to his colleagues' increasingly ambitious dreams, he snorted, "Why, you fellas are crazy."[3]

Shadid also anticipated hard times ahead, but he was convinced that Group Health had veered "down the wrong path" for different reasons. When not preaching the virtues of cooperative medicine, he spent hours in his room at the Roosevelt quizzing Shoudy about Group Health's plans for Renton and beyond. Shoudy remembered that Shadid was "very meticulous" in calculating the numbers of members and doctors needed to achieve various development scenarios, but he remained skeptical about their feasibility.

"That's all fine, but how are you going to get the doctors?" Shadid asked Shoudy. He knew from his own bitter experience in Elk City that the King County Medical Society would blacklist any physicians who challenged its de facto monopoly on prepaid healthcare. Shoudy replied that he had already begun exploring purchase of an existing clinic (which one is not identified), but this did not satisfy Shadid. "You can buy out a local clinic, but what are you going to do after that?" Shoudy declared that Group Health would sue the American Medical Society if it had to. "Oh, boy, that's going to be a tough go," Shadid said prophetically. "That's going to be very tough."

Shadid also thought Group Health's plan of coverage was too liberal. He strongly discouraged Shoudy from including prescriptions in any coverage, because "you need to have the profits from your drug store to get you over the rough spots." Shoudy stuck to his guns: "I don't want them [members] to pay for anything; they will get full coverage. That's our first plank—full coverage. Our second plank is group practice. Our third plank is co-op membership."[4]

Despite his reservations, Shadid gamely preached the Group Health gospel night after winter night through mid-January 1946.

His lectures in Renton, Rainier Vista, Highpoint, and elsewhere around Seattle were so powerful that witnesses remembered them vividly half a century later; they also remembered the doctors who occasionally showed up to heckle the Elk City crusader. It made great theater, but it did not necessarily sell memberships in a hypothetical co-op hospital.[5]

After an initial burst of sales, membership applications slowed to a trickle. When Shoudy expressed his disappointment with the results, Shadid confessed, "I knew that was coming. In our territory, we didn't sign up anybody until we got a salesman on the job." He added, "If you want $100 from them, you have to go and take it away from them. That's the only way you'll get a membership."[6]

The Board thought it had hired a salesman in the person of John Nordmark, upon whom it conferred the title first of "education director" and then "executive director and manager of the corporation." It paid him $300 a month and hired Johneye Ritter to staff an office next door to Jacobson & Associates, an accounting firm specializing in co-ops, in downtown Seattle's Arcade Building.

Nordmark contracted with at least two salesmen, Messrs. Townsend and Schwiese, but Group Health's Board members and true believers were its most effective outreach, importuning friends and colleagues, and even going door-to-door in their neighborhoods. Such word-of-mouth marketing could reach only a limited audience (only 33 memberships had been signed by May). As receipts dwindled and expenses mounted, Group Health's supporters dipped into their own pockets to pay the bills. Pacific Supply and the IAM made substantial donations, as did individuals such as Sidney Gerber and Ernie Conrad. It wasn't enough, and the Board had to let Nordmark go in April, and Ritter was left to staff Group Health's lonely office.[7]

Cash flow was not the struggling Co-op's only problem. Its dream of acquiring the Renton hospital hit a bureaucratic roadblock almost immediately. Still flush with optimism, the Board approved an official offer of $125,000 for the hospital on January 11, 1946. After an initially friendly consultation, officials of the

Federal Works Administration (FWA) responded that such an offer "did not represent what the corporation was able to pay." Heedless of this realistic assessment, the Board upped its offer to $175,000, of which the Grange and Puget Sound Co-op pledged $1,000. The government replied that it could only deal with a "public agency."

Group Health was not the only suitor wooing the FWA. A local "war memorial" organization made its own bid for the hospital, and a group of Renton citizens organized the Valley Medical Foundation, which ultimately leased the hospital for a year, but could not make a go of it. In truth, not all of Renton's community leaders were sympathetic to Group Health, and the town's medical community was openly hostile.

Despite this, Group Health encouraged the Valley group in the hope that the Co-op's future doctors might have access to the hospital. Jack Cluck and Mandel Nieder, among others, also advised local citizens on how to form a "public hospital district" on the basis of a 1945 state law modeled on the Grange's public utility district statute. Such a district would permit direct citizen ownership and operation of the Renton hospital through elected commissioners, but this strategy offered no immediate break in Group Health's stalemate with the federal government.[8]

As the Board grappled with its shrinking options during a meeting on March 14, 1946, Jack Cluck mentioned that he had to be in Kirkland by 8 p.m. to represent Group Health in a community forum on healthcare.[9]

This was held at the old Lake Washington High School and sponsored by the East Side Forum with the topic, "How can our community provide an adequate medical program?" Cluck joined a panel including a Mr. Messenger, an official from the Social Security Administration (the Murray-Wagner-Dingle Bill to expand Social Security to cover universal healthcare was then being debated in Congress); Dr. Shelby Jerrod from the King County Medical Society; and Dr. William MacColl, representing the Medical Security Clinic (MSC). This last was Seattle's largest private prepaid health plan, after King County Medical, and one of the city's few group practices.[10]

The evolution of the Medical Security Clinic paralleled that of medical practice in Washington State. From the day of its founding, the clinic had been the center of a bitter controversy over the ethics, economics, and social role of healthcare.

Modern medicine seems to have been around forever, but it is barely a century old as a scientific methodology and professional culture. Before the great discoveries of Pasteur, Lister, Roentgen, and other pioneers imposed an exacting empirical discipline on medical understanding and technique, virtually anyone with a passing knowledge of anatomy and pharmacy could—and did—pass himself off as a physician. Until the late 1800s, the degree of "Doctor of Medicine" rarely entailed more than a year of postgraduate study. At even the best schools, there just wasn't that much to learn.

Scientific and clinical research expanded medical knowledge exponentially, and also the cost, in both money and effort, of a medical education. Newer, better-trained physicians banded together in national, state, and local medical societies to drive the quacks, shamans, and "irregular" physicians from the infirmary, and, not coincidentally, to secure for themselves the unique prestige and lucrative compensation due the only legitimate practitioners of the healing arts.

A medical society was organized in 1873 for the Territory of Washington. It lobbied to include regulation of medicine in the first state constitution of 1889, and to establish a state examining board during the legislative session the following year. The new Washington State Medical Society (later Association) had to overcome a veto by the state's first governor, Elisha P. Ferry, who felt that the Medical Practice Act of 1890 conferred too much power upon the profession's self-appointed watchdogs.

Thus, politics played a defining role in the organization of this state's medical practice from the very beginning. Distrust of the medical profession was fueled by the experiences of workers facing the rigors and physical dangers of employment in the state's railroads, mines, forests, mills, and farms. For most of them, healthcare was a luxury far beyond their financial reach. Their experience of healthcare was limited chiefly to the less than tender, loving care offered by "company doctors."

Corporations had a financial, if not humanitarian, interest in keeping their workers at least healthy enough to do their jobs. Railroads and lumber mills hired or contracted doctors and docked employees' pay envelopes to fund minimal care, chiefly patching up work place injuries. Some workers organized their own benevolent societies, notably the Seattle-based Fraternal Order of Eagles, to contract services from doctors and to organize pensions, insurance, and membership welfare programs.

While damned by established physicians, these "contract medicine" jobs offered young doctors a shortcut to founding practices in the Pacific Northwest. Among those who would answer the call were Drs. Thomas B. Curran, James R. Yoccum, Albert W. Bridge, and James Tate Mason. They were among the best; unfortunately, most contract docs generally offered little care beyond patching up work place injuries, which left the vast majority of state citizens with no healthcare outside of a few county or church-sponsored charity hospitals.

The situation began to improve in 1911, when the state legislature passed one of the nation's most sweeping workmen's compensation acts for on-the-job accidents. This was expanded in 1917 to finance medical and hospital care for workers through "enforced" contributions to a state fund. These mandates expanded the market for contract medicine to supply low-cost services to corporations, fraternal orders, and workers.

Yoccum and Curran were ready to meet the demand. They teamed up in 1916 to establish the Western Clinic in Tacoma (dubbed "Choke 'em and Cure 'em" by its logger patients), and Dr. Bridge founded his own Bridge Clinic in the same city. Dr. Mason had similar ideas and in 1920, after a stint as King County's medical supervisor, he joined with Dr. John Blackford and the radiologist Dr. Maurice Dwyer to found a group practice clinic and small hospital in Seattle. Mason and Blackford's daughters shared the same first name, so they dubbed the new clinic "Virginia Mason."

The spread of contract medicine had led the American Medical Association (AMA) in 1916 to endorse a national system of mandatory health insurance as an antidote to the spread of such practices. Four years later, the AMA had a change of heart about national healthcare, but not contract medicine. Solo physicians intensified their attacks on contract doctors and clinics for undermining private practice. Like their national parent, the King and Pierce county medical societies decided to freeze out contract medicine by shunning its practitioners as "unethical." Pierce County went further by organizing a medical bureau to compete with contract clinics head-to-head, but King County held back.

This did not impede Dr. Curran or prevent him from establishing a State Clinic in Seattle in 1931. Dr. Bridge also expanded into the state's largest city that year, and both operations built up substantial contract enrollments serving local companies and workers despite the Depression and the medical community's hostility.

By this time, prepaid healthcare was beginning to spread nationwide, and even the most conservative physicians were forced to see the writing on the wall. The nation's first Blue Cross surgical insurance plan was established in Texas in 1929, not far from where Dr. Shadid was organizing his cooperative hospital. In 1932, a major foundation study endorsed both prepaid health insurance and group practice as essential to making healthcare affordable for most Americans. The following year, the King County Medical Society reluctantly established its own industrial subsidiary, the King County Medical Service Corporation.

On the national scene, the deepening Depression fueled new demands for government-sponsored healthcare. The U.S. Committee on Economic Security endorsed mandatory health insurance, as well as old-age pensions, but the AMA's "unyielding opposition" forced President Roosevelt to drop healthcare from his final blueprint for Social Security in 1935. The Washington Commonwealth Federation's own proposals for state health plans were also defeated. These were only the first skirmishes in a war that has yet to run its course.

In 1938, the California Medical Association launched the nation's first "Blue Shield" program of prepaid doctor care. That same year, Henry and Edgar Kaiser took over management of the construction of the massive Grand Coulee Dam in Eastern Washington. They bankrolled Dr. Sidney Garfield so he could organize healthcare for the project's 15,000 workers and their families, and thereby laid the foundation for the path-breaking Northern and Kaiser Permanente health plans.[11]

The Medical Society's campaign against contract medicine did not ease. It even threatened to expell Dr. Tate Mason on the eve of his election as president of the AMA in 1936, unless he abandoned his industrial contracts (Mason did, and thereby gave the new Medical Bureau its first major infusion of patients). Peer pressure also forced Dr. Hubbard Buckner, a prominent orthopedist, to abandon plans for his own prepaid practice in downtown Seattle in 1938. At the same moment, Dr. Curran surrendered to the Medical Society and sold his State Clinic to its nonphysician manager, Leslie G. Pendergast, and he in turn leased the suite of offices that Dr. Buckner had renovated but never occupied on the second floor of downtown Seattle's Securities Building.

Pendergast called his new operation the "Medical Security Clinic" and later acquired St. Luke's Hospital on Capitol Hill to serve an enrollment swelling with defense workers. Although lay control of hospital boards was common, the audacity of someone without an M.D. after his name owning and running a full healthcare program sent the Medical Society into new paroxysms of rage. Such defiance would have to be dealt with sooner or later.[12]

Pendergast was an able manager, aided by Rudy Molzan as controller, and the outbreak of World War II gave him plenty of business. The novelty of a prepaid group practice allowed Pendergast to attract physicians at opposite poles of their careers: young idealists seeking a better system of medical service, and older practitioners seeking stable incomes. By 1941, Medical Security had a staff of 10, including a pair each of internists and obstetricians, a surgeon, a dermatologist, and general practioners, not counting nurses, pharmacists, and lab technicians.

What Pendergast didn't have was a pediatrician, so he advertised nationally for applicants. On the far side of the continent, a young pediatrician named William Alexander MacColl—better known to his friends as "Sandy," the Scottish diminutive for his middle name—was looking for a new assignment that might allow him to put his ideals into practice.

Sandy MacColl was then finishing his residency at the New England Medical Center, chiefly caring for Boston's indigent children. He was an ardent believer in group practice, by which physicians and specialists teamed up to provide comprehensive care on the model of the famed Mayo Clinic. MacColl was also an outspoken critic of conventional medical practice, and he was already disgusted with what he had seen of fee-for-service economics. "I did not think that one should capitalize on other people's illness," he later recalled, so he put out feelers for a position with a group practice. A New York agency responded that a man named Pendergast from Seattle would be in town to interview pediatricians for his prepaid clinic.

When MacColl met Pendergast, the latter was candid about his strained relations with the local medical society, which created a problem since MacColl had not passed his board examinations. Pendergast agreed to pay MacColl's airfare to Seattle so he could take his license exams before joining the MSC staff. MacColl and his wife Sylvia had never been west of Pennsylvania, and they decided Seattle would be an adventure. The day MacColl made his reservation, the radio announced that Japanese aircraft had bombed the U.S. Pacific Fleet at Pearl Harbor.

MacColl won his Washington license and began practicing at Medical Security in March 1942. He was impressed with the facilities at the Securities Building and at St. Luke's, as well as with his colleagues' skills and motives. He fell into a demanding but not uncomfortable routine of seeing 25 to 30 patients per day, plus rotating night and weekend duties. Then, in late summer, Uncle Sam sent his "greetings" and MacColl found himself serving in Florida as a psychiatrist. He figured that the army "did not need pediatricians or proctologists that day," so he was assigned to the next "p" specialty in the alphabetical rotation.[13]

The army decommissioned MacColl following V-E day in 1945, and he returned to Seattle to resume his practice at the Medical Security Clinic. He found that the war had been very good for MSC. Enrollment reached nearly 20,000 individuals, mostly workers engaged in building ships and airplanes for the armed forces. It had also established four satellite clinics in Renton, Kirkland, Winslow, and Ravensdale, a village in southeast King County, between 1942 and 1945.

With the war's end now clearly in sight, Leslie Pendergast did not like the view. He calculated that the armistice would decimate his clinic's defense industry contracts, so he was happy to entertain an offer from six of his physicians to take MSC off his hands.

The purchasers were Drs. George W. Beeler, Lester L. Long, Charles E. Maas, Edgar N. Layton, and father and son E. and Rod Janson. On September 27, 1945—virtually the same moment that Group Health's founders were meeting across town—they paid $45,000 for all of MSC's stock held by Pendergast and his wife. The doctors also took an option on St. Luke's Hospital, which they exercised the following January, and acquired MSC's suburban clinic properties.[14]

The new doctors' group was as idealistic in its way as the unionists, grangers, and cooperators backing Group Health. As Dr. MacColl later wrote in his seminal book, *Group Practice and Prepayment of Medical Care*, he and many of his colleagues sought "a system of family care in which the interests of the patient and the physician were parallel and directed towards a goal of good care, health maintenance, and preventive services. They wanted the whole system to be supported by monthly payments of a group of people large enough to underwrite the cost of services desired."[15]

In the same book, MacColl described a dozen advantages of group practice, obviously drawing on his own experiences. "The free interplay of a company of professionals, sharing their knowledge and responsibility, is one of the most appealing features of a mature physicians' group," he declared. This is particularly attractive for the young physician who "soon learns that he does not need to hesitate to call for help when he is uncertain." It allows "the physician to apply himself unreservedly to those tasks for which he is best trained...without indulging in the pot-boiling type of care often found necessary in private practice in order to pay the rent."

Within the group, "The specialist...is the specialist, and his function in the group does not require that he be a family physician as well. Conversely, the generalist... can use his particular talent for over-all responsibility for the care of the patient." The two do not compete, rather "the 'we' is important. The primary thought is that the patient gets the care he needs at the hands of the person best qualified to provide it."

The prepaid group practice gives physicians time and resources to stay current with new medical developments, it imposes high standards on its members, and it allows for reasonable schedules and the sharing of emergency and late-night duties. The practice assures the physician a good income while giving him or her "relief from the business of medicine." At the same time, "The doctor is free to practice the best medicine."

MacColl concluded, "Perhaps the most satisfying aspect of these programs is that the physician is a member of *the family of doctors for the family of patients* " (original emphasis).[16]

Back in 1946, the Medical Security Clinic and Group Health Cooperative each possessed what the other needed. MSC had a family of doctors but it was worried that its enrollment would quickly evaporate with peacetime. Group Health had a family of patients, but it had no physicians to care for them.

The two groups had not been entirely unaware of each other. MSC had actively solicited contracts from IAM and other unions involved in founding Group Health, and MSC lab director John Kloeck attended one of Dr. Shadid's lectures during the winter of 1945-46. Shadid reportedly encouraged MSC staff to contact Group Health's organizers, and he appears to have met Dr. Beeler, who served as MSC's director, but with less than salubrious effects (see next chapter). Jack Cluck must have known something of MSC, since it represented thousands of area workers, but he appears not to have met any of its staff before before his accidental encounter with Sandy MacColl on March 14, 1946.[17]

Cluck and MacColl formed the instant camaraderie of two partisans meeting in the midst of battle against a common enemy, in this case, the medical establishment. "The audience jumped all over the King County Medical Society doctor," Cluck recalled. "He was lucky to get out of there in one piece."

After their foe had fled the field, the two men retired to chat. As MacColl later remembered, "The cooperative Jack described that night was very interesting to me. After the forum, the two of us went out to have a beer and discuss the merging of our operations. The Cooperative was a lay organization looking for doctors and facilities, and the Medical Security Clinic was a doctors' organization looking for administrators and a population base. It seemed almost inevitable that the two would merge."[18]

Inevitable, perhaps, but not easy.

Chapter 3

The First Alliance

1946

*Writing Bylaws ~ Skeptics and Communists ~
Debating the Deal ~ Group Health Buys the
Medical Security Clinic*

*D*espite the instant sympatico felt by Jack Cluck and Sandy
MacColl, and John Kloeck's independent urgings that
Medical Security Clinic Executive Committee chairman
Dr. H. M. "Monte" Hardwicke should meet with Addison
Shoudy, Group Health and MSC were slow to approach each
other formally.[1]

Many members of the Group Health Board of Trustees were
still dedicated to the acquisition of Renton's federal hospital, although Shoudy, for one, still regarded the plan as "monkey-
doodle." Some trustees also saw "indications" that the medical
establishment was "heeding public opinion and becoming more
friendly" to Group Health's efforts.[2]

For their part, the new physician-owners of the Medical Security Clinic hoped that the departure of Leslie Pendergast would
ease the King County Medical Society's hostility toward their
program and allow them to expand. Despite postwar layoffs,
MSC had contracts with some 350 companies and served approximately 17,000 individuals. Its owners felt confident enough
to exercise their option to purchase the 55-bed St. Luke's Hospital from Leslie Pendergast on January 31, 1946. At the same time,
MSC sold off its satellite clinics in Renton, Kirkland, Winslow,

and Ravensdale between September 1945 and May 1946. By summer, MSC staff numbered 15 physicians under the direction of general manager/chief of staff Dr. George Beeler, a former member of the King County Medical Society's ethics committee.[3]

Finally, on June 7, the Group Health Board authorized Jack Cluck and Ad Shoudy to "confer with the doctors who own the Medical Security [Clinic] and get their attitude toward group medicine [and] also explore possibilities of working out a mutually satisfactory deal between the Cooperative and the shareholders of the clinic." At the same meeting, the Board expanded itself to nine trustees by adding Al Annibal, a leader of the local postal workers union, and veteran cooperator Bernard Pearce.[4]

Some of the early meetings between the two organizations were held at Ivar's Acres of Clams Restaurant on Pier 54 (an appropriate setting since restaurateur Ivar Haglund was a longtime friend of socialist and progressive causes). The key participants were Cluck, Shoudy, MacColl, Long, and Hardwicke, and their interpersonal chemistry was positive enough for Group Health's Board to authorize formal negotiations on July 17, 1946.[5]

Getting definitive financial data from Dr. Beeler was another matter. Beeler would not permit Group Health to inspect the clinic's books, so Shoudy got around him by working with a sympathetic doctor who "knew what was going on" and conveyed information to Group Health. Beeler's reticence is surprising given his attendance at the founding convention of the Cooperative (later Group) Health Federation of America, chaired by Dr. Shadid in August 1946 in Two Harbors, Minnesota, home of the Community Health Cooperative founded two years earlier.

Based on his participation, Beeler later wrote, he and his staff "quickly realized that cooperative medicine paralleled" their own support of prepaid group practice emphasizing prevention, and that this inspired "contact with the laymen's cooperative group in Seattle." He also came away from this convention convinced that a medical cooperative had to incorporate "guarantees that no person, no thing, no corporate setup, or sets of bylaws come between the doctor and his patient." In this view, Beeler and

Shadid were diametrically opposed, which may have poisoned Shadid's later opinion of the MSC purchase.[6]

During the summer, the negotiators settled on a purchase price of $190,000, below which Beeler would not go. Cluck and the Co-op's accountant, Walter Jacobson, advised that this was much too high, but Shoudy argued that "we could make the deal with them and then come back to them in a year's time and see if we could cut the price." Even if the price was $100,000 too high, Shoudy reasoned, "we could live with it better than we could build from the ground up."[7]

Shoudy's logic prevailed on August 14, 1946, when the Group Health Board voted in principle to purchase Medical Security Clinic. In addition to accepting Beeler's inflated valuation, the Board agreed to preserve the professional autonomy of the medical staff. Both issues would have to be revisited, but for the moment Group Health and MSC were elated. Four new salesmen were hired and sent forth to sign up members for what would finally be a functioning medical cooperative, while Dr. Beeler assured the Board that his doctors "will soon be able to become members of the AMA."[8]

Enthusiasm for the purchase was not universal. Word of Group Health's negotiations with MSC had already set off alarms in several quarters. In July, Dr. Kingsley Roberts, head of the National Research Department of Cooperatives, cautioned the Board "to take time to be careful in the formulation of an agreement with any group of doctors." On the other side, the aeromechanics union officially blessed the purchase on August 30. The Board felt confident as it drafted bylaws for adoption at the Cooperative's first formal membership meeting on September 4, 1946.[9]

The assembly was convened in the county commissioners' chambers on the fourth floor of the County-City Building (now the King County Courthouse). Shoudy arrived a few minutes late and wondered if he had found the right room "because the first two people I saw were habitual drunks that I knew. Then there were all kinds of cripples around the hall." The cause, Shoudy realized, was that word had gotten out on the street that

Group Health would take Dr. Shadid's advice and enroll anyone regardless of medical condition. "It looked like we had them
all that evening," he recalled. When Tom Bevan escorted Shoudy
into the room, the latter whispered, "We're two blocks from the
[train] depot. Don't you think we had better leave town?"[10]

They didn't. As treasurer, Shoudy addressed the group on
the Co-op's finances to date. Its assets consisted of $11,992.66 in
receipts, $9,697.66 in trust, and $592.50 cash on hand, while liabilities included $47.39 in outstanding bills, $1,546.42 in salaries owing, and $3,000 in loans from Pacific Supply, the Grange,
and IAM. Shoudy went on to describe the facilities of the Medical Security Clinic, noting that Group Health had to raise an
immediate down payment of $20,000.

Bernie Pearce then reviewed the draft bylaws. The preamble
declared:

> This organization shall endeavor:
> a. To develop some of the most outstanding hospitals and medical
> centers to be found anywhere, with special attention devoted to
> preventive medicine.
> b. To serve the greatest possible number of people in the Puget
> Sound Area upon the consumers' cooperative plan.
> c. To place matters of medical practice under the direction of phy-
> sicians on the staff employed by it and to afford strong incentive
> for the best possible performance on their part.
> d. To recognize other employees of the cooperative for purposes of
> collective bargaining and to provide incentive, adequate compen-
> sation and fair working conditions for them.
> e. To educate the public as to the value of the cooperative method
> of health protection, and to promote other projects in the interest
> of public health.

This preamble contained the central ideas, virtually the genetic code, that would guide Group Health's future evolution in
its commitments to quality care, preventive medicine, aggressive regional outreach, cooperatism, physician autonomy, workers' rights, health education, and public health advocacy. The
first version's unintentional omission of another key principle,

nondiscrimination, would be corrected a few weeks later.

The bylaws' membership clause expressed the cooperative movement's lofty idealism by setting high expectations for participants. Group Health was "open to persons who believe sincerely in its purposes and who show their willingness to devote the necessary time and personal attention to have this cooperative function properly in accordance with democratic, cooperative principles." A person did not merely join Group Health to obtain better or cheaper healthcare, one pledged allegiance to the cooperative cause and a unique social and economic community.

Significantly, the bylaws gave the Board (or membership meetings) the right to approve or reject any membership application. The adoption of the bylaws that evening also barred admission of new "life members" unless they submitted to a medical examination. Thus, the cards of all original life or charter members note that they joined prior to September 4, 1946, and any pre-existing conditions are therefore covered.

The members also approved monthly dues of $3 per adult family member and $1.50 each for up to four dependent children, with no charge for additional children. The membership fee remained $100, of which at least $25 had to be paid in order to qualify for a vote in the Cooperative's affairs.

(This was a lot of money in 1946, and it was recognized at the outset that Group Health was not a solution to the healthcare needs of the poor. This financial requirement also had the unintended benefit of creating a membership dominated by skilled workers and middle-class professionals, who tended to be more pragmatic, and probably helped the Board prevail in the debates to come by restricting the number of lower-income voters with more radical outlooks.)

Jack Cluck rose to describe the purchase contract for MSC. The minutes record that the membership instructed the negotiating committee to add clauses banning "discrimination among doctors because of race, color, sex, religious belief, or political convictions" and establishing that the "need of a doctor's service rather than the length of his employment should determine the order of dismissal."[11]

The discussion was more heated than the written record shows. As Shoudy recalled the meeting, a woman rose to denounce the deal, declaring that she had written to Shadid on the matter and he had replied, "Under no circumstances do any business with the Medical Security Clinic." Shadid, she said, had met the MSC director, Dr. Beeler, and "thought he was a big bag of wind." Despite this opposition, the assembled members authorized the Board to conclude the purchase of MSC. Time ran out before the members could formally elect the Board of Trustees under the new bylaws, and the membership meeting was recessed. The continuing session was originally set for October 1, then rescheduled for the 17th. The delay would give MSC skeptics time to ponder and organize.[12]

Medical Security Clinic's doctors already regarded themselves as the medical staff of Group Health when they met on September 5 to elect the Cooperative's first chief of staff, former University of West Virginia Medical School instructor Dr. John Osborne McNeel. Group Health's acting trustees similarly viewed the merger as a *fait accompli*, and they invited leading critics of the purchase to their September 13 meeting in the Arcade Building "to hear and refute criticisms of the actions taken by the Board."[13]

At the same meeting, the Board named Bob Mitchell education director, fulfilling his old dream of a more settled job promoting cooperative healthcare. As his first assignment, the Board instructed Mitchell to write Dr. Shadid to explain the MSC deal and, they hoped, win his endorsement.[14]

This ploy proved disastrous. Shadid replied to Mitchell in a letter dated September 23. It was blunt and uncompromising:

Dear Bob:

I read your letter and confidential report and I am sorry to say that I cannot approve of the deal with the Medical Security Clinic. I would not want a hospital that I cannot enlarge readily. The 50 beds that you have in the hospital is not large enough to hospitalize the 7500 contract holders and their families much less take care of new cooperative members.

I do not care to commit the Co-op to pay $30,000 annually for office rent although Dr. Beaver [sic, presumably Beeler] told me the office rent was $5000 a month; neither do I see why you should have a drug inventory of $20,000.00.

I cannot get myself to agree to pay $50,000 for good will.

In your confidential report you give the doctors autonomy and make them self-governing. I do not see where the Board of Directors have much voice in administration.

I visualized building a cooperative hospital with offices for all the doctors on the first floor, building it in a way that you can add to it. There is always a desire on the part of members to take some short cut when they fail to achieve their purpose right away. For the money you are going to pay for the hospital [St. Luke's], equipment, good will, etc., I can build a new 60 bed hospital and equip it to suit the purpose.

I prophesy that if this deal goes through you will never build a new hospital and never achieve the success you anticipate. I would rather give up the idea of a cooperative hospital in Seattle altogether than to commit myself to endorsing this deal for I honestly believe it is pregnant with disappointment.

Bob, I would rather build a cooperative hospital for 2,000 families or even 1,000 families and start small than to go into a deal of this sort. Great things come from small beginnings. There is no short cut to success. This letter is confidential and I do not have the total confidence in the deal that you seem to have. I would like to give this deal my endorsement, but I am afraid that it will kill the cooperative medicine movement in the Northwest.

A copy of this letter goes to Charlie Baker [director of Pacific Supply Cooperative and future president of the National Association of Cooperatives].

Affectionately yours

[Signed] M. Shadid, M.D.

P.S. The next depression will destroy this Co-op.[15]

Shadid's fusillade of criticisms did not remain confidential for long. Whether through Baker or some other conduit, Shadid's letter fell into the hands of leading critics of the MSC purchase, who dubbed themselves simply, "The Committee." They included Carolyn Hurley, a veteran cooperative organizer from

Alberta and labor and civil rights activist; the Rev. Robert Shaw, pastor of the Bothell Methodist Church and a well-known progressive spokesman; Harry Meyers, owner of the Bremerton Oil Company; Fred Post, an attorney and member of the (Quaker) Friends Service Committee; and Byron Ela, a high school teacher and chairman of the University Discussion Group. The foregoing would later challenge the Board's own slate of trustees.

On October 4, The Committee sent copies of Shadid's letter to the entire Group Health membership, along with a statement of their own objections. The Committee's letter, signed by Hurley, ended by urging members to contact trustees to "demand the contract [with MSC] not be signed until another membership meeting is called. We must have free and frank discussion and understanding else this movement will be killed at birth."[16]

Two days before the membership meeting, The Committee fired another broadside, a manifesto two legal pages long detailing the points of opposition expressed by members who had "literally swamped" The Committee with calls and letters. Among these were the following:

That the proposed contract with the Medical Securities [sic] Clinic constitutes a major business transaction, in so much as the purchase price is nearly a quarter of a million dollars; and that we should have several times greater membership before giving consideration to a purchase of this magnitude....

That the hospital we are being asked to purchase is not a modern structure, and is not primarily designed as a hospital-clinic.

That the price we are being asked to pay is based on the present inflationary valuations....

That the present Board of the Medical Cooperative is a temporary, self-appointed one, not having been elected by the membership...[which] should not have presumed to carry on negotiations looking toward committing the members of the co-op to a long term contract...

That the present Board has conducted secret negotiations...not in accord with sound cooperative proceedure [sic].

...That the present contract removes doctors from the control of the co-op...

THAT THIS PROCEEDURE IS STRONGLY OPPOSED BY DR. SHADID (who favors direct hiring and firing control by the co-op) AND THAT THIS PROCEEDURE IS NOT EMPLOYED BY ANY OTHER SUCCESSFUL MEDICAL CO-0P [original emphasis].[17]

Both sides rallied their forces for a showdown at 8 p.m. on October 17 in the auditorium of Broadway High School (now Seattle Central Community College). After approving relatively minor amendments to the bylaws, the attendees turned to the main event. After considerable parliamentary jockeying, an hour was allotted for the two sides' champions to make their cases, with Shoudy speaking for the MSC purchase and the Rev. Shaw speaking against.[18]

Detailed minutes were not kept of what Jack Cluck later called a "very warm discussion," but we can reconstruct the clash with confidence. On one side was arrayed a powerful trilateral coalition of the Grange, IAM, and major co-ops, as represented on the acting Board. It is important to note that they were unified and adamant, for, surely, the hesitation or defection of any one of these interests would have doomed the purchase. After a year of meetings and false starts, they knew that buying Medical Security was Group Health's last shot at launching a real medical cooperative.

The opposition was more diverse, ranging from cooperative purists to people simply uneasy with the cost and implications of the MSC purchase. "Idealistically prompted persons felt that we were not following traditional Rochdale principles," recalled Jack Cluck. "They had the notion that if you're adopting a mortgage procedure to get outside capital [to buy the hospital], you're departing from the principle that members should put up the capital." There was also "some fear that raising capital on the projected scale, small at the time but large in their eyes, would endanger the enterprise, too."

Many critics were based in the Rev. Fred Shorter's left-wing Church of the People in the University District, a congregation that included Marxists of both Trotskyist and Stalinist stripes. This aggravated old grievances and suspicions among liberals, labor leaders, and cooperators who had battled "card-carrying Communists" in the Washington Commonwealth Federation and had helped the IAM and other unions purge communists as early as 1940.

Martha Wiberg, who served on the Board nominating committee and would later staff Group Health's first Renton clinic, felt that the attendance on October 17 was "peppered with Communists" bent on "discouraging anything that was for the benefit of the people [lest] they would become so satisfied with conditions that they wouldn't revolt." David and Laura Harstein blamed William Pennock, a well-known party member, and "Townsendites" for leading the charge against the MSC, although Pennock was not a Group Health member and supporters of Dr. Francis Townsend's pension-based "recovery plan" of the 1930s had long since scattered.

Despite this anticommunist rhetoric, the battle over the MSC contract was not a left-right confrontation. Not all or even most of the Board's critics were communists or fellow travelers or otherwise ideologically motivated. They pointed out many practical problems with the deal, with what would prove to be prophetic accuracy, and they had legitimate reason for anxiety. As Walter H. Philipp, a merchant seaman and Rainier Co-op member, explained, many MSC opponents "had come into Group Health and persuaded their friends to do so on the explicit understanding that Dr. Shadid's advice would be followed." Now his advice was being explicitly ignored.

At the same time, many of the Board's members and supporters had impeccable left-wing credentials of their own. The Harsteins readily confess, "Of course, we were radical. We felt that we were doing something that was experimental and worthwhile [that] would be the wave of the future." Bernie Pearce was an avowed socialist who had been forced out of the public utility movement by an expose in the *Seattle Post-Intelligencer*. "I had a big mouth in those days," he later recalled, and "I did a lot of the talking on the floor that night" on behalf of the MSC purchase.[19]

After much ventilating, it was moved "to refer the final vote

on the purchase to a subsequent meeting of the membership after members receive copies of the doctor's agreement and the
manager contracts." This motion carried, effectively repudiat-
ing the acting Board and potentially scuttling the purchase.

Either out of confusion or parliamentary calculation, Mandel
Nieder had voted with the majority and against the Board, which
he in fact supported. He then "announced that due to a misun-
derstanding he had voted improperly on the motion to refer the
purchase proposal to a subsequent meeting and moved a vote
of reconsideration," which only a voter on the prevailing side
may do. Upon reconsideration, the motion giving the membership the final say was reversed. A further motion referring the
purchase "to the permanent board with power to act" then
passed.

The acting Board had won, but time ran out for its election
on a permanent basis. The Broadway High School janitors, impatient to finish their work, doused the auditorium's lights and
shooed the squabbling cooperators out into the night. They
would meet again in a week's time.[20]

Opponents of the MSC purchase regrouped and revised their
strategy. Their only hope was to elect enough trustees to slow, if
not stop, the deal. The Rev. Shaw wrote to all Group Health
members on October 21. "We have been charged by some with
being obstructionists," he explained. "That is not true. We have
been forced into opposition by the Board's haste." Shaw decried
the membership's ignorance of details and artificial time pressure imposed on it to consummate the MSC purchase. "There is
no emergency except in the minds of Board members."

The solution advocated by Shaw was election of a new Board
"who believe in full and free democracy" and "will adhere to
Rochdale consumer cooperative principles." He proposed that
this new Board should then negotiate with both MSC *and* King
County Medical and sign with "whichever will give us the better deal" until Group Health had enough members to allow it to
"build our *own modern* hospital and employ our *own* doctors"
[original emphasis]. Shaw had also not given up hope of acquiring Renton's hospital, which he asserted could be bought

for $100,000 in just two months' time (events proved him wrong on this point). As to the MSC purchase, Shaw thundered, "This mongrel mixture of frenzied finance…, this hodgepodge of dubious capitalism and adulterated consumer's cooperation we want none of."[21]

The final round commenced at 7:30 p.m. on October 24, 1946, back in the county commissioners' chambers where the "membership meeting" had begun six weeks earlier. The timing was ironic: Several trustees were simultaneously helping to incorporate the new Pacific Northwest Cooperative Hospital Federation at a convention in the Frye Hotel.[22]

Their absence was not a handicap, for the meeting turned out to be an anticlimax. Shaw and Shoudy led their respective forces in rehashing the MSC purchase, which took over one and a half hours, but no motions were made to undo or amend the previous session's approval of the MSC purchase. Some time after 9:30, members turned their attention to the election of the permanent Board of Trustees.

Dissidents nominated only three Board candidates—Harry Meyers, Byron Ela, and Carolyn Hurley—and all lost to the "official" slate of Alfred Annibal, Charles Berger (a leader of the Boilermakers union), Tom Bevan, Ad Shoudy, Sid Schaudies, Bob Scott, Bob Wells, Ella Williams, and Fred Nelson. Except for Hurley, who received 46 votes, none of the protesters—including the Rev. Shaw's write-in bid—received more than three votes, compared with a range of 94 to 106 votes for each of the incumbents.

The would-be revolution had ended in a rout. Ella Williams was no doubt grateful when she typed the conclusion of her minutes: "There being no further business the meeting was adjourned."[23]

Chapter 4

The Honeymoon

1947 ~ 1948

*Group Health Takes Over ~ Two Cooperatives
in One ~ Building a District System ~
Financial Ups and Downs ~ Solidarity with
Labor ~ Exit Addison Shoudy*

While Group Health and Medical Security were still negotiating, Dr. Beeler told Frank Hart, the maintenance engineer at St. Luke's Hospital, "I want you to clean this place up real good. Make it look real sharp, now, because there's a new group."

"Oh, you mean the co-op that's in the Arcade building," Hart responded. "Gee whiz, are they coming to buy this joint?" For a $5 bonus, he and his assistant, Charlie Quarles, agreed to spruce up St. Luke's as best they could. "There wasn't nothing hardly the matter," Hart remembered, "except that it was so old, it was antique, and it was small." The hospital was also fueled by a 1910-vintage boiler dubbed "Old Smokey" because it exhaled clouds of soot that often settled on freshly washed laundry hanging in Capitol Hill yards, triggering telephone calls from irate housewives.[1]

Hart and his crew must have done their job well. On the evening of November 7, Group Health trustees joined Dr. Beeler and his medical staff for a celebratory dinner at the Broiler Restaurant. Enthusiastic speeches were delivered by Beeler, Jack Cluck, Bob Mitchell, Ad Shoudy, and other attendees. All agreed the meeting would undoubtedly "prove to have been an his-

toric one, as marking this pioneer movement in strictly cooperative medicine in the Pacific Northwest."[2]

Next day, the Board formally approved the purchase resolutions for MSC at a "final" price of $199, 995.54, and assumed the
balance of the St. Luke's mortgage, then about $50,000. Unfortu-
nately, Group Health's checking account was shy $6,125 needed
to make the initial $20,000 down payment, so each trustee signed
a note pledging his or her personal credit for the balance. They
didn't know if the MSC shareholders would accept the note.[3]

Bernard Pearce personally delivered the cash and guarantee. "I remember taking the $13,000 in my hot little hand to Dr.
Beeler," along with the trustees' pledge. "And I said, 'This is
what we've got. Will you take it?'" Beeler did, and it would not
be the last time that the sellers would have to adjust to fiscal
realities.[4]

Despite the shortage of funds, spirits were high. On the same
day, November 8, Drs. Harmon Truax, MacColl, and Hardwicke
(constituting the MSC executive committee) and chief of staff
Dr. McNeel signed an enthusiastic letter on behalf of the clinic's
physicians, who were "proud and happy to greet the members"
of Group Health. Indirectly addressing the critics of the MSC
purchase, the letter declared, "The division of 'we' and 'you' is
purely artificial. A cooperative is a unit and as such indivisible."[5]

This was not quite the case organizationally. Group Health's
purchase of MSC represented more a merger in which the original parties retained some degree of independent identity and
authority. The new Group Health was, in effect, two cooperatives—one for the members and one for the doctors, conjoined
for mutual benefit. It would take several years for each to master the art of symbiosis.

Stock and operating agreements were formally executed by
Group Health and MSC's six stockholders on November 12, 1946.
The former Medical Security Clinic and St. Luke's Hospital began accepting Group Health members on November 15. Before
the day was done, Trygve Erickson entered the world and history as "the first born under the Group Health ownership of St.
Luke's Hospital," according to Group Health's inaugural mem-

ber magazine, *Cooperative Health,* published the following spring.[6]

(This was not quite technically true. On the advice of Jack Cluck, Group Health postponed its formal takeover of MSC's clients and assets until January 1, 1947. The honor of being the first baby born at St. Luke's *under Group Health management* belongs to Roger Paulson, who arrived January 13, 1947.)[7]

During December, trustees and their new medical staff hammered out a document describing the fundamental "Policies and Organization" for Group Health. In the spirit of the bylaws, they agreed that the Co-op should "First, be of the greatest possible service to its members and users, and Second, contribute in every way possible to the development of the cooperative movement as a democratic way of doing business."

In the organizational hierarchy, the membership "in meeting assembled" exercised "supreme control." The Board was responsible to the membership and the bylaws, and it controlled "the affairs of the cooperative." The position of general manager was established as "directly responsible to the board," and this position in turn supervised various department heads for "organization and research, business control, education, facilities, and medical service." In a significant acknowledgment of the general manager's authority, the Board placed its own executive secretary, Bernie Pearce, under this position's direction.

The medical service department enjoyed special status under the new policies and under Group Health's contracts with former MSC and newly hired physicians. The professional departments such as pharmacy and laboratory services were placed under the authority of the chief of the medical staff, who was elected by the employed physicians and other selected medical professionals. The medical staff adopted its own bylaws governing the election of the chief of staff, standards for hiring and dismissal, and other ethical and professional criteria.[8]

If the medical staff was allowed to manage its own affairs, it was not exempt from the sacrifices needed to keep the Co-op afloat. On December 18, the Board cut the physicians' total monthly payroll by 15 percent, or $2,500, to control Group Health's rapidly rising deficit. The cuts did not prevent most of

MSC's staff from transferring to Group Health (only two physicians appear to have dropped out). Dr. George Beeler continued in his former MSC role as general manager, assisted by Rudy Molzan as controller, and Dr. McNeel remained chief of staff, overseeing 13 other physicians and the lab director, John Kloeck. Ruth Brown, MSC's pharmacist since 1943, also stayed on and later became famous for her "all-girl pharmacy."[9]

On January 1, 1947, Beeler posted a notice on the St. Luke's bulletin board announcing that the hospital was now under Group Health's management. At a later staff banquet, Beeler told the staff, "From now on, I'm not your boss anymore. I'm just an employee. The Cooperative has taken over the hospital and the clinic and the pharmacy."[10]

Tom Bevan quickly negotiated union contracts with Group Health's new staff. Since nurses did not yet have a union of their own, their interests were represented by the Service Employees International Union. Office and Professional Employees International Union was the other major bargaining unit. Group Health thus became the region's first—and only—private hospital to establish a "union shop."[11]

Those first days united the staff, trustees, and members in the solidarity of a shared adventure, which let them overlook the perils of their situation. "We were told their financial status," remembered Doris Ptolemy, an MSC clerk who stuck with Group Health for another 30 years, but she was confident the Cooperative could succeed. "Maybe somebody looking from the outside might have had a little more skeptical outlook, but from the inside we knew we could do it." There was some trepidation, however. Frank Hart reports that when the first paychecks were issued on Group Health's account, "To tell you the truth about it, we didn't think they would cash them." The checks were good, but just barely.[12]

Dr. Gustav Bansmer was one of the first new doctors to join the Cooperative in 1947. He was typical of the new generation of physicians who had, in Sandy MacColl's phrase, "just come out of the army, which, after all, was a group practice, prepaid kind of thing." Group Health's appeal to youthful idealists was sweetened by the promise of a steady paycheck in those turbulent postwar days of high unemployment and runaway inflation, when thousands of newly decommissioned military doctors were competing for practices and hospital staff postings.

Bansmer was recruited from Pennsylvania's Valley Forge Hospital by Dr. Harmon Truax with the promise of a salary of $500 per month (compared with the $150 he was currently making). In April 1947, he drove across the continent and arrived in Seattle virtually penniless after "being relieved of what little money [he] had" by a Montana state patrolman who stopped him for speeding. Local banks refused to lend to a Group Health employee, and an appeal to Rudy Molzan produced only about $10 since Group Health was also "low on cash." Bansmer roomed with another new recruit, Dr. John Quinn, who found them "a cheap restaurant down at the Pike Place Market, and we scrounged enough money to keep the cars running."

Bansmer's new colleagues displayed an uneven range of skills and some singular eccentricities. One was a "real dandy" who made his rounds with a revolver tucked in his belt. His bedside manner consisted chiefly of telling patients, "Keep your mouth shut and your bowels open and you will be OK." When this doctor volunteered to go on recruiting trips and later wired for funds, the medical staff "decided that he would be rewarded with enough money to find another job."

Another surgeon was chronically late for operations, due, Bansmer said, to "fondness for long chain alopathic hydrocarbons, commonly known as alcohol." Assisted by Bansmer, this doctor removed a bone spur from one patient's foot. Everything went well but for the problem that they had the wrong foot. When the patient pointed out the error, an embarrassed Bansmer gamely assured her, "Don't worry, lady. We'll keep on operating until we get the right foot." After the second operation, the patient sent the surgeon an expensive fishing rod in appreciation, along with two cartons of Camel cigarettes for Dr. Bansmer.[13]

Needless to say, elevating the quality of the medical staff was an early and urgent priority for the Cooperative and its better doctors. Like a chain, a group medical practice is only as strong as its weakest link, and Group Health acted quickly to dismiss physicians who did not meet its high standards. Despite the Medical Society's continuing refusal to admit Group Health doctors and the novelty of cooperative medicine, Group Health was able to attract topnotch replacements. Part of the reason was its deference to professional needs and requests. It was in everyone's best interest at Group Health, according to MacColl, to hire "good, well-educated, up-to-date physicians to take care of them." Therefore, Group Health's doctor contracts and policies accommodated postgraduate study and leaves, reasonable rotation schedules for night and weekend shifts, and whatever else it took to assure that "the staff be in good shape at all times."[14]

St. Luke's Hospital's physical shape was another matter. The rooms were small, and patients and gurneys were often parked in the hallways. The old hospital had been built early in the century, when electric lighting was still feeble, so its operating room was built with a glass roof to let in sunlight. It also let in rain, irrigating a garden of moss and mildew in dark corners, and John Kloeck complained that the room's hygiene was compromised. Despite this and other deficiencies, a representative of the AMA's Council on Medical Services assured Group Health during a visit on January 16, 1947, that "chances are good" for accreditation.[15]

The building's main drawback was the lack of space for a walk-in clinic. This forced doctors and patients to shuttle between the hospital and Group Health's downtown clinic in the Securities Building. The Cooperative's first capital priorities were clear, but modernizing the hospital and relocating the clinic to Capitol Hill would take money, and money would take new members.

The previous fall's battle over the MSC purchase produced surprisingly light casualties in terms of lost members. Bernie Pearce estimated that only 12 percent of Group Health's members, or about 50 families, turned in their cards. New recruits took their place and the rolls listed 363 members on December 13. Twenty more signed up by January 1. (GHC reported its memberships on the basis of families, not individuals, so the actual number of people served was greater than these figures suggest.)[16]

As Director of Education, Bob Mitchell reorganized the membership program with the goal of reaching a total enrollment of 800 by the end of 1947, and the Board extended the deadline for charter member sign-up (without a medical exam and restrictions) to January 15. No prospect was too remote: Mitchell once tracked down a potential member through her father in Coeur d'Alene, Idaho. His assistant, Bill Jordan, was equally tenacious, manning telephones all day and making late-night forays to round up recruits. Jordan also edited the monthly *Group Health News*, which began publishing in January 1947, and produced the April 1947 edition of *Cooperative Health*, a one-time slick magazine designed to introduce current and prospective members to Group Health.[17]

This magazine featured essays by Drs. Beeler, McNeel, and Hardwicke on the virtues of group practice and preventive healthcare. The most enthusiastic pitch was penned by Bob Mitchell, who praised the cooperative way as "the freest kind of enterprise." He compared Group Health to the Pilgrims, "turning back to the God-given instinct—neighbor helping neighbor to build and provide better health to enjoy freedom from fear, freedom from exploitation, freedom from economic chaos, freedom from sickness" by banishing "the element of greed and profit."

It was Bob Mitchell's last stem-winder for the cooperative cause and Group Health. In early May, having barely begun the job he dreamed of back in the early 1940s, when he and Ad Shoudy first united to promote a cooperative health program, Mitchell suffered a fatal heart attack while working on his new house in Renton. The entire national cooperative movement mourned the loss of one of its most ardent champions.[18]

Group Health pressed on, signing up members catch-as-catch-can but in growing numbers. The program had special appeal for military veterans, who were now flooding the job market or attending college with the aid of the GI bill. Being in uniform represented the first exposure to systematic healthcare for many, and, in the opinion of the charter member and merchant seaman Walter Philipp, "They felt this worked out so well that we really should have this kind of medical service available for the consumer, under the consumer's control."[19]

Bill Jordan promoted Group Health through meetings, brochures, and newsletters, but word of mouth remained the most effective sales medium. Irwin Johnson, for example, joined after hearing two women talking about Group Health on the bus. "They extolled the virtues of a wonderful new clinic that offered complete care for a fixed monthly fee." Not all the gossip was positive: When Mrs. Eugene Lux told her employers, a group of doctors, that she and her husband were considering joining Group Health, "They explained to her that Group Health was a Communist front, that the doctors were all quacks." For many people at that time, trustee Bob Scott remembers, "Anything that was not a profit operation was ipso facto a Communist one."[20]

Memberships had passed 500 by the time of the first semiannual membership meeting on April 25, 1947, but these were not enough to balance the dwindling number of industrial enrollees inherited from Medical Security. Group Health also confronted a new set of problems. First, charter members were taxing staff and resources for their unrestricted care, and second, the postwar baby boom was starting to rumble through St. Luke's delivery room. Group Health was losing $3,000 a month trying to keep up with the demand for its services. The Board proposed drastic measures: imposing a "temporary" waiver on treatment of charter members' pre-existing conditions, closing membership to people over the age of 65, and charging a $75 fee for maternity care. The membership overwhelmingly approved these reforms when it reconvened on May 12.[21]

Group Health's mounting deficit also forced MSC's original stockholders to take a second, more realistic look at the price they had set for the clinic's assets and contracts—as Addison Shoudy had predicted a year earlier. At the membership meeting held in Renton on October 18, the Board announced that a new agreement had lowered the outstanding sales price to $100,000, of which $75,000 was to be paid off in two equal installments due that November 15, and the following March 1. The Board took out a trust mortgage secured by the sale of $100,000 in "Pioneer Bonds" at 3 percent interest. In addition to cutting their original price by $80,000, the MSC shareholders accepted $25,000 in bonds for the balance.[22]

The Pioneer Bond campaign was an audacious proposal for a tiny organization living from hand to mouth, but Group Health had new reasons to believe it could succeed. Under the guidance of Jack Fortnum, Bob Mitchell's temporary successor, and Bill Jordan, the membership program had been reorganized on the basis of districts, much like a political campaign. The decentralized approach dramatically increased member participation and signed up 400 new recruits during the summer and fall. The Board believed that the new bonds could be sold in the same way, but it saw even greater potential in the district system as a "definite means for democratic participation."[23]

The Board also acted to improve Group Health's internal management. Dr. Beeler, although an enthusiastic convert to cooperatism, proved less than able as an administrator. He graciously accepted a new title as Group Health's cooperative organizer, and soon relocated to eastern Washington. The Board launched a formal search for a permanent replacement while the accountant Lewis Jones and, later, Rudy Molzan, agreed to serve in the interim. Board membership also changed in the fall as Al Annibal and Charles Berger's seats were taken by D. M. Johnson and Frank Stewart.[24]

The year 1947 closed on three upbeat notes with the proceeds from the sale of $20,000 worth of bonds in the bank, an enrollment of more than 1,000, and Renton voters' approval of a new Public Hospital District and Commission on December 16. The last gave Group Health leaders hope that they might finally get to use, if not own, the federal hospital they had coveted for so long.25

While the purchase and integration of the Medical Security Clinic had dominated Group Health's attention for the past 18 months, the Board never abandoned its dream of establishing clinics in Renton, Enumclaw, and Pierce County. It also went as far as drawing up papers to take over the Kitsap Cooperative Hospital Association. (This plan appears to have collapsed after voters rejected a hospital district for Bremerton in fall 1948.)[26]

Of these possible clinic sites, Renton had first claim on Group Health's attention. The Cooperative had 376 members in the "Renton trade area" by April, and the transportation system of the day made treks to downtown Seattle or Capitol Hill inconvenient for working-class families in the South End. Renton was also the stronghold of many of the union and Grange leaders who had helped found Group Health and upon whose continued support the Cooperative's survival depended.27

Group Health maintained its own formal bid for Renton's surplus federal hospital, but it dropped active negotiations in favor of other local efforts. Initially, it provided counsel and encouragement to the new Valley Medical Foundation, which leased the hospital for one year beginning in 1946, but the Foundation fell under the sway of the King County Medical Society and excluded Group Health physicians. When federal authorities rejected the Foundation's bid to purchase the hospital for "lack of standing in the community," Group Health's attention shifted to organizing a public hospital district under a 1945 state law written by State Representative U. S. Ford, an Olympic Peninsula physician and ally of progressive causes.[28]

In anticipation of access to the Renton Hospital (which opened under public district control in 1949), Group Health rented a small house in the town from trustee Sid Schaudies and opened its first satellite clinic on July 6, 1948. Chief of staff Dr. McNeel assigned himself to Renton, assisted by nurse-in-charge Elizabeth Owens and receptionist Martha Wiberg. McNeel's double duties soon became a problem, so a newly recruited physician, Raymond Bunker, took his place in Renton after a few months.29

On March 22, 1948, Group Health's Board finally winnowed 50 applications for its general manager down to one: a young hospital administrator named Don Northrop. It also reorganized its management and marketing plans along new lines proposed by the consulting firm of Ward, Fish, and DeForest. George

Belding and, later, Morris Seim were hired to train and deploy a force of professional salesmen, while Bill Jordan "activated" the new district system and established formal Neighborhood Advisory Councils to promote bonds and memberships while also advising Group Health on member needs and desires.[30]

These efforts met with instant and startling success as membership nearly tripled to 2,811 by year's end. While some effort was made to market group contracts, Group Health's "industrial" enrollment was allowed to decline to fewer than 8,000, chiefly through attrition or conversion to individual Cooperative memberships. It was a matter of priorities, and full Co-op members—along with their $100 initiation fees—were deemed more important than group contract enrollees.[31]

At the same time, Group Health remained loyal to "parent" organizations such as the International Association of Machinists. When IAM took its Boeing workers out on strike for 130 days during 1948, Group Health granted them membership "extensions" with deferred payments. This gesture of solidarity cemented Group Health's ties with organized labor, but it did not endear the Cooperative to company executives. Relations remained cool between Boeing and Group Health for more than 20 years to come.[32]

Overall, the picture only brightened in 1948. The hospital won accreditation from the American Medical Society despite the hostility of the local medical establishment (see next chapter), but its shortcomings remained. With more than 7,000 hospital admissions during 1947, including 403 major operations and 328 deliveries, and a swelling enrollment in 1948, the staff and Board recognized early on that expanding and modernizing the hospital was the top capital priority. On July 22, the Board approved construction of a 30-bed addition to be financed through the capital portion of membership fees.[33]

On August 6, Group Health hosted Cooperative League director Jerry Voorhis, who had recently lost his seat in Congress in a vicious, Red-baiting campaign to Richard Nixon. Voorhis proclaimed the Seattle cooperative "the most hopeful sign in the whole country for the solution of the health problem in this country."

At the November 17 annual meeting, general manager Don Northrop reported the good news that Group Health had paid off Medical Security Clinic's shareholders in full the previous month. At the same meeting, architect and "Review Committee" chairman George Bolotin cautioned that "although this difficult period has been safely passed, our organization is growing rapidly and constantly facing new problems."[34]

The membership approved two bylaw changes. One authorized Group Health to provide services on contract to members of similar health cooperatives, such as those being organized in Kitsap and Pierce counties (but nothing came of this approach to regional expansion). The other addressed a problem created by Group Health's promise to refund a member's full $100 fee if he or she left the Seattle area. The new bylaw broke the fee into a nonrefundable $25 for enrollment and a $75 "lifetime" capital contribution which could be redeemed.[35]

Ernie Conrad, chair of the Board nominations committee, presented new trustees William Birnbaum, a University of Washington professor of mathematics and statistics, and Ron Fredlund, an accountant, and incumbents Sid Schaudies, Nettie Jean Ross Cawley, and Bob Scott for election. The last succeeded Tom Bevan to become Group Health's second president and head of an organization that had in only a year grown from less than zero into a health service with assets of nearly $300,000, doing more than three-quarters of a million dollars in business.[36]

At this meeting, Addison Shoudy took his leave from the Board to devote himself full-time to the Cooperative Health Federation of America, which was then pursuing delicate negotiations with the AMA. (In 1954, Shoudy moved to the Lake Stevens area, where he established a store and published the local community newspaper until his death in 1993.) Shoudy left Group Health confident in its survival. As a veritable Northwest "Johnny Appleseed" of cooperatism, he was no doubt especially proud when employees and members founded their own Group Health

Credit Union on December 6, 1948, and Group Health helped organize the Cascade Cooperative League on December 14.[37]

The success of Group Health and the cooperative movement seemed assured—but not everyone looked upon this with favor, least of all the King County Medical Society.

Chapter 5

Group Health v. King County Medical Society

1949 ~ 1951

A Case of Pneumonia ~ Fellow "Mavericks" at Virginia Mason ~ A Friend at the AMA ~ Twenty Points ~ Jack Cluck for the Plaintiffs ~ A Historic Ruling

Group Health's celebration of voters' approval of Renton Public Hospital District Number 1 was short-lived. Soon after the hospital began operating in 1949, Group Health applied for admission privileges. At the behest of the King County Medical Society, the hospital's medical staff threatened a boycott if Group Health doctors were allowed to use the facility. The staff's position was opposed by Frank Hanley, one of the three newly elected hospital commissioners, but his colleagues Elmo Wright and Rudolph Seppi "turned out to be rather unfriendly in permitting access to the Cooperative," in Group Health attorney Jack Cluck's phrase. They voted to grant hospital privileges only to Medical Society members, effectively freezing out Group Health doctors. The physicians at Group Health might have swallowed this latest snub but for one incident that transformed the nuisance of Medical Society exclusion into a life-threatening peril for one of their patients.[1]

Early in 1949, the Seattle area was struck by a brutal winter storm. In Renton, Amos Huseland's teenage son caught a cold that quickly worsened. Huseland, who had joined Group Health in 1946 (member number 117) after hearing one of Dr. Shadid's lectures, took his boy to Dr. Raymond Bunker at the Renton Branch Clinic. Bunker immediately diagnosed the problem as pneumonia and called the Renton Hospital to arrange an emergency admission.

This was not possible, the hospital staff explained, because Dr. Bunker was not a member of the King County Medical Society. If, however, Mr. Huseland turned the case over to one of the hospital's doctors, his son would be admitted. Huseland angrily refused to surrender the right to choose his own doctor, and, as court records later described his actions, drove his son 15 miles north to Group Health Hospital "despite harsh winter conditions, with heavy snow and icy roads."[2]

The boy recovered but the Renton Hospital staff and, by extension, the Medical Society had gone too far. After months of hesitation, Group Health's physicians agreed with the Board that there was only one course of action left: It was time to take on the King County Medical Society.

Group Health's grievances against the Medical Society had been piling up from the Cooperative's inception, and Dr. Michael Shadid had long been an object of the medical establishment's special enmity. In the 1930s, only the intercession of Oklahoma's populist governor, "Alfalfa Bill" Murray, saved Shadid's license from being revoked by the state legislature. Shadid counter-attacked by suing the Oklahoma Medical Society and by heaping scorn on the "American Meddlers Association" in his pamphlets and lectures.[3]

Alarmed by Shadid's popularity during his 1945 speaking tour, the King County Medical Society attempted to abort the formation of any health cooperatives by offering its own contract plan to the state Grange and the International Association of Machinists. When this failed—the Society's Medical Service Corporation could not match the coverage or rates proposed by Shadid—the Society resorted to other tactics.[4]

In February 1946, the *Grange News* reported that King and Kitsap "county medical societies have launched a campaign combatting organization of co-op hospitals." Six months later, the *Grange News* disclosed that the King County Medical Society had circulated a letter to Renton-area physicians asking for donations to buy the federal hospital and "thereby prevent acquisition by a 'socialistic' group." In March 1947, the King County Medical Society's own *Bulletin* complained about an "undesirable contract group working in South King County." It was the Society's first printed acknowledgment of Group Health's existence.[5]

Group Health physicians endured extraordinary abuse from their colleagues in the Medical Society. "There were a lot of dirty digs passed around," Dr. William MacColl remembered. "And it even affected my children. We were living up in Ravenna at the time. Some of the children wanted to play, and they said, 'Well, your dad's unethical. We can't play with you.'"

During a dinner forum on healthcare sponsored by *The Seattle Times* in 1947, a physician refused to be seated across from MacColl. "I'll be damned if I'll sit at a table with that radical!" he announced loudly, so the host dispatched him to another dining room. At another community meeting on healthcare, MacColl found himself seated beneath a banner reading, "Compulsion: It's the Key to Collectivism." MacColl couldn't resist tweaking his fellow speaker, a Society member, by pointing out that the AMA had just levied a compulsory fee on members to fund its campaign against socialized medicine.[6]

Such confrontations might have been dismissed but for their consequences for Group Health and its patients. Foremost, the Medical Society's denial of memberships was making it increasingly difficult for the Cooperative to recruit competent physicians. Despite the hiring of Drs. Charlotte Bansmer (Gustav Bansmer's sister), Raymond Bunker, Louis Murphy, and Frank Foglianno, and optometrist Adalbert Kaminski, the total medical staff had increased by only one since 1947. Meanwhile, enrollment was soaring toward 16,000 by the end of 1949, taxing the ability of the staff to keep up with patient needs.[7]

Because "we felt at that time that we could not afford to practice poor medicine," Dr. G. Bansmer recalled, "I must say we were under a great deal of emotional strain." This was compounded when Group Health physicians found themselves unable to buy malpractice insurance through any American company. They finally secured coverage through Lloyds of London, but only up to $5,000. Beyond even this, one major insurance underwriter made a key exception to its rule prohibiting physician policyholders testifying against their medical colleagues: They were free to criticize Group Health doctors.[8]

These physicians found themselves not only ostracized and placed in financial jeopardy, but their patients were denied essential services. A few Society members quietly performed services for Group Health on the side, and Bansmer compared such secret liaisons to "having an affair." It was impossible to hide relationships with hospitals, however. In addition to Renton Hospital, Swedish, Seattle General, and other major hospitals refused staff privileges and assistance to Group Health doctors and admission to their patients. The Virginia Mason Clinic was the one notable exception.[9]

Mason physicians had themselves been shunned by the Medical Society for the sin of group practice, which fee-for-service physicians excoriated as "closed panels" that restricted patients' freedom to choose any doctor. The Society had gone so far as to threaten Dr. James Tate Mason with expulsion on the eve of his election to the presidency of the AMA in order to force him to turn over his industrial contracts to the Medical Bureau (which gave the Bureau its first clients). This history created an instant sympathy between Group Health and Mason medical staffs as "maverick organizations," notes Virginia Mason's official history. "Virginia Mason maintained an open-door policy for Group Health physicians," and both staffs began to share resources for collaborative services such as radiation therapy and pathology.[10]

Group Health had another important ally in Dr. Edwin Turner, first dean of the University of Washington's new School of Medicine and Dentistry, which opened on October 2, 1946. The State Medical Society had tenaciously opposed the school's creation from the outset, and when its establishment appeared inevitable, the Society lobbied the legislature to limit enrollment to only 50 students a year. The Medical Society's posture may seem shortsighted today, but it was governed by the basic logic of supply and demand. With thousands of physicians returning from military duty, the last thing established practitioners wanted was a school turning out hundreds of bright young competitors right in their own backyard.[11]

Such conflicts between "town and gown" were not unprecedented, but if the Society viewed the School as a menace, Dr. Turner had to be its worst nightmare. He was a vocal critic of traditional medical practice by solo physicians collecting fees for service. "The fee system will never work," he once told Ernie Conrad, and he "supported the idea of Group Health all the way along." In 1952, when UW psychologist Charles Strother was invited to join the Group Health Board, he consulted with Turner. He found the dean "very supportive. He felt this was a good direction for medicine to take and he really encouraged my going on [the Board], so I did."[12]

With such powerful support, Group Health's physicians understandably harbored hope that the Medical Society would eventually relax its opposition to the Cooperative. National trends also gave grounds for some cautious optimism as the American Medical Association gradually softened its stand against prepayment and group practice.

The AMA endorsed prepaid, doctor-managed insurance programs on the "Blue Shield" model in 1942. The following year, the U.S. Supreme Court ruled against the AMA for trying to strangle the new Group Health Association of Washington, D.C., and some thought that "organized medicine" had learned its lesson. Following the war, the AMA focused its fire on the threat of "socialized medicine" via the government, not independent health plans. In 1946, it successfully lobbied in Congress to block passage of the Wagner-Murray-Dingle bill for national health insurance. This defeat only intensified agitation for healthcare reform, a cause President Truman loudly championed during his 1948 campaign for re-election. "The AMA suddenly declared itself eager to promote the formation of alternative medical care mechanisms," Dr. MacColl later wrote, "to offset pressure for 'socialized medicine.'"[13]

At the same time, the cooperative health movement gained strength. New York City's Health Insurance Plan was launched in 1947, a culmination of planning begun under Mayor Fiorello LaGuardia four years earlier. It was one of 35 new health cooperatives organized that year, including Group Health. In 1948, the National Health Assembly, a commission appointed by President Truman, endorsed the elimination of legal and regulatory barriers faced by health cooperatives, and U.S. Senator Hubert Humphrey later proposed federal financing for health co-ops.[14]

Group Health Hospital was an accidental beneficiary of the debate within the AMA over alternative health programs. Curious about the delay in accreditation since the Hospital's January "registration," Ad Shoudy and fellow trustee Frank Stewart, a former Kaiser employee with medical contacts, decided to drop in on AMA's headquarters while attending a meeting of the Cooperative Health Federation of America in Chicago.

Initially, they encountered a bureaucratic runaround, with assurances from an aide that "it's being studied." That evening, the same aide paid a surprise visit to Shoudy and Stewart at their hotel. He was disgruntled at not being promoted to a better job at the AMA, so he gave them a more candid report on Group Health's application. "Your inspection by the team that came into Seattle will never be passed by this group here because the Seattle Medical Association [*sic*] has put a stop to it." The aide promised to help Shoudy meet the AMA's manager the next morning in an effort to overcome the hurdle.

Shoudy was nervous when he was ushered into the office of AMA manager, Dr. George F. Lull, without an appointment. "I hit the wrong pew, I guess, coming in like this," he confessed, but Lull liked what Shoudy told him about Group Health. He had his own confession: "I believe in group practice and prepaid medicine."

Shoudy replied, "You don't say that too loud around here, do you?"

"No, I don't," Lull admitted. "I am kind of feeling my way. Because I know that is what is coming."

Lull moved Group Health Hospital's accreditation from the bottom of the AMA in-basket to the top and promised to "see it through." He did, and the Hospital won approval on July 26, 1948.[15]

With Truman's re-election that November, the battle over socialized medicine resumed. Against this backdrop, Dr. Shadid and other representatives of the Cooperative Health Federation of America, including Group Health's chief of staff Dr. John McNeel, initiated a series of quiet conversations with AMA officials. Months of negotiation ultimately yielded agreement on 21 ethical and organizational criteria by which a prepaid health plan run by nonphysicians might gain AMA approval. These principles specified that such programs should be nonprofit, financially responsible, subject to inspection and accreditation, and be structured to offer members "free choice among participating physicians" and prevent any "interference by the governing body with the medical staff in the practice of medicine."[16]

The last of these 21 principles made the previous 20 criteria binding on local medical societies as the "standard guide for evaluation." When the AMA's House of Delegates took up the package at its Chicago convention, everything but the principle of mandatory local conformity was adopted on June 4, 1949. Passage of what became known as the "Twenty Points" drew no cheers from reform advocates because, as Shadid noted, "Many societies indicated that twenty points or no twenty points, they would not work with cooperatives." Allowing local discretion had "the practical effect," Dr. MacColl later wrote, "of nullifying the whole effort."[17]

While the AMA debated the Twenty Points, Group Health doctors made a final push for Medical Society recognition. Their first disappointment came on April 29, when the Society rejected the transfer of chief of staff Dr. John McNeel's membership from Virginia, which he had requested nearly two years earlier. Soon after, Dr. Bansmer was told in so many words that he was ineligible because he worked for Group Health. "I was told essentially to bug off. This was just another part of the nice treatment we got."[18]

Dr. Beeler then offered his services in an effort to mediate a solution. On the evening of June 7, three days after adoption of the Twenty Points, he hosted a dinner attended by several Group Health physicians and Medical Society trustees. The latter were candid and told Beeler and his companions that if Group Health were accepted, "the economy of medical practice in Seattle would be badly disturbed." Even when Group Health physicians voted officially two weeks later to oppose "any compulsory government health program," it made no dent whatsoever in the Medical Society's armor. Dr. Bansmer and his colleagues concluded, "We were not going to get anywhere with these meetings."[19]

Finally, Dr. McNeel wrote to Dr. Charles Watt, president of the King County Medical Society, on August 10, 1949. He firmly insisted that the Society sit down with Group Health to "establish a procedure by which this group may be recognized as an approved consumer-supported Health Plan" before the end of the month. August 31 came and went with no progress, and Jack Cluck got the green light to sue the King County Medical Society.[20]

Cluck's essential theory was that the Society, its members, and hospitals were participating in a conscious conspiracy to monopolize contracts for the King County Medical Service Corporation, which acted as a broker for doctors belonging to the Society's Medical Bureau. By declaring "contract medicine" to be "unethical" unless it was provided by participants in the Bureau, the Society intentionally sought to prevent any doctors from competing with its own healthcare plan.

Only "ethical" doctors could join the Society, thereby excluding any physician who dared to challenge the Medical Bureau's monopoly. Since it was also unethical for any Society member to assist a physician who was not a member of the Society, the rule denied Group Health and other contract healthcare providers (the Bridge Clinic was then the only other service in Seattle) access to hospitals and consulting specialists without expressly discriminating against such groups.

Passage of the AMA's Twenty Points made it all the more clear that promotion of economic advantage, not ethical conduct, was the real object of the Society's policies and actions. This principle of restraint of trade by a "trust" of physicians had been the basis of the U.S. Supreme Court's 1943 ruling in behalf of the Group Health Association of Washington, D.C. It was also the basis of a successful litigation brought by the federal government in 1948 against the Oregon Medical Association for excluding co-op physicians who worked in that state and, crucially, across state lines.[21]

Unfortunately, Group Health's complaint did not fall under federal jurisdiction, and Washington did not have its own fair trade statute. Group Health and its political allies tried to remedy this in Olympia by passing House Bill 185. The February 1949 issue of *Group Health News* urged Group Health members to write their legislators in support of the bill, because "passage would make it much easier for us to press an anti-monopoly suit—in case such a suit is deemed expedient."

The proposed law failed, so Cluck had to fall back on Article XXII, Section 22 of the Washington State Constitution, which prohibits monopolies and trusts from "fixing the price or limiting the production...of any product or commodity." He knew it would be a stretch, however, to get a court to recognize medical care as a "product or commodity."

British Common Law, which is recognized in American courts, offered a more compelling if historically distant precedent: the 1919 case of one Dr. Pratt versus the British Medical Society. Pratt was employed by the Coventry Provident Dispensary, which served about 20,000 prepaid subscribers. He was one of several new physicians hired when the previous staff walked out in a dispute with management. The local Medical Society ordered its members to boycott Coventry in support of the former staff, and retaliated against Pratt and other new physicians by expelling and formally "ostracizing" them.

Pratt sued for reinstatement and damages. The British judge held that the Society's rules "are in restraint of trade, and are void upon the ground of public policy. They gravely, and in my view unnecessarily, interfere with the freedom of medical men in the pursuit of their calling, and they are, I think, injurious to the interest of the community at large."[22]

Group Health filed its suit in King County Superior Court on November 25, 1949. To make his case, Cluck organized Group Health's staff and physicians in an intensive research program to document the activities of the King County Medical Society, individual physicians, and most major hospitals. (Group Health did not sue the AMA in recognition of the value of the Twenty Points and Dr. Lull's help behind the scenes.) Members and friends of Group Health went to work raising the $25,000 needed to bring the case to trial.[23]

"In our abundant free time," Bansmer later joked, "we had the delightful chore of reading their newsletters and bulletins and things like that." The effort was not wasted. It yielded a whole armory of smoking guns, including an article in a 1937 Society *Bulletin* declaring that "the success of this [Medical Bureau] plan depends upon the Bureau having a monopoly of the contract practice." This was to be accomplished by "declaring it unethical for any members to consult or assist a man engaged" in non-Bureau contract medicine. Such examples of unfair competition, conspiracy, and other efforts to control the practice of medicine for economic gain ultimately filled 23 volumes of evidence.[24]

Group Health cleared the first legal hurdle in January 1950 when Judge Roger Meakim found it had sufficient cause for a suit. The trial opened on May 24 before Judge Howard Findley. Cluck's meticulous examination of scores of witnesses, and the Society's aggressive defense stretched out over five weeks.[25]

Group Health was stunned on July 14, when Judge Findley dismissed its suit. Cluck and client were even more flabbergasted when they read Findley's memorandum of opinion, in which he declared, "The evidence in this case fails to show malice or ill will on the part of the defendants...[or] to establish a conspiracy or combination, the object of which was to injure the plaintiffs."

Findley continued, "I can come to no other conclusion than what the defendants did was done by them bona fide in the protection not only of their own interests, but those of their profession and the welfare of humanity, and to that end they adopted such reasonable rules and regulations as were calculated to maintain and advance the standards of the medical profession."[26]

Findley had essentially conceded the facts of exclusion and collusion, but he refused to interpret them as an economic conspiracy. This gave Cluck hope for an appeal to the State Supreme Court, but both Group Health's Board and its physicians were reluctant to proceed. Cluck won them over by promising to limit Group Health's costs to $5,000.[27]

Cluck then prepared an elegant appellant's brief that ran to 292 pages of tightly reasoned citation and argument. The Medical Society and its remaining codefendants (Swedish Hospital was dropped from the case) were equally meticulous, recognizing that "the magnitude of the case, the seriousness of the issues" had national implications.[28]

The State Supeme Court heard oral arguments on June 27 and then began its deliberations. Shoudy, for one, never doubted the outcome because he trusted the fairness of Supreme Court Justice Frederick G. Hamley, whose candidacy for the Seattle City Council years earlier he had supported. Another vocal friend and former cooperative supporter, Justice Finley, recused himself, as did Justice Olson.[29]

The unanimous ruling of the remaining seven Justices was announced on November 17, 1951. Written by Justice Hamley, the decision began by declaring, "This action brings to a head the long and vigorous struggle of the King County Medical Society to curb independent medical and hospital services in King County. In late years the battle has been waged chiefly against Group Health Cooperative of Puget Sound." The Supreme Court went on to find for Group Health on virtually all of its allegations. While the Court did not grant financial damages, it took the extraordinary step of placing the Society under effective probation for three years, during which any further interference with Group Health would be deemed contempt of court.[30]

Dr. Bansmer remembered when the news of the decision reached Seattle. "One Group Health member used to run a liquor store on 4th Avenue and we tried to drain the place. We did have enough sense to take a cab and go home," he added.

"It was back to work as usual the next day."[31]

Chapter 6

Growing Pains

1950 ~ 1952

Too Many Patients, Too Few Doctors ~
Expanding on Capitol Hill, Holding on in
Renton ~ Trustee Elections by District ~ The
Red Scare ~ A Fight over Physicals ~
Management Falters and Dr. McNeel Departs

*T*hings were not quite as usual at Group Health, for the Cooperative had changed in many ways during the two years it took to battle the Medical Society in court. Foremost, it had grown dramatically. The new district-based sales strategy worked beyond anyone's wildest expectations. Cooperative memberships leapt from 2,811 families at the end of 1948 to 3,958 at the end of 1949, surpassing Group Health's industrial contract enrollment. By the end of 1952, Group Health served 22,440 individual Co-op members, compared with 9,761 group contractees.[1]

The largest share of group business, more than 2,200 enrollees, was constituted by a contract with the International Longshoremen and Warehousemen's Union, first signed in 1951. The ILWU's representative to Group Health, Goldie Krantz, pressed the Board relentlessly to extend coverage to another 2,500 worker dependents. This represented nearly $17,000 in monthly income for the cash-starved Cooperative, but Group Health's managing director, Don Northrop, feared that covering such a huge group would require dropping other contracts. He warned against "placing all our eggs in one basket" at an unknown cost in service. (Krantz prevailed in 1953, and, as Northrop predicted, Group Health lost money on the contract.)[2]

Dr. Gustav Bansmer had helped to solicit the ILWU contract on the theory that the enrollees would be "for the most part healthy young males." Before long, however, the waiting list for hernia operations numbered as many as 50. "When we had time, we'd go ahead and do them," Bansmer remembered. "What the heck, they weren't hard to do." At the same time he and his colleagues opposed adding ILWU dependents.[3]

Group Health's 17 physicians were already drowning beneath the flood of new Cooperative members. Dr. John Quinn grumbled, "All that you are selling are policies to the lame, the halt, and the blind." Bansmer echoed most of Group Health's physicians when he complained, "They can't keep loading all these people on our necks."[4]

The problem was that the hiring of new physicians lagged far behind the growth in membership. In January 1951, chief of staff Dr. John McNeel cited three factors for Group Health's inability to recruit additional staff: the Medical Society's hostility, "deficiencies" in Group Health's facilities, and the Korean War draft. The last of these was outside Group Health's control, and the fighting would not wind down until July 1953.[5]

The first was only partially relieved by Group Health's legal victory. Although the Medical Society officially inducted the Cooperative's physicians into membership in July 1952, Group Health remained the target of medical establishment enmity. Private doctors and their patients spread snide gibes about "Group Death," despite the fact that the Cooperative's patient mortality rate was half the national average. Dr. William MacColl later compared the relationship between the Group Health and the Medical Society to "the partners in a shotgun wedding; we are getting along all right in spite of some of the sharp comments of the inlaws."[6]

Physical expansion and improvement bogged down after Group Health Hospital (the name "St. Luke's" was retired in July 1948) opened its new 30-bed north wing on August 9, 1950. Plans for a further expansion, including a clinic and doctors' offices, ran into neighborhood opposition led by a local church and some merchants who feared Group Health's impacts on traffic and parking. Estimated construction costs eventually soared to $500,000. Lenders weren't interested in the project, and Board president Bob Scott told the April 1950 annual meeting "that no financial organization seems to be willing to buck the reactionary forces that do not want us to succeed in this building program." Group Health's own bond sales, while impressive, fell far short of the cost of the new "West Wing."[7]

Meanwhile, Group Health's landlord at the Securities Building hiked the monthly clinic rent from $1,000 to $3,500, and the swelling enrollment made shuttling staff and patients between downtown and Capitol Hill all the more inefficient. As a last resort, Group Health began negotiating with a Mrs. Westover to purchase her Costa Vista apartment building at the corner of 15th Avenue and John Street. Talks dragged on for over a year, and she demanded that Group Health find her a comparable income property to support her retirement.[8]

Such a building was finally found on Queen Anne Hill in February 1951, and the deal for Costa Vista was closed for a total of $154,000. It ultimately cost another $260,000 to remodel the building, which Seattle First National Bank agreed to finance with a trust mortgage. The new clinic opened on June 16, 1952. Group Health also bought two parking lots and later signed a lease-purchase agreement for a drug store across John Street, into which it moved its pharmacy.[9]

Progress on the new clinic did little to relieve the pressure on the medical staff, which had increased to only 23 by mid-1952 to serve 27,700 enrollees, not counting dependents. It also left important constituencies within the membership unsatisfied. They wanted the "branch clinics" that they felt they had been promised since Group Health's inception.[10]

Ideas had previously been floated for clinics in White Center and Enumclaw. Following the failure of the Kitsap hospital district in November 1948, the Board considered purchasing a Poulsbo clinic that the Kitsap County Cooperative Health Association had equipped at a cost of $40,000. But Group Health couldn't spare any physicians or the $20,000 in annual operating costs to serve a few hundred members. Not long after, a group of Tacoma residents approached Group Health for inclusion and, possibly, a future clinic.[11]

Next, the Board briefly entertained a proposal from the North End Co-op to establish a clinic in a new center it was building at North 47th Street and Stone Way, but nothing came of the idea. At the same time, Group Health members on Vashon Island demanded refunds because they found it inconvenient to commute to the mainland for medical care.[12]

The most strident demands for a clinic came from the one locality that already had one, Renton. They wanted something more than a converted house staffed by a single physician, a nurse, and a receptionist. The medical staff agreed that branch clinics should have a minimum of four physicians on duty, and since Group Health could spare only one, they argued that the Renton Clinic should be closed. This almost happened when Renton's lone physician, Dr. Warner, resigned, in January 1951.[13]

The Board refused to shutter Renton. The area represented a tenth of Group Health's Cooperative membership and included some of its most active supporters. Renton's clout was magnified by a crucial reform of Group Health's governance: the creation of districts for nominating a majority of Board seats.

When Jack Fortnum first suggested creating districts as a way to organize membership sales in 1947, Addison Shoudy recognized that they might also provide a foundation for member democracy. The idea was endorsed in principle at the November 17, 1948, membership meeting. The following June, the Board and members discussed three options: a 15-member board with 11 districts, an 11-member board with 7 districts, and a 9-member board with 5 districts. (These were later dubbed "nominating areas" to avoid confusion with smaller membership districts. New lines were drawn in 1954 to add a sixth nominating area, and in 1955, two more nominating districts were established to expand the Board to 11 members.)

Group Health's first district-based board election was held on November 5, 1949, and the existing board resigned so that the Cooperative could begin with a clean slate. District nominees Virgil Chadwick, George Hunter, D. M. Johnson, Bob Scott, and Bob Wells were elected, along with at-large candidates Tom Bevan, William Birnbaum, Jean Ross Cawley, and John King (the election of a West Seattle representative was delayed until 1950).[14]

There is no question that the new district system revitalized consumer participation in Group Health, but this fact gave some cause for anxiety. Jack Cluck and other members of the newly formed Americans for Democratic Action (ADA) worried that the districts opened a door to communist infiltration, a topic then very much in the news.

The postwar Red scare is today identified with Wisconsin Senator Joseph McCarthy, but he actually entered the scene relatively late and the first steps to identify and ostracize members of the Communist Party were taken by liberal Democrats—not conservative Republicans. The purges began in 1947 when President Truman signed an executive order demanding loyalty oaths from federal employees. Inspired by liberals such as Hubert Humphrey, activist Democrats organized the ADA to drive Communists and "fellow-travellers" from the party and labor unions. Even the American Civil Liberties Union expelled communists—including long-time leaders—from its ranks.

Also in 1947, while the House Un-American Activities Committee launched sweeping investigations of Hollywood and the State Department, local Red hunters won approval of the Joint Legislative Fact-Finding Committee on Un-American Activities. Chaired by State Representative Albert Canwell of Okanogan, this committee conducted three years of hearings chiefly targeted on ferreting out subversives among Seattle organizations and on the faculty of the University of Washington.

Group Health never fell under direct scrutiny, but several former allies from the days of the Washington Commonwealth and Church of the People became star attractions in Canwell's circus. The FBI interviewed new trustee Aubrey Davis and others about "Communist members" of Group Health (which amused Davis since he was then himself a security officer for the Wage Stabilization Board). "They were very impatient with me," Davis recalled, when he refused to betray his colleagues.

The paranoia was so pervasive that Bill Jordan, director of Group Health's membership services, feared he might be subpoenaed simply because he once subscribed to the Washington Commonwealth's newsletter, which had been edited by a communist, Terry Pettus. The FBI also quizzed Jordan about Group

Health leaders Julius Draznin and Bob Wells, but suspicion within and without Group Health focused foremost on William Pennock, whom many Group Health leaders suspected as having helped organize opposition to the Cooperative's purchase of the Medical Security Clinic.

Following approval of the new district system, the Board took special care to review membership applications with an eye to detecting and blackballing any potential "troublemakers." On September 19, 1950, Pennock's name appeared on the roster of applicants, and the Board voted three to one to reject him.

It is unknown whether Pennock approached Group Health or was in fact solicited by its ever-eager sales staff. In the case of activist attorney John Caughlan, it was Group Health that came to him, and he was frankly surprised. He was already notorious for representing Communist Party head Earl Browder in appealing the city government's revocation of permission to lecture at the Civic Auditorium (this cost him his post as secretary of the local ACLU chapter). He never heard back on his application, and when he inquired, he was informed that it had been rejected because he was a communist (he wasn't) and the Board feared a "take-over." "Communists should be so smart," Caughlan later joked.

Pennock decided to press the issue and asked for reconsideration. This prompted a heated debate among members of the Board Executive Committee on March 15, 1951. Don Northrop explained that Pennock had been rejected because of "questionable activities, associations and public statements and because of actual incidents with which [trustees] Mr. King and Mr. Scott were acquainted." Bob Wells and architect George Bolotin questioned the ethics of "an individual being denied because of his political convictions." Paul Goodin replied that Pennock had been a "disrupting influence in any organization with which he was associated." Wells and Bolotin were unpersuaded, and the committee referred the matter back to the full Board.

The Board took up the matter nine days later. Ben Asia, a new trustee and longtime attorney for unions and cooperatives, joined Bolotin and Wells in defending Pennock's application, but they were outvoted. The matter was revived one more time, when a Mr. Jacobson (possibly Group Health accountant Walter Jacobson) questioned the rejection at the April membership meeting. Board president Bob Scott explained that "by his past actions [Pennock] could be expected to use the democratic procedures and principles of this organization" to advance causes other than healthcare. Scott and the majority of the trustees tried to draw a line between a person's political views, which were not the proper concern of the Cooperative, and a person's *behavior* as a member of the organization, which was a legitimate issue if it would likely prove disruptive. This delicate distinction left some unconvinced.

Julius Draznin, a veteran member, took exception "on the basis that applicants should not be discriminated [against] on the basis of race, religion or political conviction." He pointed out that Group Health's contract with the Longshoremen's Union might fail to meet the Board's test, since it (and its leader, Harry Bridges) had "been accused of being Communistically controlled." The minutes also identify Lyle Mercer and Annie Koppel as speaking for Pennock, and Addison Shoudy remembered that he and Ben Asia also defended him in the discussion. "And right away, we got branded as Communists," Shoudy added.

The membership finally agreed with Hilde Birnbaum that "with that climate, a Communist in Group Health was just not acceptable." They upheld the Board in rejecting Pennock's application, but there was no celebration. "I think a lot of members were sort of shamefaced about that time and later," recalled Aubrey Davis. "[They] didn't feel too good about that. It never happened again."

Not long after his rejection by Group Health, William Pennock was prosecuted under the Smith Act for advocating the violent overthrow of the government. During the trial, in which John Caughlan served as his attorney, the years of harassment and exclusion finally proved too much to bear. On August 3, 1953, William Pennock took a fatal overdose of drugs.[15]

The district system created a forum for other political debates of a more conventional, but no less passionate, variety.

Members living north and south of central Seattle intensified their appeals for local clinics, and trustees such as Ben Asia stepped up pressure for preventive health programs, particularly annual physical examinations, which they felt were receiving short shrift from the medical staff.

This charge exasperated some of the medical staff. Dr. MacColl complained, "This is where fact and mythology clash. You can have everybody in for a physical exam once a month and what would you prevent?" Dr. Quinn tried to explain to the Board that "We are doing these things...but we don't separate them from ordinary medical practice."[16]

Board advocates were not convinced. In November 1950, chief of staff Dr. McNeel announced that a "preventive medical program has finally falteringly been gotten underway" with the hiring of a specialist, Dr. Irving Nieman. At the same time, Group Health hired its first public health nurse, Ruth Stoneman, and it increased the health education content in its monthly *News & Information* magazine.[17]

Dr. Nieman made his first report to the Board on December 28, 1950. He defined preventive medicine as "that branch of the art and science which deals with the <u>application</u> of any principles which may be expected to protect the individual from illness, minimize the ill-effects of disease, prolong life and promote good health [original emphasis]." Nieman further divided "preventive medical practice" into strategies for communicable and noncommunicable diseases. The former relied on vaccinations, education, and sanitation, while the latter relied chiefly on early diagnosis.[18]

Nieman later systematized his recommendations in a program of one-time "multi-phasic examinations" (chest X-ray, blood test, etc.) and vaccinations to establish a baseline for each Group Health member. This was offered as a substitute for annual physical exams, which the medical staff regarded as useless and distracting rituals, but the plan encountered much member resistance.

Such debates over preventive healthcare were unique to Group Health and helped to establish its leadership in the field, but they also managed to rub some Group Health doctors the wrong way. Their frustration was compounded by the Cooperative's rapid growth, the inability to recruit new staff, delays in opening a new central clinic, and stalled negotiations over salaries and pensions. Some physicians also resented the Board's forays into electoral politics, its open advocacy of a compulsory national health insurance program, and its efforts to organize other cooperatives.

These grievances were exacerbated by serious deficiencies in Group Health's administrative systems. To remedy these, Stanley Erickson conducted a detailed program audit in late 1950. Building on an earlier survey conducted by Dr. Richard Weinerman for the University of California—Berkeley School of Public Health, Erickson's report spotlighted serious flaws in purchasing, billing, record-keeping, personnel, and other vital management functions, and he outlined a series of concrete reforms. On a more fundamental level, Erickson proposed that administrative leadership should be divided between a "managing director" and a "medical director" elected by the staff.

Erickson's recommendation was supported by Don Northrop, who noted that the former medical director (presumably Dr. Beeler) had attempted to "control and dictate to the Board." The Board approved the Erickson Plan on February 24, 1951. Only newly elected trustee Paul Goodin dissented, saying he feared that the division of administration "would create friction rather than eliminate it."

He was right. The medical staff had its own ideas, which Dr. Nieman summed up in a memorandum dated March 12, 1951. At the urging of Dr. McNeel, he outlined several reforms including an immediate three-month moratorium on new memberships. On the issue of administrative authority, Nieman declared "there should be a single controlling administrator who should be medically trained and not be expected to practice medicine."[19]

Three days after Nieman's memo arrived, Dr. McNeel tendered his resignation as chief of staff. His letter offered little concrete cause, beyond the Cooperative's by now well-documented administrative failings. He made one enigmatic allusion to a "minority of the participants who abuse the use of the service, but under the difficult conditions which the doctors have to work, this small minority seems like a very large number, indeed. This results in the greatest degree of unhappiness which exists in the professional staff and, I might add, the lay staff as well."

McNeel's letter exudes an aura of profound mental and emotional exhaustion. He hoped his resignation would let in "new blood in trying to revamp" Group Health. He closed by prodding the Board to consider the issues raised by Nieman "urgently and immediately" because "they too are a part and parcel of the uneasiness and friction and lack of coordination tending toward the major schism in the organization."[20]

The Board, which was preoccupied with the Pennock affair and the Medical Society lawsuit at the time, seemed to be at a loss at how to react to McNeel's resignation. The medical staff elected Dr. John Quinn its new chief, and McNeel remained on staff until July, when he left to apply for a post at the Labor Health Institute in St. Louis, and died shortly thereafter.[21]

Word of internal dissension began to spread among the membership, and Bill Jordan warned the Board that a "dangerous situation was developing with rumors." A crisis was averted for the moment, and that November's membership meeting was a festive occasion, coming only two days after the Supreme Court ruling in favor of Group Health. Dr. Weinerman lectured on group practice and Dr. Bernice Sachs, wife of Group Health's new chief of surgery, Dr. Allan Sachs, gave a popular talk on psychosomatic medicine, after which the Cooperative pledged to help organize a "city psychiatric clinic." The membership elected two new members to the board, IAM leader John Carruth and federal housing official Aubrey Davis. It agreed that two annual meetings per year were one too many, and voted not to convene again until April 1953.[22]

This was good, because new president Paul Goodin and the Board would need all the breathing room they could get.

Chapter 7

Childhood's End

1952 ~ 1955

A Surgeon Is Cut and a Director Departs ~ The
Board and Medical Staff Go to the Mat ~ Hilde
Birnbaum Fights Discrimination ~ Dr. MacColl
Delivers a Healthy Cooperative

*I*f the staff of Group Health was pulling long hours for little
pay, it couldn't fault the Board for not equaling its commitment. Bob Scott later recalled, "We had many, many meetings just on the details of operation of the clinic." Trustees would
meet "until 10 or 12 o'clock at night and they'd adjourn down to
the Blackhawk Tavern" and "sit and talk for another two hours.
Some of those meetings would run to 2 o'clock in the morning,
sometimes only one night a week, sometimes two or three
nights."[1]

This tremendous expenditure of volunteer effort was not
without its drawbacks. The Board involved itself in every facet
of Group Health, and its participation was not always welcome
or necessarily constructive.

Board-staff relations began to sour anew early in 1952. In
January, trustees ignored Dr. Quinn's objections to approve coverage for Longshoremen's dependents and to make a contribution to former trustee Fred Nelson's campaign for Renton Hospital Commissioner. The following month, the Board pressed the
medical staff to hire a "health educator" to augment the preventive medicine program and to implement a "family doctor" program, both of which it opposed.[2]

Meanwhile, no agreement had yet been reached on a new medical staff contract. Dr. MacColl fired back, "Staff puts out a good day's work in the interest of keeping the cost of medical care down and then sees the budget whittled into by numerous auxilliary functions such as the Cascade [Cooperative] League and other things not actually related to medical service." Dr. Quinn also attacked the Board's expenditures on cooperative organizing and political campaigns, which he estimated as having already cost between $8,000 and $10,000.[3]

Amid this rancorous debate, Dr. Quinn informed Dr. Allan Sachs that eight of his colleagues had asked for his resignation and that the medical staff would conduct a hearing on March 17. Sachs had joined the staff as chief of surgery two years earlier, and, at the time, it was regarded as a coup to recruit a board-certified surgeon who would defy the Medical Society's blacklist.

Sachs ignored the summons and instead contacted his allies on the Board. The staff delayed its hearing until March 25, at which time it voted 17 to 5 to dismiss Sachs. The grievances against Sachs only tangentially concerned his skill and competence, although he was implicated in at least one incident involving a minor surgical error. The real issue was his personality, which even his defenders conceded could be "difficult."[4]

Dr. Charlotte Bansmer recalled "He wasn't a person with a very pleasant personality." He had the "attitude that he was running the department and everything that he said was the law." Her view might be discounted since her brother Gustav was one of Sachs' loudest critics and his likely successor, but others agreed with her assessment.

Lab director John Kloeck served as secretary for the medical staff meetings and reported, "The surgeons who worked with [Sachs], by and large, were the ones who had the most objections." Aubrey Davis admits, "The more I knew him, the more I understood how the medical staff was unhappy with him."

The real issue was Sachs' compatibility within a small and overworked cadre of physicians. Even Sachs' wife Bernice conceded, "Allan was a very forthright person who doesn't pull any punches, and created a lot of hostility and resentment." She added, "Medical people who have not gotten their [specialty] certification, which is the imprimatur of respectability and acceptability, take umbrage at being criticized for their work. And so I think there was a lot of bad feeling on both sides."[5]

A delegation of trustees met with the medical staff on March 21, but the lines of contention only hardened. The issue of Sachs' dismissal was taken up by the full Board on March 27, and after that, in Kloeck's words, "it became the Italian Parliament." Davis remembered, "Al didn't think their [other surgeons'] standards were high enough." Board members "thought to fire a guy who was being critical of your standards was a poor thing to do. And that's one of the reasons why we reacted as we did."

Jack Cluck advised the Board that the medical staff had acted legally (indeed, he had reviewed the staff's procedures at the doctors' request) and the Board's special committee on the new medical staff contract, which was still under negotiation, could see no recourse. John Carruth commented, the "important thing was not the legality of the procedure but whether the decision was based on facts, coolly and impartially considered."[6]

While the Board debated what to do, word of the dismissal spread through the membership, and many thought that Sachs had been singled out for being Jewish. Gustav Bansmer was awakened by late-night callers who accused of him of being "nothing but a Nazi," and his sister remembered, "It got quite ugly." Dr. Alfred Magar, for one, dismissed the charges of anti-Semitism: "One of the most active persons against [Sachs] was a fellow religious."[7]

The Board convened for a special meeting on April 5, 1951. After Dr. Sachs pleaded his case, the Board resolved that it "does not give status to the action of the medical staff," despite clear contract language establishing the staff's right to remove its own members on a two-thirds majority vote. The Board allowed Sachs to resign effective that day and awarded him three months' salary as severance. At the same meeting, the Board rubbed salt in the staff's wounds by pointedly noting that the current contract would expire in fewer than two years. By now the issue was no longer Sachs, but whether or not, as Dr. Magar put it, "the medical staff [was] going to accept interference from the lay board."[8]

This was the crux of a constitutional crisis, for Group Health was really two cooperatives in one. The self-governing medical staff was responsible for the conduct of its own members and for the delivery of healthcare services. It accepted the authority of the Board (and through it, the membership) in matters involving overall management and finances, including critical decisions on who and how many to serve, but the staff drew the line when it came to medical personnel and practice. In crossing this frontier, trustees risked upsetting Group Health's internal balance of power and sundering the Cooperative.

The Board was not united, however, in overruling the staff. On April 30, it conducted a roll call vote on the question of whether the staff had acted within its contract rights. John King, George Hunter, Nettie Jean Cawley, and Bob Scott voted in the affirmative; Ben Asia, George Bolotin, Aubrey Davis, and Paul Goodin voted nay. John Carruth was absent.[9]

This division created a stalemate, and the dispute settled into a kind of trench warfare over the next several months. Meanwhile, several members of the Board decided to open a new front by launching an assault on Don Northrop and his management. This battle had also been brewing for some time.

In April of 1951, the Board praised Northrop for his progress in implementing the reforms outlined by Stan Erickson, but the next month, Dr. McNeel delivered a "bill of particulars" detailing management shortcomings along with his letter of resignation from the medical staff. As chair of the Finance and Management Committee, Ben Asia investigated McNeel's critique. Northrop replied on May 25, 1951, with a four-page defense, which concluded, "I do not wish my answers to these charges to be misconstrued that management feels everything is running smoothly—this is far from the case." He felt that "with time and further counseling as to our aims and goals, we will achieve a well integrated organization."[10]

Following their election in November 1951, Aubrey Davis and new Board president Paul Goodin joined with Ben Asia in renewing the pressure on Northrop. A special organizational survey was conducted by three experienced managers, Kenneth McClaskey, Gilbert Rolfe, and Don Redfern, recruited from the membership. They delivered their findings in May 1952, reporting that Erickson's recommendations "in the main have not been actuated" and "there does not presently exist a 'sound structure of organization within which the Cooperative can expand gracefully,'" as called for by the Erickson plan. At the same time, the report rejected Erickson's "dual-head" scheme for administration in favor of a "unit-head."[11]

This report was taken up by the Board at a special all-day meeting on Saturday, July 12, 1952. It also considered critical reports delivered by subcommittees on budget and purchasing, whose respective chairs, Ernie Conrad and Derwin Demers, were in attendance. Almost from the first word, the 28 pages of minutes for this meeting read like the trancript of a trial, with Don Northrop in the dock and Aubrey Davis and Ben Asia leading the prosecution.

Over many hours, they walked through the criticisms of Northrop's administration. Some of these were as niggling as who had authority to sign checks and order towels, but they added up to a case for a management in disarray. Among trustees, only Bob Scott offered any defense, and it may be significant that Nettie Jean Cawley resigned from the Board on the day before this meeting. John King, who would later champion Northrop, was also absent.

Dr. Quinn also rallied to Northrop. "My feeling is that what has been accomplished in this organization in five years scarcely needs to be elaborated, and must be a tribute to everyone involved." Quinn also took issue with the idea of shifting to a single administrative head, which Dr. MacColl had characterized as "a two-headed monster versus Cyclops." He declared, "If it were possible at the present time to combine in one small head all that Don knows and all that I know after five years experience...that would appear desirable. I am extremely skeptical of our ability to get such a person." This said, he departed the meeting to tend to other duties.

Without claiming to be perfect, Northrop tried to justify his actions and inactions. "You have so many hours in the day to achieve the things that must be done in good administration. Add to that the hours required because of being a cooperative, put on top of that an organization that was defunct when the Co-op took over. First things are going to be selected sometimes on an emotional basis of what is confronting you at the moment, rather than what should continue to be planned." He cited the new hospital wing, where "practically every brick and chair [was] my decision."

He liked the work, Northrop said, "but I know that it is pulling me apart." No sympathy was forthcoming from Aubrey Davis: "I have spent most of my adult life evaluating management per se, and one thing I have learned is that management which is poorly planned and poorly organized is always putting out fires and never has time to get properly organized."

After many hours of interrogation, Northrop tried to get to the heart of matters. "I feel today that this [organizational survey] is an objective report but I feel some people are not laying on the table just what is on their minds. I should know if I am the man for the job." If not, "I will present to you today my resignation orally to do with as you see fit."

Davis agreed, "What we have got to decide now is the issue that Mr. Northrop has squarely put to us." The Board then went into executive session (of which no minutes were taken). When it reconvened on the record, Northrop left the room, and his lone champion, Bob Scott, moved that no action be taken. This did not muster even a courtesy second. George Hunter joined him on a second motion to put Northrop on probation, but this failed. Finally, the Board voted 5-2 to accept Northrop's resignation.

Bob Scott warned his colleagues "that the action of the board would not be favorably accepted by the staff and intimated that they would resign en masse." He tendered his own resignation and left (he was persuaded to return to the Board).

Northrop returned to the room and graciously agreed to stay on until September 15. "To avoid personal embarrassment," he also suggested that the Board report officially that he had resigned because of a decision to "change to a single medical director type of organization" in which he declined to accept a lesser role. The Board agreed with this, and called Dr. Quinn to schedule a special meeting with the staff on Monday to "prevent the spread of unfounded rumors."[12]

The storm broke immediately. On July 15, Quinn wrote Goodin to express the staff's view. He praised Northrop's leadership in Group Heath's "history-making explorations into the uncharted field of consumer-sponsored medical care" and his "singular devotion to the fundamental objectives of what has become nationally known as cooperative medicine."

Quinn faulted trustees for having "failed to give clearly defined directives to the Manager" and for having "in many instances, trespassed into the fields of operation and management." He reported that "the staff regards the present action as precipitous, ill-conceived, destructive, and reflecting a grave error in judgment" and cautioned that the staff would "suffer in its professional activities if it lacks confidence in the wisdom of the Board." To avoid this, he urged the Board "to reconsider its decision promptly before further damage is done."[13]

A similar plea was also written by a committee of the nursing and clerical staff, and Dr. Sandy MacColl wrote a letter on the issue to the full membership. This fueled scrutiny by the Board of Review, a special committee of members charged with monitoring Board activities between membership meetings. The Renton District also empaneled its own Special Investigating Committee to examine "the difficulties between the Board of Trustees and the Medical Staff."[14]

At the Board's next meeting on July 31, John King moved to rescind acceptance of Northrop's resignation, but he garnered only one other vote. Recognizing how explosive the situation had become, Paul Goodin took the unprecedented (and technically illegal) step of inviting three members of the medical staff to sit on the Board. The staff accepted "unanimously and enthusiastically" and assigned Drs. Charlotte Bansmer, Harmon Truax, and Alfred Magar.[15]

This was the first step toward a cease-fire. The next was taken when Northrop's tenure was extended to November, giving the staff and Board time to work out their differences on the new unit head. The staff felt that this medical director should be filled by an M.D. and that it should have the right to recall, if not appoint, the individual. The issue was assigned to a special Joint Conference Committee (JCC) of Board and staff members charged with negotiating a new medical staff contract. The JCC would soon prove to be a crucial innovation in re-establishing Board-Staff communications and provide a less politically charged forum for resolving jurisdictional disputes.

In September 1952, Dr. Quinn stepped down as chief of staff, and Dr. Sandy MacColl took his place. The following month, Dr. Charles Strother was named to fill Cawley's vacant seat. Both appointments would contribute dramatically to restoring peace within the Cooperative.

On October 25, the Board approved formalizing the Joint Conference Committee, composed of three trustees and three medical staff members, as a permanent body "to review and make recommendations on all proposals in which there is a medical interest" and to handle any appeals from the medical staff "from actions of the Medical Director." It also approved formation of a permanent Medical Advisory Committee to evaluate staff performance.[16]

MacColl advised the Board that he and the medical staff would accept his appointment to assume "for an arbitrary period the responsibilities of the Managing Director." The issue was tabled for the moment, but MacColl's willingness to take the post pointed toward a reconciliation.

On November 19, Dr. Raymond Bunker presented a new staff proposal for an executive director jointly hired by the Board and staff. The scheme also "pledged" the Board to recall the director if two-thirds of the staff requested it to do so. This led to another marathon Board meeting six days later, which was attended by a large number of member observers and physicians.

"Bud" Asia was hostile to the staff's right of recalling the director, because "responsibility should not be divided from authority." In his view, responsibility rested with the Board, but the proposal vested real administrative authority in the medical staff. He also felt the arrangement would hamstring the director and restrict his actions only to those approved of by staff.

MacColl replied that he was "somewhat at a loss to match Bud's eloquence." He added, "If we were running an army or a steel mill I would be inclined to agree. This organization was constructed from the very beginning on the sense of parallelism of interest and mutual confidence."

After several hours of deliberation, Aubrey Davis offered a substitute motion that retained the recall right but allowed either the Board or staff to end the "trial period" for the new arrangement on 90 days' notice. It was, he said, "the only hope I see for coming out of this whole." The arrangement was premised on the selection of Dr. MacColl as the interim executive director and the hiring of an administrative director, for which position John James had already been interviewed. William Birnbaum dubbed it a "gentlemen's agreement," and the motion ultimately passed with only Asia and George Bolotin dissenting.[17]

The final element of the new truce was approved on December 30, when the Board approved a new Joint Executive Committee including three staff members to review matters before they were presented to the full Board. Ben Asia remained doubtful about sharing so much power with the staff and offered to resign, but he was dissuaded.

Dr. J. H. Millhouse was introduced as the new chief of staff at the same meeting and the Board approved a new pension plan for the medical staff. In keeping with the renewed spirit of unity between the staff and the Board, it was a fitting moment to dissolve the Medical Security Clinic corporation, which had been maintained as a paper entity for the past five years. Paul Goodin took the opportunity to close his tumultuous two-year term as president, and turned the gavel over to Aubrey Davis. John Carruth, who would become a prophetic advocate of new information systems at Group Health, was elected vice president.[18]

Don Northrop formally departed Group Health on January 15, 1953. In his new role as executive director, Dr. MacColl took to describing himself as "the man in the middle." It was a position he was reluctant to occupy. "I was drafted," he later explained. "It was an impossible position. Nobody in his right mind would have accepted it because" the director had to be "acceptable to most of the staff and the board, but their acceptance could be withdrawn at any time by either side."[19]

This did not prevent Dr. MacColl from being quite blunt, even "insulting" in the view of one trustee, when an issue called for firmness. "I think on both sides, [people] felt they couldn't be sure of him," Aubrey Davis said later. "He filled a spot at the time which had to be filled and was very difficult. I don't know anyone who could have filled it better, but it wasn't a permanent fix."[20]

MacColl was not alone in the middle. Charles Strother became the glue that held together the Joint Conference Committee, which usually thrashed out the most divisive issues before they reached the Board. Davis compared it to "a permanent, ongoing labor negotiation" in which "anything either party wanted to bring up was fair game."[21]

Although Strother was not an M.D., he enjoyed a dual appointment with the UW School of Medicine and the Department of Psychology. "He was clearly an intellectual and social equal with the medical staff," says Davis. He remembered one stormy JCC meeting: "Chuck was really offended, but I don't think he was as offended as he looked. He got up and said I can't negotiate with you any more, got up and walked out of the meeting. They were thunderstruck." The sides then quickly reached agreement on the issue at hand.[22]

Strother later wrote, "One very important factor" in weathering the storm was "the fact that the medical staff, too, was composed of idealists, held together for its part by a joint commitment to a new pattern of medical care delivery." He recalled that staff-Board tensions "cooled down fairly quickly, and for that Sandy MacColl deserves a great deal of credit."[23]

In February, the Special Investigating Committee formed by Renton district members reported that while "rather serious problems have existed during the past year, most of them have been resolved; therefore there is little need for alarm on the part of the membership at this time." At the same time, the report admitted "the truce between the board and the staff is still somewhat uneasy." It saw one benefit from the battles: "They have stimulated a new interest in the Co-op's affairs on the part of members who want to make sure that Group Health continues as a cooperative rather than as a medical care corporation, run from the top."[24]

The new equilibrium was tested almost immediately by the ghost of an incident from a year earlier. Amid the turmoil over Dr. Allan Sachs in the spring of 1952, the medical staff also turned down an application from an African-American physician, Dr. Blanche Lavizzo. "She appeared to be perfectly well qualified," Dr. Charlotte Bansmer remembers, and she won acceptance on the medical staff's first vote. Then it was decided that a quorum was not present. On the second vote, the staff again voted to hire her by 10 votes to 8, but this majority was three short of the two-thirds required.[25]

Bansmer later recalled that the debate was dominated by a member of the staff from the South who "claimed he knew about Southern black schools [Lavizzo had recently taken her degree from a such a college] and claimed they were of lower academic quality." Bansmer said others felt Dr. Lavizzo "would be a problem making house calls," by dint of both her race and sex. Dr. Gustav Bansmer, for example, made his sister's house calls. Chief of staff Dr. Quinn polled the staff and found that a third had voted *for* Lavizzo chiefly because she was black, and only one opponent admitted racial bias. The Joint Executive Committee later investigated the issue and concluded that prejudice had not been a "deciding factor."[26]

In the medical staff's defense, it should be noted that Dr. Robert Joyner, an African-American general practitioner, did not feel that he encountered any discrimination when he sought a position at Group Health in 1950. "I applied because I knew they didn't have any blacks on the staff," he later related. He remembered being interviewed by a Virginian, presumably chief of staff Dr. John McNeel, who seemed very open to his joining the staff.

Dr. Joyner was not hired, however, because he required a part-time position in order to develop his own clinic in Seattle's Central Area.[27]

Dr. Lavizzo took her rejection to the local chapters of the NAACP and Urban League and filed a complaint with the state's Fair Employment Practices Commission (one of the nation's first such agencies, and later chaired by Group Health stalwart Sidney Gerber). The charges arrived before the Board in February 1953 and became a major issue at the annual meeting in April.

There, Ted Astley rose to urge a reaffirmation of the "very important principle" of nondiscrimination as it applied "not only to membership in the Cooperative but to the hiring of employees and acquisition of medical staff membership." He advocated special effort to hire "competent Negro doctors" and Asian-Americans.[28]

Hilde Birnbaum dedicated herself to this cause, following her election to the Board at the same meeting. She later noted, "Group Health was the first and probably the only desegregated hospital and health facility in the area," yet it had become the target of a discrimination charge. She was especially sensitive to the paradox, having left her native Germany in 1933, shortly after Hitler came to power. Her efforts to help German Jews escape won her the distinction of being declared an "enemy of the Reich" in 1937.

Armed with degrees in both the law and economics, Hilde Birnbaum was a longtime advocate and student of the cooperative movement, and she was also the wife of former trustee William Birnbaum. Her candidacy for the Board was personally recruited by Dr. MacColl, who feared that the Nominating Committee was "stacked somewhat against the physicians." The Committee interviewed her but did not put her name up for election. She was well known in the movement thanks to her columns in the Cascade League's *Cooperative News*, so her nomination was secured by a petition of members.

Birnbaum faulted her husband for failing to secure strong antidiscrimination language in the original medical staff contract, and she set out to correct the omission. When Birnbaum found herself the swing vote during negotiations for the new contract, she used her leverage to insert this clause: "In the selection and dismissal of staff members there shall be no discrimination on any basis other than professional competence and personal character."

Meanwhile, Dr. Lavizzo was offered the chance to fill a new vacancy; she declined and her discrimination complaint became moot, although several African-Americans dropped their Group Health membership in protest. Dr. Lavizzo went on to become a distinguished pediatrician on the staff of Children's Orthopedic Hospital, and later founded the Odessa Brown Clinic to serve Seattle's inner-city children.

Had the Lavizzo incident not occurred amid the crisis between the Board and medical staff, it might have had a happier outcome. As it was, an important opportunity for social leadership was lost. Group Health did not hire an African-American nurse until 1956, when Gertrude Dawson joined the staff. Thirteen years later, the medical staff recruited its first African-American physician, Dr. James Garrison, and launched a concerted affirmative action program to balance the racial ledger.[29]

Following the 1953 annual meeting, the new Board included Ernie Conrad and William Cowan, a Renton member nominated by petition, in addition to Hilde Birnbaum. The body re-elected Aubrey Davis as president and turned its attention to a familiar set of issues: the medical staff contract, budget and costs, continued overcrowding and overwork at the hospital and central clinic, and the perennial problem of branch clinics.

The first was resolved in October. The staff also agreed to a capitation formula based on the size of the enrollment for the distribution of the lapsed salaries of doctors who left the staff among those who remained. Group Health's physicians continued to resist full capitation, however, as the basis for general compensation for several more years.[30]

By April, enrollment had passed 35,000, of whom more than two-thirds were full Cooperative members. Aubrey Davis warned that such "growth is not necessarily an unmixed blessing." The medical staff saw no blessing, mixed or otherwise. Although the staff had increased to 23 physicians, the rising enrollment pushed the family doctor/patient ratio past 1:1800 by mid-1953. At Dr. MacColl's urging, the Board agreed to cap enrollment at 35,000 until the staff could expand to catch up. This did not prevent the Board from signing a new contract with the Longshoremen's Union to cover more than 1,300 dependents. To compensate, the Board later voted to drop small groups numbering fewer than 25 members, a plan Don Northrop had suggested nearly two years earlier.[31]

The situation in Renton became critical again in the summer when Dr. Joseph Alter flatly refused to staff the tiny clinic any longer. Dr. MacColl recommended shutting down the operation, but the Board was persuaded by William Cowan's impassioned plea to save the clinic. It didn't hurt his cause that nearly 5,000 members resided in the Renton service area. In November, the Board acquired the Renton City Club property for $31,000, and later retained architect Paul Hayden Kirk to design a model facility. While planning and financing proceeded, Group Health purchased the existing Keigwin Clinic as an interim facility.[32]

Some 3,500 North End members also kept up the pressure for their own branch clinic. In the spring of 1953, a poll showed that the Northgate area was the most popular location for a future clinic and the staff began exploring sites.[33]

A long-held ambition was fulfilled in summer 1953 when Group Health incorporated an independent cooperative to provide dental services and hired Dr. Harry Kraft, D.D.S. The new Group Health Dental Co-op moved into a building just a few doors from its namesake hospital and clinic. It opened for business on July 15 when Dr. Delbert Miller and his family arrived for their first checkups.[34]

Group Health ended the year with a total enrollment of 35,824. It had also run up an operating surplus of $33,000, but its accountants forecast a deficit of nearly a quarter of a million dollars in 1954. To remedy this, the Board approved a 10 percent increase in dues and charges, which took effect the following February. In the final months of 1953, the medical staff also welcomed five new physicians, but the new chief of staff, Dr. Alfred Magar, cautioned that during the year Group Health had actually replaced only 13 of 14 doctors lost during the year.[35]

Despite the pressure of work and finances, the staff-Board peace held as Dr. MacColl's directorship continued into 1954. Many of the veterans of the previous year's battles dropped away, including Ben Asia and Paul Goodin. John Spiller, H. Donald Gouge and Warren Morgens joined the Board, and Charles Strother was elected president in April. The refreshingly uneventful year was notable chiefly for the launching of a $250,000 bond campaign to finance the new Renton Clinic and dissolution of the Board of Review, a signal of members' growing confidence in their trustees.[36]

It also marked the end of the staffing crisis. In January 1955, Dr. Magar told the Board, "It is a pleasure to report that 1954 has been an active and a successful year." A staff of 40 doctors now served 36,000 members, representing a remarkable 7 percent of the community.[37]

At the annual meeting in April 1955, the membership expanded the Board to 11 members by creating two new nominating areas. The membership was also invited to support Group Health's new Auxilliary, organized by Fay Miller and Pauline Hillier and later chaired by Harla Fox. Felix Reisner (later replaced by Art Siegal) and Myron Ernst were elected trustees, and Hilde Birnbaum became the first woman to wield the president's gavel at Group Health, a rare position of power for women in healthcare, then or now.[38]

Dr. MacColl was now entering the 28th month of his "one-year" assignment as executive director, and he was eager to return to his duties as a pediatrician. The press of his administrative responsibilities did not prevent him from performing one crucial medical service in 1955.

The big healthcare news of that year was Dr. Jonas Salk's revolutionary polio vaccine. "Infantile paralysis" was a ruthless killer and crippler of young adults as well as children, and the news of a long-sought vaccine was greeted in the mid-1950s with the same impatient eagerness that a cure for cancer or AIDS might receive today. With much fanfare, the federal government and various foundations rushed the vaccine into distribution.

Dr. MacColl was not convinced that this was wise. "There

was something about the way it was done that irked me and made me suspicious." He consulted Dr. Bud Evans at the UW School of Medicine, who said, "I think the vaccine's good, but I'm not sure it's going to be safe on this mass basis so soon." Officials from the state Health Department and National Centers for Disease Control concurred, so MacColl told the medical staff he wanted to go slow. He calculated that Group Health's population might experience 10 cases of polio at the most that summer—the same number that could result from a single vial of bad vaccine.

MacColl resisted increasing pressure from trustees and members to begin vaccinations during the summer. He was gratified when the wife of a trustee reported that she had defended Group Health's doctors to skeptics by pointing out "they're not in it for the money."

MacColl kept "hanging tough" even as the vaccine arrived at Group Health's pharmacy. Then came the reports he had hoped not to hear: some shipments were in fact tainted. He got the serial numbers of the bad lots from the state, and discovered that Group Health had received *five* vials of potentially lethal vaccine. Dr. MacColl did not authorize vaccinations until new supplies were received from a Canadian manufacturer and certified safe.[39]

This episode was one of the last in Dr. MacColl's tenure as executive director. A nation-wide search had yielded several candidates for his successor, but this predictably triggered a new tug of war between the staff and Board. The former wanted a medical doctor, while the latter wanted a person who would not bend to the staff's will.

Fortunately, Dr. Strother had quietly recruited the perfect compromise: Dr. John A. Kahl (pronounced "kale," like the lettuce), former head of the Washington State Department of Health. He was an M.D. and had earned both a degree and wide professional acclaim in public health, which satisfied the medical staff. He was also a proven public administrator accustomed to working with elected officials and citizen boards. Even with these qualifications, it proved a hard sell. Hilde Birnbaum remembered that she "kept the Board in session until they said yes, until two in the morning" of June 3, 1955.[40]

Dr. MacColl gratefully relinquished his position on June 29 in order to return to pediatrics. He told the Board and medical staff, "I don't believe we have yet learned to work together as smoothly as we eventually will." MacColl regretted "leaving challenges unsolved, but the compensation is that I shall still be a part of Group Health and continue to work in the primary direction in which this organization is committed and to which I long ago committed myself."[41]

It was fitting that Group Health's first and most beloved pediatrician had helped guide the squalling Cooperative through the final years of its childhood. Now beginning its 10th year, Group Health was ready to enter a robust and remarkably untroubled adolescence.

Chapter 8

Salad Days

1955 ~ 1960

*Dr. Kahl Takes Charge ~ Renton Gets a Real Clinic
~ A Philosophy of Preventive Care ~ Growing
Enrollment and Deficits ~ Northgate Clinic Opens ~
An Outside Evaluation ~ The Medicare Debate ~ A
New Hospital on Capitol Hill*

*D*r. John A. Kahl began his 10-year shift as Group Health executive director in August 1955. His hiring was "a great coup," according to Aubrey Davis. "He had an M.D. after his name, which meant that the medical staff could live with him. He was a non-political guy, but he understood our culture well enough, and his values were consistent because he came from a public health background."[1]

Art Siegal, who was appointed to the Board a few months before Dr. Kahl's hiring, later described Group Health's new director as "an energetic, emotional man who was totally dedicated to his work. There were no strawmen or windmills that he was afraid of, and he would charge off on a project, working long hours. He had an instinct for knowing when to forge ahead and when to consolidate."[2]

Dr. Kahl demonstrated this instinct from the start. One of his first acts was to ask the Board to eliminate John James' position as administrative director. James had already left (when the Board refused his request for a leave of absence) and Kahl felt no need for such assistance. It was clear that as an administrator, Dr. Kahl was a solo practitioner.[3]

Kahl plunged immediately into the central issue of growth.

He undertook a detailed review of the Board's policies and plans, going back to 1952, when Don Northrop had forecast that Group Health enrollment might reach 33,000 by 1970. With enrollment pushing 38,000 in the fall of 1955, it was clear that Group Health needed to rethink some key assumptions.

The Board had tacitly accepted that Group Health would grow to 70,000 when it approved a five-stage facilities expansion plan in February 1955. Kahl thought even this was unrealistically conservative and that the Cooperative should plan on reaching 80,000 within 10 years, which would seriously overload its hospital and central clinic.[4]

The news was not all bad. The perennial problem of the Renton Clinic had been solved at least temporarily, although not as originally planned. In late 1953, the Board had purchased the Renton City Club site for construction of a new clinic. The following year, it approved a $250,000 bond issue to finance a new facility to be custom-designed by Group Health's still skeptical physicians.

Amid planning for the new Renton clinic, the Board learned that Dr. Charles Kiegwin was willing to sell his private Renton Medical Center. Dr. Kiegwin died in a plane crash shortly after negotiations commenced, but Group Health was able to reach agreement with his widow in the spring of 1954. After remodeling to accommodate six physicians and space for Dental Co-op staff, Group Health's first true Renton Clinic opened on June 11, 1954, at a total cost of $65,000.[5]

With Renton members satisfied for a fraction of the projected cost, the Board shifted its sights to North Seattle, where enrollment was surging. In July 1955, the Board approved purchase of the Perkins site near the new Northgate Shopping Center. Two months later, it asked architect Paul Kirk to design a state-of-the-art clinic based on the physician specifications originally drawn up for Renton.

Paul Kirk's selection might have been influenced by a new and very active member of Group Health, Victor Steinbrueck, who would later make his mark leading the 1972 campaign to save the Pike Place Market from urban renewal. Steinbrueck worked in Kirk's firm when not teaching architecture at the UW. He had run for trustee in 1954 (losing to Warren Morgens) and advised the Board on plans to expand and remodel Group Health's hospital. Based in part on his counsel, the Board retained Young, Richardson, Carleton, & Detlie as architects for the hospital project in April 1955.[6]

The hospital was the focus of Dr. Kahl's immediate concern in late 1955. Eighty-two beds were crammed into space suitable for 60. This did not prevent the hospital from winning full accreditation that July, shortly after the retirement of Kathleen Sumption, its longtime supervisor. She was succeeded by Marian Gillespie, who would also serve a long tenure.

The Board had tentatively committed to adding 20 beds to the current 82, which would provide the minimum capacity for an enrollment of 40,000. Kahl argued that this left Group Health's membership "stationary." Based on calculations of efficient staffing and facilities, he declared, "If it is decided that we should grow, it would seem practical to do it in units of 40,000—in other words, if we are going to grow beyond 40,000, we should plan for a goal of 80,000 members."

By this logic, what Group Health really needed was an additional 100 beds, and the architects had estimated that building a new addition of this size would cost only 25 percent more than remodeling or replacing the existing hospital. The best approach in Kahl's opinion was to build a completely new 150-bed hospital in two stages, beginning on Group Health property immediately south of John Street. When the first stage was ready, the old hospital would be demolished and replaced. The two wings could be united if the city government approved vacation of John Street, or, in the worst case, linked by a tunnel or a skybridge. This plan, with an estimated price tag of $2.5 million, was adopted by the Board with the goal of reaching an enrollment of up to 100,000.[7]

This commitment was another giant leap of financial faith. Sales of bonds previously authorized for the Renton Clinic had stalled that winter at about $170,000, and the finance charges for a loan or mortgage were prohibitive—assuming any lender would gamble a couple of million dollars on the still "radical" Cooperative. The only alternative was to raise Co-op members' one-time $75 capital dues by another $100, which would yield $3 million for the hospital, Northgate, and clinic improvements.

An earlier proposal for higher capital dues had sparked a debate among trustees over whether to levy the new assessment on the Board's authority or to submit the plan for membership approval. In August, Aubrey Davis warned his colleagues that to fail to consult members "would be a mistake of the first magnitude." After several months of discussion, the Board agreed to schedule a special membership meeting, but many trustees feared that members would not be able to grasp the technical issues involved, let alone vote to more than double their capital dues (group plan enrollees were not affected).

The capital dues plan presented by the Board gave members the option of either paying a lump sum of $100 or paying $1 per month over 120 months. More than 500 members assembled in the Chamber of Commerce's downtown auditorium on November 29, 1955, and carefully reviewed the capital plan and proposed assessment. After two hours, the motion to raise capital dues to $175 passed with only two "nay" votes cast. Both Group Health's coffers and its internal democracy had been greatly enriched.[8]

By the annual meeting on April 11, 1956, more than 3,000 members had paid their additional capital dues in full, and another 10,000 had elected the installment plan. At the same meeting, members paid their respects to Ernie Conrad, who retired from the Board.[9]

Dr. Kahl used this occasion to outline his philosophy on an issue of keen concern to most members, preventive medicine. He reviewed Group Health's prenatal and Well Child programs, which were already yielding dramatic statistical improvements in pediatric health compared to national averages. As to adults, Kahl cited the need for good diet and "preventing obesity, which can cause some of our more important chronic diseases." Kahl's failure to mention tobacco is understandable since the national alarm over cigarettes would not be rung for several more years—and he was himself a smoker.

Combined with public health programs to protect water, food, and the air, Kahl explained, "All of this is a program of 'primary prevention.'" Kahl knew full well that what his audience really cared about was implementing a program giving each member "a routine annual physical examination." Such exams were an article of popular faith thanks to relentless propaganda from groups such as the American Cancer Society, and a complete waste of time from the point of view of practicing physicians.

"We at times confuse the problem of 'early detection' of disease, or perhaps I should say 'secondary prevention,'" Kahl continued. "This is the prevention not of the disease, but of the occurrence of disability or premature death" resulting from chronic illnesses. Medical knowledge was still too limited to treat many such diseases, but "we may at times prevent progress to a point" where the patient suffers permanent harm or death.

"In the field of prevention," Kahl told Group Health members, "the individual himself must assume some responsibility for his own health" by getting vaccinations, eating a balanced diet, and avoiding environmental risks. "And so it is in the early detection of chronic diseases...he must assume responsibility for noting any changes in his health" and bring them to a doctor's attention. "Under these conditions, no one should wait for a routine examination, but seek medical care promptly."

Not only were annual physicals of little value in this context, Kahl said, but they were enormously expensive. With thorough exams then costing as much as $150, Kahl calculated that even more modest "health evaluations" for Group Health's 27,000 current adult enrollment would require seven full-time physicians and cost $95,000 just for staffing. There was another cost: "I have seen it repeatedly happen, where a physician has been required to do routine physical examinations of ostensibly healthy people—the physician soon tires of the program" because it fails to offer "sufficient professional challenge."

The alternative Kahl proposed (and later implemented) was to intensify Group Health's education efforts and to offer periodic "health inventories" for "people not under medical care during the year." Such an inventory would consist of a detailed questionnaire, chest X-ray, and blood and urine tests. Significantly, Kahl proposed "pelvic and breast examinations in the female—as well as eventually using the Papinicoleau [sic] pelvic smear for detection of early cancer." So-called Pap smears (named for the American physician, Dr. George Papinicolaou, who invented the test) were then a new procedure, and Group Health was one of the first medical institutions in the world to offer them as a routine—and free—service.

Kahl concluded his remarks with a plea: "If you will give us your cooperation by being patient, I believe we can work out a practical solution which will in turn do what you want done, and at the same time make it professionally interesting to our medical staff, and economical for all." These were not the last words to be spoken on the subject of annual physicals, but they proved decisive in the long run.[10]

Over the next year, capital dues gave Group Health more than enough to pay off its existing $90,000 mortgages on the clinic and hospital and to buy additional parking lots and the nearby Lou Anne Apartments, a graceful structure designed and built by Frederick Anhalt, to which it relocated its administrative offices. Unfortunately, the hospital expansion plan hit a speed bump when several neighbors and the local Methodist Church protested the closure of John Street. Group Health won a five-to-three victory on the City Council in August 1956, but Mayor Gordon Clinton vetoed the ordinance, claiming that the city was not adequately indemnified from any liability created by the street vacation.[11]

Group Health had other problems with the municipal government at the time. The city had approved a healthcare benefit for its employees to begin in 1956, but it offered them only one "choice": King County Medical. Group Health organized a letter and petition drive to broaden the program, and finally prevailed on October 1, when the city approved it as an "alternative" plan. Group Health would have to fight this same battle in Olympia, where King County Medical promoted laws and rules to freeze out any competitors.[12]

Group Health began its 10th year of operation with nearly

42,000 individual enrollees, three-fourths of whom were full Co-op members, and an annual operating budget in excess of $2.7 million. The Board approved a new membership agreement expanding services and began distributing distinctive green and yellow decals to be attached to members' automobile windshields so that emergency workers would know where to take them (and nonmember passengers) in case of an accident.[13]

The membership gathered to celebrate Group Health's first decade in grand style at the Olympic Hotel on April 6, 1957. As they reflected on the past, members also offered a preview of issues to come by passing a resolution urging Group Health to cooperate with other agencies in studying the public health effects of insecticides, food preservatives, and radioactive fallout from A-bomb tests. The 1960s had not yet begun, but the next decade's political agenda was already taking shape at Group Health.[14]

The keynote address at the annual meeting was delivered by Dr. George Saslow, clinical professor of psychiatry at Harvard Medical School. Saslow had been invited by the Board not only to speak but to evaluate Group Health, chiefly at the behest of Drs. Charles Strother, Sandy MacColl, and Bernice Sachs, who were gently nudging Group Health into providing mental health services.

Saslow's visit was a direct consequence of a January inspection by Dr. Lester Evans, who represented the Commonwealth Fund, a major healthcare philanthropy. This earlier visit led the Board to establish a formal Research Committee, chaired by Dr. Strother with the charge of finding funding for a study of psychiatric services in a prepaid context. Strother had prepared a plan for this the previous May, but his aims were not fully supported by the medical staff. Saslow advised the Board that the staff was "quite divided within itself" over the need for mental health counseling. He suggested that Group Health might explore funding from the Public Health Service, and, on a more general level, Saslow recommended that the Co-op bring in an expert to conduct a more general "medical audit."[15]

Mental health was not Dr. Strother's sole area of interest in terms of research, it should be noted. Group Health had already assisted in several studies. A number of investigations had already been conducted, and in 1956 University of Washington public health researcher K. Warner Shaie launched a long-term study to monitor the health histories of 800 members. Such efforts would quickly grow as researchers recognized the statistical gold mine offered by Group Health's membership. (As to the area of mental health, Strother did not really make progress until he converted Dr. John Quinn to his cause some years later, and American voters elected President John Kennedy, whose family had a special concern for the mentally ill.)[16]

Meanwhile, back on East John Street, the City Council passed a new vacation ordinance on May 6, 1957, which Mayor Clinton signed two days later. Three neighbors and the Methodist Church filed suit. They lost in Superior Court on July 22, but appealed to the State Supreme Court. The legal path was not cleared for months, prompting the running joke that "somebody should give that John (meaning Dr. Kahl) a vacation."[17]

During the year, the Board committed to construction of a new South End clinic in the Burien area and began looking for a site. At the same time, it fended off renewed pressure from Kitsap and Eastside members for clinics in their areas. Trustee Chandler Redman explained to them, "We already have more problems than are desirable here at home."[18]

As enrollment climbed toward 45,000, Group Health found itself facing an unexpected problem, a projected $105,000 deficit in 1958. There were several causes, including the delay in hospital construction, but the chief culprit was inflation. As Dr. Kahl explained to the Board, the general consumer price index had risen 6 percent since the last dues increase in 1954—but medical costs had risen 13 percent. Group Health had compounded this with new services such as Pap smears, which cost $25,000 annually. Despite this cost, Dr. Kahl deemed it a worthwhile program that had already detected 11 cases of cancer in slightly more than 1,000 tests. Even a $200,000 cut in operating costs and Group Health's budgetary safety margin during 1957 could not forestall next year's anticipated shortfall.[19]

The Board took the problem to the membership in a round of district meetings during November and December. It laid out a variety of options, including a new "low option" plan with reduced benefits and charges for certain services. Nearly 1,000 members participated in the meetings, and of the 654 who cast votes, 78 percent supported a dues hike without any reduction in services or additional charges. Thus instructed—and supported—the Board voted on January 3, 1958, to raise dues roughly 20 percent across the board. At the urging of many members, as well as Dr. Kahl, it also eliminated the differential rates for married men and women, and levied a flat $6 monthly dues on all adults.[20]

Compared with the new hospital, construction of the Northgate Clinic was a snap, but costs here also increased during the "Eisenhower Recession" of the late 1950s. The building was dedicated on March 22, 1958, and its innovative design won Paul Kirk top honor from the American Institute of Architects. It also allowed its new chief of staff, Dr. Sandy MacColl, to put some distance between himself and his colleagues on Capitol Hill.[21]

Despite MacColl's efforts in holding Group Health together during its near-schism, Aubrey Davis recalled, the staff did not welcome him back as "the great hero, Cincinnatus returning to the farm." Hilde Birnbaum, who served as Board president during the late 1950s, believed that the memories of the staff-Board clashes were still too fresh for veteran doctors ever fully to trust MacColl again. "The medical staff made it very hard on him," she said, so "he went joyously" to Northgate "to get out of that."

Not everyone harbored such resentments, however, and Aubrey Davis reports that MacColl "had a great influence on young doctors as a charismatic kind of doctor-leader." Through his example and tireless advocacy of prepaid group practice, Dr. MacColl came to personify Group Health and the ideals of cooperative medicine for an entire generation of physicians in and beyond Seattle.[22]

In July, Dr. Edwin F. Daily, vice president of the Health Insurance Plan of Greater New York City, arrived to conduct the evaluation of Group Health that Dr. Saslow had suggested a year earlier. While Dr. Daily praised "the almost universal dedication of the medical staff to principles of group practice of the highest order was unquestionable and a joy to behold," his report did not give Group Health high grades in other respects.

Daily focused on medical staffing and compensation. He found Group Health doctors' average annual salary of $14,400 to be well below the average for comparable organizations (although it was well above the national average for physician income). He also felt that the Group Health pay schedule did not adequately reward advanced degrees and qualifications.

If this pleased the medical staff, Daily's recommendation that Group Health trim its staff and operate on a physician-patient ratio of 1-to-5,000 did not. They were not happy with his idea of placing all doctors' extra fee-for-service income in a special Group Health fund to offset salaries. Some doctors also opposed his idea that every enrollee "select a personal physician and that this physician make every effort to become a friendly, professional advisor to the patient," although Group Health later adopted precisely this approach.

Daily also supported adding a full-time psychiatrist, eliminating "waivers" for preexisting conditions, instituting evening office hours, encouraging doctors to seek teaching opportunities at the UW School of Medicine, and appointing an "independent Medical Board" like that contemplated in the original Joint Conference Committee compromise.

At the same time, he noted that the Cooperative offered its enrollees exceptional benefits, including all drugs and 180 days of hospitalization, for an average annual $54 contribution (including children's rates). He contrasted this with New York's Health Insurance Plan, which earned $56 per enrollee while excluding drugs and covering only 21 days of hospitalization. Group Health was obviously delivering remarkably efficient care without penalizing its patients.

Daily's report, in brief, offered something for everyone to like—and dislike. Many of his ideas, including eliminating waivers, assigning personal physicians, and providing mental health services, were ultimately implemented, but there is no instance where Dr. Daily got the credit.[23]

One of Daily's recommendations drew unanimous rejection from the Board and medical staff: consolidation of internal medicine and general practice into a single department. This would effectively diminish the status of the latter, which had been organized as a discrete unit under Dr. Joseph Alter's leadership in 1956.

General practice—or "family practice" as it was later dubbed—was held in declining esteem as medical specialties proliferated during the 1950s. Group Health was not immune to such attitudes, but Dr. Ward Miles explained, it discovered "a big repository of common illness" within the membership that did not warrant the attention of specialists. GPs "filled a niche" and "gave a flexibility to the organization that it didn't have otherwise." What began as a pragmatic innovation gradually evolved into a specialty all its own, and in the mid-1960s the Cooperative joined with the University of Washington School of Medicine to develop one of the first curricula and internships devoted to family practice.[24]

While mulling Dr. Daily's report, the Board briefly tangled over complaints that non-English-speaking immigrants were being denied membership. Hilde Birnbaum took up the cause, but she suffered a rare defeat at the hands of staff, who countered that they couldn't help people they couldn't understand. She did, however, secure the elimination of all references to a patient's race in Group Health's records.[25]

In the fall of 1958, Group Health revamped its membership magazine and unveiled *View*, edited by John Donnelly. The inaugural issue announced "Operation Zero Mortgage," a new $1 million bond issue (added to $1.5 million previously authorized) to finance the new hospital.[26]

An old wound was re-opened in the spring of 1959, when the medical staff requested funds from the Board to print its own stationery—without Group Health's name or symbol. This enraged veteran cooperators on the Board, and the staff retreated. At the same meeting, the Board ended two years of talks of an "amalgamation" with Group Health Dental, which was chronically underfunded despite serving more than 500 families from new offices near its big sister cooperative. The Board cited legal "ambiguities" in the Dental Co-op's charter (state law prevented the dental co-op from owning the equipment of its dentists), but it really feared taking on a new mouth to feed.[27]

At the annual meeting on April 11, 1959, Board president Ken McCaffree reported that Ruth Brown's "all-girl pharmacy" had dispensed its one-millionth prescription in January. Chief of staff Dr. Magar described the new organization that assigned Group Health's 57 physicians among five departments: surgery, ob-gyn, (internal) medicine, pediatrics, and general practice.

Members also learned that Operation Zero Mortgage had been a complete success, and that Group Health could finance all hospital construction costs, now $3.2 million, without borrowing a cent. On June 1, 1959, Rabbi Raphael Levine and Mayor Clinton helped new Board president Myron Ernst turn over the first spadeful of earth for the new hospital.[28]

A few months later, the Board purchased a lot for the Burien Clinic at First Avenue South and South 146th Street, and later retained Bassetti & Morse architects to design a new building. The location did not please West Seattle members, but the Board could find no better site. What really annoyed Group Health's South End constituents was the Board's long-standing decision to build a new Central Clinic before their branch clinic. This became one of several hot issues when the Board found itself having to consult the membership over how to handle another projected deficit, this time nearly $350,000.[29]

On December 10, the Board convened in the Eastside YMCA to debate its budget and rate options. Despite concerns over aspects of Group Health's planning, the 47 members who attended unanimously supported a dues increase. The Board voted to increase dues by $1 on adults and by $.25 on children, to raise $380,000. It also resigned itself to medical inflation as a new, permanent fact of life and approved consideration of dues adjustments as a routine element of Group Health's annual budgeting.[30]

An old friend returned in April 1960 to keynote Group Health's 13th annual meeting. Jerry Voorhis, director of the Cooperative League, USA, addressed the plight of America's elderly. Of the 16 million citizens over the age of 64, four-fifths eked out their livings on $2,000 a year or less. This put medical care out of the reach of all but a fortunate few, and even benevolent organizations like Group Health refused to accept members over the age of 60.

Voorhis joined with the Board to urge members to write their Congressional representatives in support of the Forand Bill, which would add healthcare to Social Security benefits. first introduced by Representative Aime Forand of Rhode Island in February 1959, this plan was immediately condemned by the AMA as "the first giant step toward socialized medicine." On the other side stood the newly reorganized Group Health Association of America, created in July 1959 when the older Group Health Federation merged with the Labor Health Association. ("Cooperative" had been dropped from the Federation's name in 1956 when it voted to admit noncooperatives such as Kaiser Permanente.)

House Ways & Means Chair Wilbur Mills later offered his own bill to include healthcare as part of federally funded welfare programs, and debate gained intensity as the 1960 elections approached. A new ingredient was added in May 1960 by the man who had taken away Voorhis' seat in Congress 14 years earlier. Vice President Richard Nixon, no doubt with an eye on his own presidential candidacy, joined with Arthur Flemming, Secretary of Health, Education, and Welfare, to offer a more modest program. Their proposal drew fire from both the left and right, and though it went nowhere in Congress, it did introduce a new word into the political vocabulary: Medicare.

Group Health was in the thick of the battle, naturally. In March 1960, Dr. Kahl represented Group Health at the National Forum on Positive Health for Older People in Miami. The Board had endorsed the "principles" of the Forand Bill back in July 1959, but the Cooperative was not unified. Some on the medical staff later opposed incorporation of healthcare into Social Security as creating a "bureaucratic nightmare." Even some trustees feared that the system might encourage an ethic of "let George pay for it" in financing healthcare. This debate would continue for another five years.[31]

A different kind of reform immediately affected Group Health's fortunes in 1960 when federal employees became eligible for health benefits on July 1. The number of Group Health members who worked for the national government more than doubled to 7,000 and pushed total Group Health enrollment past 60,000 by year's end.[32]

The highlight of 1960 came on October 8 with the dedication of the new 173-bed hospital. In a gesture of reconciliation, the Reverend Fred Hunt, pastor of the Capitol Hill Methodist Church, which had opposed the project, offered the invocation (although Hilde Birnbaum remembered that the hospital's neighbors were still bickering as they posed for ceremonial photographs). Assembled dignitaries included Mayor Clinton, State Attorney General John O'Connell, University of Washington School of Medicine dean Dr. George Aagard, and the executive secretary of the Washington State Hospital Association, John Bigelow. They joined Board president George Bolotin and chief of staff Dr. Alfred Magar to unveil a plaque dedicating the hospital to the "15,000 Cooperative families and friends through whose efforts this institution was made possible."[33]

It had taken four years and $3.5 million to create what Dr. Magar called "truly a physical and spiritual monument." Thousands of members and neighbors joined in the celebration of another example of Group Health's remarkable powers of perseverance.

As the new decade began, the Cooperative would need them.

Chapter 9

New Frontiers

1961 ~ 1965

Members Choose Full Coverage over Lower Cost ~
Growth Falters ~ A Friendly Rival Scouts Seattle ~
The Limits of Cooperatism ~ The Medical Staff
Accepts Capitation ~ Group Plans and Marketing
Boost Enrollment ~ Dr. Kahl Passes Away

A few weeks after Group Health dedicated its hospital, Americans went to the polls to elect a president. John F. Kennedy's narrow victory over Richard M. Nixon was hailed as a political and generational watershed, the dawn of a new decade of youthful vigor and social innovation. For the nation and for Group Health, the 1960s promised unlimited possibilities.

For the latter, at least, the return to reality was swift.

Despite a 13 percent surge in enrollment during 1960, mostly fueled by federal employees, the Board again found itself facing a projected deficit of nearly half a million dollars in the coming year. This resulted from general inflation of medical costs and new expenses added by the hospital's opening.

The Board that grappled with these numbers was missing two of its senior officers: Charles Strother and Hilde Birnbaum had both left in July to pursue yearlong sabbaticals. W. Karl Campbell, John Philbin, and Louis Weinzirl were appointed to fill Board vacancies, joining Lyle Mercer, elected in April 1960, as the newest trustees.[1]

They developed two proposals for the membership's review. The first maintained benefits but raised adult dues by more than

14 percent to $8 per month, and levied an extra 50 cents a month on women to reflect their higher demand on services (excluding obstetrics, which was still subject to a separate charge). As an alternative to an across-the-board dues increase, the Board also offered a plan for optional "limited Group Health medical coverage" at the current dues, offset by direct charges for certain services.[2]

This choice was presented to the Cooperative's 14,000-plus member families via a written ballot and a new round of district meetings in January 1961. Ironically, the Board had become concerned about lagging participation during the previous year and commissioned a task force, chaired by Carl Munson, to suggest improvements. While the Board later acted to strengthen the role of the Joint District Council, the threat of another dues hike proved to be the best medicine for lackluster attendance at district meetings.[3]

At these meetings, members offered a variety of counterproposals for reducing the deficit, including greater use of licensed practical nurses (LPNs) to perform medical procedures such as giving medication. They also suggested charging for the first doctor's visit of each year to discourage "unnecessary usage" of Group Health services. Dr. Kahl responded that expanding LPN duties threatened to undermine the quality of care (it was actually illegal until the following July). As to the second idea, he replied that there was little abuse under the present system and a first-visit charge "would not deter the person who feels…a need for medical care, even though it may be more emotional than real."

Other members questioned the priority placed on a new Central Clinic versus the Burien Clinic, and many raised the old issue of annual physical exams. In particular, some wanted to know why Group Health was not providing company-sponsored health coverage to Boeing workers. Kahl explained that Group Health would become hostage to the wild fluctuations in Boeing's payroll, forcing the Co-op to invest in new facilities and staff that would be idled during a major downturn in company employment. He didn't mention that relations between the Co-op and Boeing were still cool a dozen years after the 1948 aerome-chanics strike.[4]

Despite these concerns and cavils, the vast majority of the membership endorsed the dues increase, and again rejected the notion of a limited-care option. By March 1961, a total of 6,861 member families had returned their ballots. Of these, 6,538 voted in favor of the dues increase for full benefits, 203 supported the optional plan, and 20 quit.[5]

No sooner had Group Health cleared this hurdle than it faced a new and unexpected variant on the old problem of growth—that is, the lack of it. New enrollment declined precipitously during the first half of 1961, with only 675 new sign-ups versus the 1,800 anticipated. Without federal workers, the net growth would have been negligible. At the same time, the metropolitan population was growing dramatically, with the effect of reducing Group Health's market share from 14 percent to 10 percent.[6]

The bad news was delivered by Dr. H. Frank Newman, Group Health's new "assistant director for medical affairs." Late in 1960, Dr. Kahl had recognized the necessity for administrative help. While he retained direct responsibility for the hospital, he redefined Rudy Molzan's job as "assistant director for business affairs," and established the new assistant directorship for medical affairs. To fill this slot, Kahl recruited a man with credentials and skills very similar to his own. Dr. Newman, at age 35, had already risen to assistant director at the King County Health Department.[7]

That Dr. Newman's portfolio at Group Health also included enrollment was not accidental, he explained later, since the "medical staff was threatened by growth." Newman recalled, "Their greatest concern was that we could anticipate whatever growth we had as accurately as possible, so that we could get enough staff on board to take care of it." Early in 1961, the staff included 65 physicians, four optometrists, and one other associate. Thus, the physician-patient ratio was below the 1-to-1,000 cap, but any dramatic enrollment gain could upset it.[8]

Thus, slow growth might have been welcomed by the medical staff, but it had other consequences. Sales of bonds lagged, forcing the Board to dip into operating funds to pay construction costs, and member participation in district meetings evaporated, threatening the Co-op's democratic base. The dearth of new enrollment also put Group Health in a classic actuarial bind: It needed to recruit younger, healthier members to help subsidize the cost of older members who consumed more services.

At this moment, a new threat appeared on the horizon. During the summer of 1961, Dr. Kahl had the first of several conversations with Dr. Ernest Saward and other officials of Kaiser Permanente, based in Portland, Oregon. This was the region's oldest prepaid healthcare organization, but its Washington State enrollment was limited chiefly to the Vancouver and Hanford areas. Kaiser officials asked if Group Health was really serious about limiting itself to 80,000 enrollees, with emphasis on full Co-op members versus groups. If so, Kaiser would be delighted to enter the Seattle area to pursue what it viewed as a lucrative market for group enrollment.

Dr. Newman reported that during a tour of Group Health, Kaiser representatives broached the idea of the Co-op "joining forces with them, and becoming part of the Kaiser organization." Group Health's Board and staff recoiled from the suggestion, fearing the loss of the Co-op's own identity and the sacrifice of its consumer democracy. Kaiser deferred to Group Health's judgment, and the two groups entered an informal reciprocity agreement to treat each other's patients in emergencies.[9]

It was all very friendly and fraternal, but the implication was clear: If Group Health did not begin to pursue group contracts, somebody else would. This triggered a long debate within the organization. The notion of fighting for members was new and unwelcome for trustees, who had confidently chosen to ignore the marketing efforts of King County Medical. When in the summer of 1960 a trustee had commented on the sudden appearance of "billboards of competing medical care programs," Hilde Birnbaum sniffed that such signs were "undesirable" (a lighted sign for the hospital was later approved only on the condition that it be "tasteful"). She preferred "dignified news releases" to promote Group Health. It took another year for the Board to

"Crusading Doctor" Michael Shadid (left) came to Seattle in
1945 at the invitation of Addison Shoudy, who is also shown
below (right) planning Group Health Cooperative's sales
strategy with its first president, Tom Bevan (center), and
Dick Powell.

Ruth Brown serves a customer at Group Health's original downtown pharmacy. The first chief of staff Dr. John McNeel (front row, center) poses with his medical staff in 1946.

Most of the Medical Security Clinic's nursing and clerical staff shifted to Group Health Cooperative in 1946. St. Luke's Hospital is shown shortly after its expansion in 1950.

An early map guided holders of Group Health membership cards to the Cooperative's growing complex on Seattle's Capitol Hill.

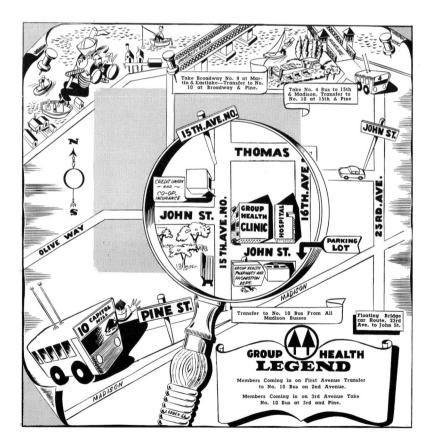

Bill Jordan (top) took
member card #1 in
1946. Dr. George
Beeler served as
Group Health
Cooperative's first
director. Jack Cluck
defeated the King
County Medical
Society in court.

**GROUP HEALTH
COOPERATIVE**

*Brings You
A Family*

HEALTH PLAN

WITH COMPLETE, ONE-PRICE
Health Care For the Whole Family

Medical • Surgical • Hospital
Preventive • Cooperative

GROUP HEALTH COOPERATIVE OF PUGET SOUND
Renton Clinic   415 Third Ave.
Phone 3487

Nurse Elise Cook and Dr. Sandy MacColl show off the first GHC babies: Trygve Eriskson (left), Wendy Lou Hougen, Joanna Marie Jenner, and Roger Paulsen. Dr. Harry Kraft, DDS, examines one of the Dental Co-op's first patients.

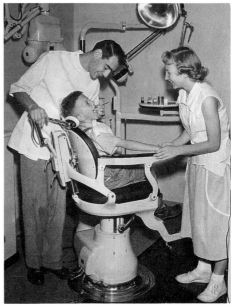

This cartoon promoted an early bond drive, which raised funds to purchase the Costa Vista Apartments for the original Capitol Hill clinic. Below, Dr. Charlotte Bansmer (far right) checks a member of the Hemmen family, a virtual cooperative in itself.

Aubrey Davis (right) joined the Board of Trustees in 1951 and has been a leader ever since. Veteran cooperators Chester Kingsbury (left) and Lyle Mercer have helped to safeguard the organization's democratic values (photo: Kim Zumwalt).

Dr. Bernice Sachs and Charles Strother, PhD, (below right) championed mental health services. Ernie Conrad's financial insights helped the Cooperative squeeze through many a tight spot.

Soggy weather did not dampen Cooperative chair Hilde Birnbaum's (opposite page) enthusiasm as she joined City Councilmember David Levine (left) and County Commissioner Dean McLean to break ground for the original Northgate Clinic (below) in March 1957. Art Siegal (top) and Bob Scott devoted long hours as early trustees.

Dr. Alfred Magar served as chief of staff from 1953 to 1961. He appears below (front right) standing with Group Health Cooperative director Dr. John Kahl and the medical staff in 1957.

Dr. John Quinn (right) was one of the first new doctors recruited by Group Health. Dr. Daniel Arst, pictured with a patient, served as chief of staff in the early 1960s.

Dr. Richard Handschin (top) organized Group Health Cooperative's first research efforts. Dr. Arthur Schultz led the medical staff from 1965 to 1970.

Dr. Robert Glenn Hartquist was chief of staff from 1971 to 1976. Director Dr. Frank Newman (center) and controller Rudy Molzan consult with hospital supervisor Marian Gillespie shortly before her retirement in 1970.

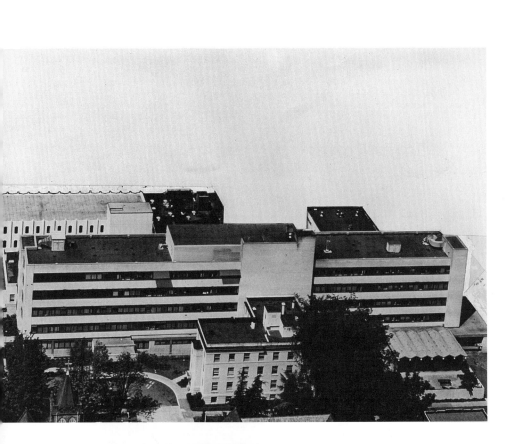

*As head of the Cooperative
League, U.S.A., Jerry Voorhis
praised Group Health
Cooperative in 1948 "as the
most hopeful sign in the whole
country" for healthcare reform.
By the time he retired in 1966,
GHC's Capitol Hill facilities
had expanded from the tiny St.
Luke's (foreground) into a
major hospital-clinic complex.*

authorize management to "recommend what is ethical, possible and desirable to improve our image in the community," and empanel a Select Committee "to prepare an advertising and public relations policy."[10]

The Board also resisted pleas for new facilities. Kitsap residents renewed their petition for a clinic, and Eastside members offered to sign up 3,000 new members to finance their own facility. The Board politely declined both offers and stuck to its plan to build a new Central Clinic followed by one in Burien.[11]

Also during 1961, Group Health took the first serious steps toward offering mental health services, a field then being promoted nationally by the Kennedy family. The National Institute on Mental Health encouraged Group Health in pursuing Dr. Strother's idea for a pilot project study grant, and the Co-op joined with other groups in promoting creation of a city psychiatric clinic.[12]

Group Health also joined with the Group Health Dental Co-op and Credit Union and the Nationwide Insurance Company to discuss creating a new federation to succeed the defunct Cascade League. Support for this was divided; some objected to Nationwide's participation because it was a mutual company, not a true co-op, and others feared that Group Health might be harmed by imprudent promotions such as an earlier, disastrous marketing campaign for low-cost home freezers. For its part, the medical staff remained opposed to any affiliation with nonmedical co-ops.[13]

Despite these misgivings, the Board endorsed joining the new Puget Sound Cooperative League in principle on December 20, 1961. At the same meeting, Lyle Mercer led Group Health's left wing in striking a blow against an old foe, the Chamber of Commerce. Group Health's membership in this "capitalist" association had long rankled movement purists, and they used the Chamber's proposed 50 percent dues increase to win a vote to allow Group Health's membership to lapse. This battle would be refought many times.[14]

Group Health began 1962 with a new medical chief of staff, cardiologist Dr. Daniel B. Arst. He succeeded Dr. Magar at a moment when events again vindicated the staff's innate conservatism. Group Health physicians had delayed introduction of the new Sabin oral polio vaccine to see if problems arose elsewhere. They did, and Group Health members were once again spared exposure to a potentially dangerous vaccine.[15]

The main event in Seattle that April was the opening of the Century 21 World's Fair. Along with many other local businesses, Group Health was invited to sign a guarantee of $10,000 to underwrite the fair's expenses if it failed to break even. The Co-op thought this was a little steep and pledged $5,000 (Century 21 ultimately made a small profit, and Group Health's pledge was not needed). Group Health also put out the word through national groups that members of any cooperative would be welcome at Group Health if they had a medical problem while visiting the fair. It also extended care to the fair's 238 employees as part of a special group assembled by Ernie Conrad.[16]

Also that spring, the debate over Medicare resumed with the introduction of the King-Anderson bill, which became President Kennedy's top legislative priority. Jack Cluck noted, "It is unique in our recent history for the President and the leaders of both Houses of Congress to give active leadership to legislation relating to prepaid medical care and [to be] urging groups like ours to get behind it." The Board joined other prepaid plans belonging to the Group Health Association of America in supporting the plan, but the medical staff again balked.

Dr. Kahl explained that he opposed the bill because it too closely resembled the national health programs of Great Britain and Canada, which were "failing" to provide a "high quality of medical care" while driving up costs and driving away experienced specialists. This was a red flag for cooperators such as Hilde Birnbaum, who had rejoined the Board, and Jack Cluck, who defended socialized medicine. In the end it was academic, for the King-Anderson bill ultimately died in committee under the weight of numerous hostile amendments promoted in large part by the American Medical Association.[17]

The issue of lagging enrollment growth continued to preoccupy the Board throughout 1962. In February, Board president

Art Siegal tapped Ben Asia to chair a Select Committee on Public Relations. Its real mission was much broader: "to consider whether a program directed at the community as a whole would provide a better framework for our membership contacts and our general sales effort." In other words, should Group Health expand its marketing beyond the recruitment of individual Co-op members?

The committee grappled with fundamental issues over the next seven months, asking if Group Health had "lost the cooperative spirit that distinguished its original membership" and "what actually are the opportunities for, or limits of, effective democractic action—'consumer control' —in an organization such as Group Health?" Somewhat sadly, the committee recognized "the membership today includes a smaller proportion of 'cooperatively-minded' people" and that most members "are mainly, if not entirely, concerned with the quality and kind of services provided and the cost." As to Group Health's internal democracy, a survey the previous year revealed that most newer members did not even realize that they had any rights in the Co-op's governance.

At the same time, the committee reminded the Board that Group Health had been formed with a broad and inclusive mission "to serve the greatest number of people in the Puget Sound Area upon the consumer's cooperative plan" and "to develop some of the most outstanding hospitals and medical centers to be found anywhere." This pioneering evangelism was now a marketing imperative.

The committee decided that "the achievements of Group Health probably provided the best and only arguments" for membership promotion. While it urged more aggressive sales outreach to targeted groups, such as professional associations, public employees, and Boeing workers, it ruled that paid advertising was "not to be considered." In essence, the committee concluded that improved internal and external community relations campaigns provided the best and most "ethical" means to tell Group Health's story, reinvigorate its consumer democracy, and attract new members. Most important, the committee urged the

Board to "prepare a concise statement of Group Health objectives for some manageable period—five years, perhaps."[18]

The committee's report of September 21, 1962, highlighted the growing divergence between the Board and medical staff's views toward the application of cooperative principles to healthcare delivery. The gap had been widening since July when the Joint Conference Commitee reviewed the final bylaws for the new Puget Sound Cooperative League. Dr. Arst reported that "the staff does not feel a compelling need to see a Cooperative League formed," but he was contradicted a few days later when the medical staff voted, albeit narrowly, to endorse joining the League. The Board followed suit on July 25.[19]

In October, Dr. Arst used the Select Committee's report as a wedge to reopen the cooperative issue. He said he long had a "disturbing feeling that this [cooperative] system may not be practical for a long-term medical care program." While Arst praised the "individuals who brought this organization to its present status," he mocked "the rigid adherence to cooperative principles and the dogged determination to make them work forever in healthcare." Arst pointed to Group Health's older, namesake healthcare cooperative in Washington, D.C., which, he said, had "realized that cooperative memberships would have to be a much smaller proportion of their organization if it were to continue to be successful."

He urged Group Health to undertake a similar "reappraisal and reorganization, so that this be not primarily a cooperative, but rather a successful healthcare program....We must realize that the course of events has forced, not an abandonment of the principles of Group Health Cooperative, but rather a realignment of them in the interests of continued success and service to our members." Stalwarts such as Dr. Sandy MacColl and Hilde Birnbaum took issue with Arst's views, but he was not alone in his gloomy and heretical assessment of the future of cooperatism as the central tenet at Group Health.[20]

Simultaneous with the work of the Select Committee, an Ad Hoc Committee on District Problems examined the base of Group Health's consumer participation. On October 15, committee chair

John Philbin reported that half of the Co-op's 14 districts were "inactive" and 5 of these lacked any elected officers. The cause was "the simple fact that there is little required work for the members to perform at the district level."

Philbin reminded the Board that the districts played a key marketing role by providing "a corps of active, well informed and oriented cooperative members who in turn would seek to interest others" in Group Health. The committee's remedy to district-level apathy was first outlined by health education director Wade Spalding. He proposed to replace the existing system with four districts focused on the three existing area clinics and the anticipated development of an Eastside facility (Group Health had already purchased property in Houghton, but no building plans were in place). The Board rejected this reform, but did present an eight-district plan to members for discussion at the next annual meeting.[21]

During 1962, a third group effort, dubbed "Task Force X," addressed "how best to increase the revenue" to Group Health. In August, the task force projected a $270,000 operating deficit. It proposed two alternatives: a 7 percent dues increase (Plan A) or charging $1.00 per "registration" for any Group Health visit and $.50 per prescription filled (Plan B). Dr. Arst preferred the latter, arguing "there is no plan in the world, including the British system now, that doesn't utilize some charges for service." The task force rejected a third option, eliminating prescription coverage, despite Dr. Arst's agitation for this change.[22]

The alternative plans were presented to members in the form of a ballot that fall and 8,169 families cast their votes. Plan A was preferred by 6,057, Plan B won 2,007 votes, and the rest didn't like either option. Although the membership had again overwhelmingly voted to protect their comprehensive benefits, even at the expense of a dues increase, the constituency for an alternative was growing.[23]

Group Health received one piece of financial good news late in 1962: approval of a federal Hill-Burton grant to aid expansion of the Central Clinic. The Co-op had been chasing these state-administered funds, which paid up to 40 percent of hospital and medical center construction costs, since 1956. It applied first to finance the expansion of Renton in 1958, then to add a treatment and diagnostic center to Northgate in 1960. Both were rejected, despite some frank conversations with state Health Department Director Dr. Bernard Bucove.

Finally, with the aid of State Senator Andy Hess, a grant for $295,000 was awarded in September 1962 for a diagnostic component in the Central Clinic. This drew immediate and loud protests from Group Health's old nemesis, the state medical society, which asked the state attorney-general to investigate and rescind Group Health's grant. The AMA also argued that "closed panel" organizations were not eligible for Hill-Burton grants (Group Health addressed this problem by liberalizing its bylaws to accept private patients). These protests fell on deaf ears, and the state later sweetened its grant by another $63,075.[24]

The enrollment picture was not so rosy. During the first 10 months of 1962, Group Health netted only 731 additional members (although a late surge created a year-end gain of over 2,000). On the recommendation of Task Force X, the Board voted on January 23, 1963, to place greater emphasis on group sales. The new policy bore fruit six months later with the signing of a contract with the Seattle Professional Engineering Employees Association (SPEEA), which chiefly represented engineers at Boeing.

Despite this new contract, Boeing refused to handle payroll deductions for its other workers, particularly aeromechanics. Dr. Newman recalled, "they never forgave us" for supporting IAM in the 1948 strike. "We would never have expanded our Boeing Group without the SPEEA group, and they simply would not settle their contract until they were permitted to have Group Health coverage," Newman said. A Teamster local's intransigence similarly forced that union's regional joint council to offer Group Health to its members, Newman asserted, "when they were not about to have a contract with anybody unless they could control it."[25]

Membership surged during 1963 as new group enrollees signed up at twice the rate of new Co-op members. This intensified the effect of a severe shortage of trained nurses then being experienced by Group Health and other hospitals. To fill the gap, more than 100 volunteer "nursettes" were recruited and deployed to assist professional staff.[26]

The annual meeting on April 20, 1963, marked Dr. Strother's return to the Board. The meeting also featured a debate over endorsing President Kennedy's call for a nuclear test ban treaty, but the issue was tabled. Dr. Strother was later elected vice president, while Aubrey Davis succeeded Art Siegal as president.[27]

As enrollment neared 68,000 by year's end, Dr. Kahl and the Board took a fresh look at the challenges posed by growth. Demographers projected that the metropolitan Seattle area would grow by nearly 200 percent over the next two decades and that most of these new residents would locate in the suburbs.

Dr. Kahl calculated that Group Health had adequate outpatient facilities to serve up to 90,000 members, but that its new hospital was already reaching capacity. He recommended that if Group Health were to grow beyond the 80,000 limit previously set, it should "plan for our next plateau" of 120,000. He also warned that Group Health might be reaching the limit of its ability to self-capitalize new facilities through bond sales. In particular, he feared that expanding on Capitol Hill "is going to be a tremendously expensive undertaking and may be impossible." One solution, he said, might be to develop a "second center or a second co-op" to duplicate the Capitol Hill complex at a new site.[28]

The Board was not so pessimistic on December 18, 1963, when it voted to "remove any limits now included in the Cooperative's policy on expected size and proceed to investigate at what rate the Cooperative should grow." The Rubicon had now been crossed, and Group Health would never be the same. Enrollment leapt by nearly 8,000 members during 1964, and the annual growth rate would drop below 9 percent only once during the next decade.[29]

The year 1964 was marked by steady progress and little conflict. The Board briefly entertained a proposal to buy the nearby Madison Hospital but rejected the facility as "useless." The new Burien Clinic opened on April 11, while work went ahead on the

Central Clinic expansion and new plans were prepared to expand the Renton Clinic, eliciting the usual groans from the medical staff who regarded it as a frontier outpost.[30]

The annual meeting approved a number of reforms, collapsing Group Health's 14 districts into 8 and approving absentee ballots for the election of trustees. In the most important change to Group Health's tacit constitution, the medical staff signed a new contract establishing a capitation system. Under this agreement, the staff as a whole received a lump sum based on enrollment for allocation as it chose. This made the staff responsible for its own budgeting and cost control. Dr. Newman credited Kahl for recognizing that, until capitation was adopted, "we were always going to have this adversarial relationship with the staff," which "would keep demanding more and more doctors" without regard to financial impacts. It was the final piece in the strategy to begin marketing aggressively to groups and to hold Kaiser and other potential competitors at bay.[31]

Also that spring, the first shot was fired on a new public health front, when *View* published a letter from Mrs. Millard Petersky asking that smoking be banned in Group Health waiting rooms. The magazine's next issue drew more letters, including the comment that while limiting smoking was a matter of courtesy, "nobody should be asked to give up smoking." Dr. Kahl, it should be noted, was rarely seen without a cigarette.[32]

In October 1964, Dr. Bernice Sachs was elected president of the American Medical Women's Association. This honor for Group Health's expert and leading staff champion of mental health services may have helped persuade the Joint Conference Committee to approve the hiring of a full-time psychiatrist the following month.[33]

This was also a victory for Dr. Strother, under whose renewed leadership Group Health's activities in medical and mental health research began to intensify. One of the studies marked the return of Dr. K. Warner Schaie, who had won his doctorate doing the first analysis of Group Health's membership. In 1964, he interviewed nearly 1,000 members for a detailed attitudinal study; he found them largely satisfied with the Cooperative.[34]

Dr. Strother spent much of 1964 developing a pilot study of mental health services in a prepaid plan solicited by the National Institute for Mental Health in late 1963. A year later, NIMH turned down the application but talks went on. Undaunted, Group Health made mental health and the new Seattle Crisis Clinic the subjects of its first "All-City Health Education Meeting" on January 15, 1965, and attracted more than 400 citizens.[35]

The new year saw enrollment pass 76,000, and the election of a new medical chief of staff, Dr. Arthur L. Schultz. His hallmark was the hopeful, upbeat approach he took to each new obstacle. By way of explanation, he later quoted an older practitioner of his specialty: "A neurosurgeon who deals with brain tumors needs to carry with him a formidable amount of optimism."[36]

Amid preparations for a gala open house at the new Central Clinic on April 3, 1965, it became clear that Dr. Kahl's health was in serious decline. He had suffered chronic digestive tract troubles for several years, and his condition had worsened dramatically following his wife's death the previous September. He was not eager to give up the reins, however, and it took the man who had recruited him a decade earlier, Dr. Strother, to finally persuade him to resign. Dr. Frank Newman was effectively running Group Health by the end of March, although the Board agreed to keep Dr. Kahl on salary through August.[37]

Dr. Kahl died of a stroke on July 18 before he could collect his final paycheck. Group Health mourned the man who had shepherded it through a challenging but remarkably peaceful period of growth and maturation. Under his guidance, the Cooperative had completed a new hospital, Central Clinic, and branch clinics at Northgate and Burien, while nearly doubling its enrollment and tripling its revenue.[38]

On July 31, 1965, just days after Dr. Kahl's funeral, President Lyndon B. Johnson signed the Medicare Act into law. Another revolution in healthcare was about to begin.

Chapter 10

From Medicare to HMOs

1965 ~ 1971

[handshake emblem]

*Enter Medicare ~ Dr. Newman Takes Over ~ The
Great Society –First Shots in the Abortion War ~
Taking Affirmative Action ~ The Boeing Bust Inflates
Enrollment ~ President Nixon Champions HMOs ~
America Discovers Group Health*

*D*espite lingering concerns over some of its details, Medicare was welcomed by most Group Health members,
physicians, managers, and trustees as a long-overdue
reform. After decades of agitation, the federal government had
finally taken a major step toward establishing healthcare as a
right for all to enjoy, not a luxury for the wealthy few. But Medicare would soon confirm the old adage: Be careful what you wish
for, because it might come true.

The bill signed by President Johnson offered the public a
"three-layered cake" of health reform baked in the oven of congressional compromise. Part A of Medicare covered hospitalization and some extended care costs on a reimbursement basis
through compulsory insurance paid by workers through Social
Security. Part B was a partially subsidized, voluntary program
to cover physician care. The legislation also established Medicaid, which expanded federal aid to finance healthcare for the
poor through state-administered programs.

To overcome opposition from the medical establishment, the
new law effectively institutionalized the fee-for-service system
while liberating medical services from any competitive con-
straints, which had never been terribly strong to begin with.

Rather than establishing a binding rate schedule for medical procedures, Medicare allowed doctors and hospitals to charge their "usual, customary and reasonable" fees. Since reimbursement was all but assured, these naturally began to rise.

Not only was there no incentive to control costs, Medicare created a positive impulse to raise rates in order to lift the average basis for future charges. Government subsidies, payroll deductions, and relatively painless supplemental insurance premiums insulated consumers from the reality of these escalating costs, creating an inflationary hothouse in which the fiscal temperature steadily climbed and new and expensive procedures bloomed like tropical orchids.[1]

In such a climate, Group Health was as out of place as a Douglas fir in an African jungle. Even in the absence of direct competition, the Cooperative's consumer ethos made it inherently sensitive to costs, and it practiced a very conservative brand of medicine because it operated on advance payments based on the historical expense of serving its enrollment rather than on the collection of charges for services actually delivered. Indeed, Group Health had no machinery for tracking or billing the costs of individual procedures.

These incongruities had been recognized even before Medicare became available on July 1, 1966. Group Health joined with Kaiser and other prepaid group practice programs to seek amendments and regulations that recognized their unique situation in relation to fee-for-service reimbursements. This effort was only partially successful, but Group Health's experiences and innovations under Medicare would lead to later reforms.[2]

Early in 1966, the Board of Trustees adopted a Part B plan offering Medicare participants full Group Health coverage for $6 per month and amended the membership agreement to admit members over the age of 65. (Group Health continued to deny membership to people between the ages of 60 and 65 until 1980.) Significantly, it did not impose copayments and it did not isolate Medicare patients into their own actuarial pool for purposes of setting fees. Thus, the Board reaffirmed its commitment to "community rating" for its enrollment as a whole.[3]

On January 1, 1966, Group Health welcomed its first full-time psychiatrist, Dr. Jack Brown, to the staff. Under the impetus of new federal employee health benefit mandates to provide mental health services, he set to work designing a program for all Group Health enrollees. Later that month, Dr. Bernice Sachs televised her mental health advocacy nationwide as a guest on Johnny Carson's popular "Tonight Show."[4]

Growth remained Group Health's main preoccupation. Executive director Dr. Frank Newman outlined a $5 million capital program to keep pace with enrollment, including adding 150 more beds to the hospital, expanding the Northgate Clinic, and building a new, larger Renton Clinic. The latter project earned Group Health its second Hill-Burton grant in the amount of $202,000. Newman also noted that Medicare would increase pressure to build an "extended care facility" and that Group Health should be prepared to add facilities on the Eastside and in Snohomish County.

In reviewing these plans, the Board decided that the word "clinic" was too restrictive in describing Group Health's multi-service satellite facilities and adopted a new term, "medical center." That summer, the Board purchased a 10-acre site in Lynnwood for $41,000, sold the former Keigwin clinic, and began construction of a new $1.1 million Renton Medical Center. It also reorganized its visiting nurses as Home Health Services, which greatly expanded Group Health's delivery of home nursing and physical therapy, particularly for the elderly. This program also allowed nurses to prove themselves as innovative members of the healthcare team.[5]

By now the Sixties were in full swing, and Group Health found itself confronting some new and unfamiliar issues. While the baby boom had peaked—live births dropped from 17 per 1,000 members in 1960 to 12 per 1,000 just five years later—the sexual revolution was just beginning to flower. Hilde Birnbaum argued that Group Health coverage should be broadened to include contraceptive aids such as diaphragms. She lost the first round in March 1966, but there were many more to go. Soon after, another long policy debate over "natural childbirth" procedures made its debut.[6]

View magazine reported on "Project Vietnam," a volunteer corps of Group Health physicians led by Dr. William Pope, providing medical services to civilians caught in the escalating war. The same issue of *View* also noted the mounting "drug menace" among young people.[7]

The most heated controversy of 1966 erupted over the new Puget Sound Cooperative League and its newspaper, *The Cooperator*. The tabloid was mailed to 37,000 households, most of which were Group Health members. This fact rankled more conservative Group Health physicians, who regarded the League and its paper as parasites preying on the captive market of their patients.

Their criticisms found fresh support when *The Cooperator* began selling space on its "Opinion Mart" page for outside editorial columns. There were a few grumbles when Aubrey Davis and Art Siegal bought an ad endorsing Dave Sprague's candidacy for the State Legislature, but when the John Birch Society purchased editorial space to present its own ultra-right-wing ideology, a chorus of howls rose from every quarter.

In November 1966, Dr. John Quinn fired back in a paid column of his own, but his target was not the Birch Society. He dismissed the whole idea of cooperatism as largely irrelevant: "Prepayment, group practice and good medical care are the cornerstones of Group Health and they are not unique to Co-ops." He also blasted the "cluster of satellite or in some instances saprophytic Co-ops...congregated on Capitol Hill about Group Health." (Saprophytic organisms such as fungi feed on dead matter.) No formal break with the Puget Sound Co-op League is recorded in Group Health minutes and trustee Gene Lux later took over as the League's president, but the organization withered away after a few years.[8]

Whatever the merits of Dr. Quinn's complaints, he picked an indelicate moment to air them. Cooperatism lost two of its most dedicated champions in 1966. First in April, at the 50th annual meeting of the Cooperative League, U.S.A., Jerry Voorhis announced his retirement. Then, on August 13, Dr. Michael Shadid died. He had turned leadership of the pioneering Elk

City Community Hospital over to his son a few years earlier, but it did not survive as a cooperative.

Despite his opposition to the purchase of the Medical Security Clinic in 1946, Dr. Shadid deserves credit as the physician who delivered Group Health into the world. Twenty years later, it was the largest of the brood of medical cooperatives that he had helped to birth and, for all its internal wrangling, the most faithful embodiment of the principles Dr. Shadid first articulated.[9]

On Februay 19, 1967, Group Health opened a new wing at Northgate. Based on a new 10-year plan prepared by Dr. Newman, which forecast an enrollment of 238,000 by 1976, the Board reversed its previous policy and accelerated construction at Lynnwood to relieve pressure on Northgate while delaying expansion of the Capitol Hill complex. The Co-op also committed to opening a medical center in Everett, where 3,000 pulp and paper workers were eager to sign up.[10]

Group Health's 20th annual meeting in April 1967 coincided with the Group Health Association of America's national convention in Seattle. Group Health also hosted the GHAA's "Group Health Institute," featuring scholarly presentations on preventive medicine and other topics. Shortly after this, the Board elected Dr. Charles Strother as its new president, and his long-held dream was fulfilled on July 1 when Dr. Brown formally inaugurated the new Mental Health Department.[11]

In December 1967, Group Health enrollment passed 100,000, and it added another 10,000 to its rolls—four-fifths from groups—during 1968. This rapid growth and the opening of the new Renton Medical Center on January 14 were stretching Group Health's medical staff thin. Dr. Schultz paid a visit to Northgate in April and found "a group of weary doctors" juggling 285 new charts each month on top of a load of 1,800 patients per physician. Group Health's staff shortage was compounded when Dr. Harmon Truax died suddenly in May, and the Co-op turned to the Virginia Mason Clinic for the loan of several of its staff urologists.[12]

At the 1968 annual meeting, Dr. Newman reported that nearly 14 percent of Group Health revenue was now coming from Medicare. Not coincidentally, the cost of treating its non-Medicare population was also rising by 8 percent annually, which forced a 15 percent rate boost to catch up (while monthly Medicare Part B rates were lowered by $4 to reflect higher reimbursements). Accelerating medical inflation did not prevent the Board from broadening coverage during the year. It added outpatient mental health services and home health visits to the basic menu of services, and expanded out-of-area emergency reimbursements. Group Health also eliminated all "waivers" on pre-existing conditions, but the debate over covering contraceptives continued without resolution.[13]

Under its latest (but hardly new) president, Aubrey Davis, the Board reactivated the dormant health education program with the hiring of Dr. David Chivers, and formalized Group Health's research program by naming its first director, Dr. Richard Handschin, and establishing a joint Board-Staff Research Committee. Group Health entered close cooperation with the UW School of Medicine to launch the latter's Research Center and to plan a program for general practice residencies that was launched the following June. Late in 1968, Dr. Robert M. "Burry" Pelzel transferred from Northgate to fill Dr. Newman's former post as assistant director for medical affairs.[14]

The year 1968 marked the pinnacle of President Johnson's "Great Society" initiatives as the new Demonstration Cities Act was implemented in response to the inner-city riots that had taken place in Seattle and elsewhere over the previous several years. Better known as "Model Cities," this program funded a comprehensive array of community development and social service activities, which were planned and administered by local governments and citizen groups. Group Health was invited to help put together an experimental benefit package to be offered by the Seattle Model City Community Health Board along with a King County Medical plan to low-income residents in the Central Area.[15]

President Richard Nixon's new administration slowed but did not end such social experiments in 1969. Group Health contracted with the state Department of Public Assistance to provide federally funded "Plan 8" coverage, which ultimately served more than 2,000 recipients of Aid to Families with Dependent Children. It later contracted with the federal Office of Economic Opportunity to establish a "Plan 9" health program for some 500 low-income families in rural King County. Group Health's cost of service fell 30 percent below that of other providers in such programs, and these early efforts gave it an invaluable base of data and practical experience when discussions of comprehensive healthcare reform heated up in the early 1970s.[16]

Despite its social idealism, Group Health was cautious in taking on these new obligations. "We had been under considerable pressure for not doing more for the poor," Dr. Newman recalls, "and that was difficult for us to do because we were already growing as rapidly as we could." By mid-1969, the national aerospace industry was beginning to slump and Boeing began to lay off workers. Newman told Group Health controller William Pyle, "Why don't we just go ahead and take on so many thousand Medicaid enrollees to compensate for what we think we may lose" in group enrollment. Contrary to such pessimism, Group Health did not lose group business, and in fact grew by another 10,000 enrollees during 1969.[17]

In accordance with its 10-year plan, Group Health focused its capital expansion to the north and east during 1969. While construction proceeded on the Lynnwood Medical Center, the Cooperative encountered difficulties finding a suitable location in Everett. Things also became complicated on the Eastside. The construction of a drive-in theater next to Group Health's property in Houghton ruled out that site for a new medical complex (although this might have given patients a source of free, if silent, entertainment), and community opposition stalled plans for its Bellevue location.

Meanwhile, pressure grew for Group Health to expand into Pierce County. The Board began a protracted series of talks with the Northern Pacific Benevolent Association (NPBA), which represented railroad workers and operated Tacoma's aging Mountain View Hospital. Although Board minutes record "a consensus that Group Health should take a fairly aggressive role in tying this up," management could not reach agreement with the NPBA, which was reluctant to surrender any of its autonomy.[18]

Staff recruitment began to catch up with enrollment by mid-1969, when the physician count reached 107. Expansion of the Capitol Hill complex remained on hold because of finances and neighborhood resistance, but Group Health did open a satellite clinic in the downtown Seattle Medical-Dental Building on June 29.[19]

That same month, Group Health and the UW School of Medicine offered the first family practice residencies. The two institutions also collaborated on another innovative program, "Medex," to retrain military medics returning from Vietnam as professional paramedics. The effort was conceived by Dr. Richard Smith, a UW public health professor, who enlisted Group Health's Dr. Robert Monroe as an early and enthusiastic collaborator. The program's first African-American participant, Richard Turnipseed, was later trained and employed at Group Health.[20]

While Vietnam dominated the headlines during 1969 and 1970, Group Health focused its attention on another divisive issue closer to home: abortion. The Co-op took its first step into a 20-year storm of controversy in January 1969. The Community Affairs Committee asked the Board to endorse legislation sponsored by Planned Parenthood and others to liberalize the state law, which then permitted abortions only where a pregnancy jeopardized the mother's life.

The Board reviewed the issue carefully. Trustees noted that medical opinion was growing more liberal on the issue, and that many physicians were now performing abortions in cases involving "psychiatric problems and they [were] not being prosecuted" despite the law. Fear was expressed that liberalization might make Washington "a Mecca for women seeking an abortion," but chief of staff Dr. Schultz replied that "the only way this state would become an abortion mill is if we have a lot of crooked doctors," something he doubted.

Ralph Bremer sounded a prescient note when he speculated aloud "about people who would oppose this legislation on the basis of religious belief." He answered his own question by noting that "nothing in this change prevents them from acting in accordance with their own convictions." Aubrey Davis added that, in fact, the new law "would end the imposition of private religious convictions on the general public and would leave the decision in each case to the patient and the doctor."

The Board then voted unanimously to endorse abortion reform, which became a priority for Group Health's first full-time lobbyist, Kenneth Flemming, when he was hired in March. The Board's position was aired in *View* magazine, and drew only one dissenting letter. It was a false indicator of things to come.[21]

The state legislature passed the reform bill in January 1970, subject to a referendum the following November. While the campaign over Referendum 20 became quite agitated across the state, barely a ripple was stirred at Group Health. Voters endorsed the new law by a solid majority on November 2, and the Board voted to add abortion to its basic coverage three weeks later. Rather than ending the debate, passage of the new law lit a slow fuse among religious and social conservatives inside Group Health and out.

A more immediate conflict briefly stopped construction of Group Health's expansion on Capitol Hill when "black contractors" picketed the construction site as part of city-wide protests against racial discrimination in the building trades. In September, Lyle Mercer won passage of a new policy requiring the Cooperative's contractors and subcontractors "to employ members of minority races in reasonable proportion to the distribution of population in the community."

Group Health reviewed its own employment and found that 12.4 percent of its work force belonged to minority groups. This compared well with the population at large, but the overall statistic concealed white dominance of higher-paid jobs and professions.[22]

The Co-op had by then hired its first African-American physician, Dr. James Garrison. An obstetrician with the U.S. Army at Fort Riley, Kansas, Garrison responded to a Group Health employment ad. He remembered that Dr. Schultz followed up with a phone call. "You seem well-qualified," he told Garrison.

"I better tell you something," Garrison said. "I'm black."

"I don't care if you're purple," Schultz answered, "as long as you can do the job."

Dr. Garrison was flown to Seattle and quizzed by his future colleagues during a dinner at the Swedish Club. One formulated a hypothetical problem: A patient calls Group Health in the middle of the night to report that she's gone into labor. Garrison is dispatched but the patient refuses to let him in because he's black. How would he handle this?

"I'd call another doctor and go back to bed."

This satisfied the interview committee and Garrison was hired in March 1969. He was personally very impressed by the medical staff's commitment to affirmative action, and during his 20 years at Group Health, Dr. Garrison rose to become chief of obstetrics and chief of staff of the Central Region, serving greater Seattle.[23]

In December 1970, Dr. Glenn Hartquist was elected by the medical staff, now numbering nearly 140 physicians and associates, to succeed Dr. Schultz. He had been recruited by Group Health in 1960 to help cope with the surge of federal employee enrollments. Five years later, Dr. Schultz had pointed him out and commented prophetically, "There's a bright young man, a future Chief of Staff." Indeed, he was the youngest chief of staff yet.[24]

Hartquist first proved himself an able administrator as chief of the new Downtown Medical Center. There, he pioneered the "personal physician" panel system that would later be adopted throughout Group Health. He credits Dr. Charles Wischman for "popularizing" the approach, but for Hartquist it was a necessity as he and half a dozen physicians prepared to transfer downtown from Capitol Hill in 1969. The question was, How many patients would transfer with them?

He recalled, some patients declared, "I'll never leave you, I'm going to follow you down there," and others said, "There's not enough parking down there, I hate downtown, I'd love to stay with you, but I'm going to find a doctor up here on the hill." Hartquist and his staff surveyed their patients to see how many fell into each category. "Pretty soon, each doctor had a box" of survey responses, Hartquist remembers, "and it suddenly dawned on me that this is the first time we've ever identified a practice."[25]

Boeing employment had continued its steep nosedive throughout 1970. Nearly 60,000 of the company's Puget Sound workers were pushed out or jumped, and few had parachutes. As the impact of mass layoffs rippled through the region, King County Medical lost 100,000 members, a third of its enrollment.

It was a different story at Group Health, where many laid-off workers chose "group conversion" to maintain health coverage at their own expense while they sought new jobs. Group Health was clearly a beneficiary of the economic anxiety of the period. The higher cost of its coverage vis-a-vis King County Medical (group conversion dues were even higher) was offset by its comprehensiveness, providing a measure of security in otherwise uncertain times.

To the astonishment of Dr. Newman and his forecasters, Group Health enrollment not only did not fall with "the Boeing Bust," it actually shot upward by another 14,000—and pushed group enrollment past Co-op membership for the first time since 1948. Group Health ended 1970 with a total of nearly 136,000 enrollees.[26]

Dr. Newman saw no cause for alarm as he finished a new 10-year plan in January 1971, but he reaffirmed "that a 10 percent growth represents the limit that the Co-op, with its present resources, can achieve without seriously jeopardizing service or burdening members with excessive capital and interest costs." Newman outlined possible innovations in medical benefits, technology, and organization, such as coverage of contraception, renal dialysis, and greater use of paramedical staff. With more than $11 million in new construction already under way or planned, Newman stressed the importance of determining "where we want to grow" in order to pursue a "definite program of decentralization" of specialist and hospital care as well as primary care.

Notwithstanding these challenges, Newman's tone was supremely assured. "None of these parameters [is] new—we've been involved with all of them. It's just a matter of sharpening our planning process." In this spirit, the Board invited Dr. John Hogness, an administrator at the University of Washingon School of Medicine faculty (and the University's future president), to review the new plan.[27]

In February 1971, the Board finalized new policies on family planning for submittal to members. Dr. Strother warned fellow trustees that "we are moving into a period where the distinction between medical and social is becoming more and more obscure."[28]

That month's *View* magazine featured a detailed discussion of "who is subsidizing whom" at Group Health, stimulated by the issue of whether to add "family planning" to basic coverage. An internal study concluded that within the community of Group Health members, the young subsidized the old, the young male subsidized the young female, and adults subsidized children. More to the point, the study found that "equalization" of rates would raise dues for large families and save everyone else money. *View* warned that "if large numbers of members are priced out of Group Health, the results could be disastrous."

A companion membership survey produced curiously contradictory results: While 77 percent of member responses supported adding family planning counseling to the basic plan, only 51 percent supported the newly liberalized policy on abortion. Despite this advance warning, the Board was caught unawares at the annual meeting on April 24, 1971, when anti-abortion members, led by Mrs. Jean Bennett, sponsored a resolution to repeal the Board's policy. The argument continued until 11:15 that night, and the Board was upheld in the final vote by a majority of only 141 to 113. The issue would return, but most in Group Health were focused on other matters early in 1971.[29]

The debate over healthcare reform had suddenly reignited, thanks to a most unlikely firebrand—President Richard Nixon. He had struck the first spark back in July 1969 by declaring, "Unless action is taken within the next two or three years...we will have a breakdown in our medical system." He followed up on February 18, 1971, with a call for a "new national health strategy," and introduced a new term into the medico-political vocabulary: "health maintenance organization," or "HMO" for short.

The phrase had been coined only a year earlier by Dr. Paul M. Ellwood, Jr., director of the American Rehabilitation Foundation, in a February 8, 1970, meeting with officials from the federal Department of Health, Education, and Welfare. His idea was simple: Fee-for-service reimbursements actually rewarded doctors with sick patients and punished those with healthy ones. What was needed was a new set of "structural incentives" to reverse this so that physicians and hospitals earned money for keeping their patients well, not just for treating the ill.

Ellwood argued that the government could limit its direct intervention in healthcare delivery and slow, if not halt, medical cost inflation by shifting from reimbursements for services performed to per capita contracts with comprehensive healthcare organizations. Thus, Adam Smith's "invisible hand" of market economics would shape a new "health maintenance industry," which maximized revenue by serving the most people at the lowest cost.[30]

Whereas prepaid group practice had been given short shrift in the original Medicare legislation, Dr. Newman recalls, "The Nixon Administration was very supportive of this concept and felt it was a method for controlling medical care costs." Group Health entered into talks with the Social Security Administration about an HMO amendment to Medicare as early as September 1970. In March 1971, Dr. Newman reported "strong federal interest" in Group Health joining with its Minnesota counterpart to form "Associated Group Health Plans" with the aim of organizing HMOs across the northern tier of the United States; the Board approved the concept, but nothing came of it.[31]

The following month, President Nixon released a white paper, "Health Policy for the 1970s," formally prescribing HMOs to cure the national healthcare system. Also in May, Dr. Hogness graded Group Health's 10-year plan. The Board was stunned when he flunked their efforts and warned them, "Group Health is in danger of becoming one of the conservatives of medicine, doing exactly what the 'establishment' is doing." He chided the organization for having become too inward-looking and too accustomed to "having to go it alone." It had failed to notice, Hogness said, that the "health delivery system and the attitude of the government is changing so fast that this demands a speed up of an evolutionary change."

If Group Health really believed that it was the "wave of the future," as Newman asserted, then its planning should prescribe an "aggressive, experimental approach" as the "essence of the life of this organization." Dr. Hogness believed that Group Health could offer national leadership if it accepted "its social obligation to serve as a stimulus for change in the entire healthcare system." In particular, Group Health had the opportunity, if not the duty, to pioneer new approaches to cost accounting and control, service integration, regional healthcare delivery, and training "good health system managers." In carrying out this mission, he urged the Board to establish a professional planning office.[32]

What really stung the Board was his charge that it was no longer marching in the vanguard of healthcare reform. In truth, Group Health had long practiced what others were only beginning to preach. Perhaps its nearly 25 years of experience as a de facto health maintenance organization was the real source of Group Health's "conservatism" in not joining the cheers for HMOs as the saviors of Medicare and the entire healthcare system.

Despite these misgivings, Hilde Birnbaum remembered, "Everybody thought the millenium had come." She championed reform as a guest panelist on the influential public television program "The Advocates" and commented, "If [Senator Edward] Kennedy and Nixon could agree on something with regard to healthcare, it must be coming."[33]

Unfortunately, Kennedy and Nixon could only agree that a problem existed, not on how to address it. Senator Kennedy offered his own Health Security Act (the Kennedy-Griffiths bill) to establish a national system of comprehensive health insurance. Not surprisingly, the Board of Group Health promptly endorsed the plan, which had been crafted chiefly by the Committee of

100. This group was chaired by Walter Reuther, president of the United Automobile Workers union, and its membership included Dr. Newman, who was also president of the Group Health Association of America. Senator Kennedy returned the compliment by praising Group Health as "a model for reform" during a June 1971 tour of the Co-op's new Family Health Center, which had opened on Capitol Hill the previous March. This center was managed by Gertrude Dawson, Group Health's first African-American nurse, who had played a major role in its design and supervised its nursing staff. (Dawson retired in 1984.)[34]

As Dr. Hogness had rightly noted, Group Health didn't have to worry about "having to go it alone" anymore. It was written up by such diverse magazines as *The New Republic* and Germany's *Der Spiegel*, and academics and health officials began regular pilgrimages to inspect and praise its work. "The joke was," says Dr. Hartquist, "they finally discovered what we've been all along. And many of the people in the medical community, who always saw our demise around the corner, now realized that we had some substantial standing."[35]

After this initial gush of enthusiasm, some familiar patterns reappeared in the healthcare debate. By June, the Group Heath Association of America was sounding an alarm that the Nixon administration's draft HMO criteria seemed to favor more traditional, for-profit healthcare providers. Group Health argued in vain that any new law should require consumer representation on HMO boards, and it feared that an HMO mandate could end up restricting patients' freedom to choose nonconforming institutions such as cooperatives.[36]

Hogness was proved correct on another point: Group Health had made an "invalid assumption" in thinking it could limit annual growth to 10 percent. Thanks in part to all the publicity, enrollment expanded toward 149,000 by the end of 1971 and it continued to swell in the new year. "Suddenly," Dr. Hartquist remembered, "Group Health became very popular."[37]

Too popular, it turned out, for its own good.

Chapter 11

Best Laid Plans

1972 ~ 1976

*Unexpected Guests ~ Opening in Olympia ~
Pioneering Procedures and Preventive Care
Research ~ Women's Liberation ~ Hyper-Inflation ~
Sharing Risks for Medicare ~ Patients' Rights ~
Nurses Strike ~ Dr. Newman Departs*

*T*he celebration of Group Health's 25th anniversary in 1972
was spoiled by a surprise complication: Too many people
wanted to join the birthday party. As executive director
Dr. Frank Newman put it later, "Sometimes things don't turn
out quite the way you expected them to."[1]

By the annual meeting in April, enrollment had roared past
160,000—10,000 more than Group Health had budgeted for, and
the growth showed no sign of abating. The following month,
the Board imposed a moratorium on new group plans (Co-op
memberships remained open) after a furious debate. In the end,
Newman explains, the Board "recognized that we had a crisis
and we had to do something. And the last thing you want to do
is to have your reputation suffer" by enrolling more people than
you could serve.[2]

It was a fateful decision, which created new problems down
the road. Hilde Birnbaum later admitted, "We blew it," but there
seemed to be no alternative at the moment. The cap was loos-
ened later in 1972 to accommodate 10,000 new enrollees, but
demand blew the lid off. Group Health ended the year with
173,000 enrollees, a record 16 percent gain in one year.[3]

The staff scrambled to keep up, and delays in appointments

became a major and chronic headache during 1972. Late in the year, evening clinic hours were instituted to handle the backlog, and more than 600 patients showed up on a single night in November.

For once, the problem was not a shortage of doctors. Thanks to all of the national publicity praising Group Health as the wave of the healthcare future, the Cooperative had no trouble recruiting physicians. Unfortunately, it had nowhere to put them or their patients, despite having opened the new East Wing of the Central Hospital and the adjacent Family Health Center early in 1971. Even the new Lynnwood Medical Center was quickly overwhelmed after its dedication on December 5, 1971.[4]

The only solution Dr. Newman could see was to "go ahead and get some new facilities completed as rapidly as we could." The Board was already committed to building an "extended care facility" (later dubbed the Progressive Care Facility) to provide skilled nursing services for recuperating and elderly patients on Capitol Hill, and it had targeted Federal Way, between Seattle and Tacoma, for the next medical center. Group Health was stymied, however, in its main expansion plans for Tacoma and the Eastside.[5]

Group Health's negotiations to take over the Tacoma healthcare program of the Northern Pacific Benevolent Association (NPBA) reached an impasse in 1972, and the NPBA joined with Pierce County residents to form a new "Sound Health Association." As it had done with other groups in the past, Group Health encouraged the effort and even guaranteed a $50,000 loan to help launch the Association.[6]

The Eastside situation was more complex. Delays in rezoning Group Health's Bellevue site led to a decision to pursue simultaneous planning for both it and newly acquired property in Redmond.

The most ambitious expansion during 1972 was the opening of the Olympia Medical Center. Ironically, this was less the product of careful analysis or planning than a combination of circumstances and some savvy organizers in Thurston County.

The groundwork had been laid early in 1970 with a new state

law giving state employees the option of selecting "panel medicine plans" such as Group Health for their medical benefits. Thousands of state employees working in or near the state capital of Olympia had nowhere to exercise this new right. Led by David C. Carson, a small band of these workers incorporated its own "Group Health Cooperative of Olympia" on April 2, 1970, but they had no intention of going it alone and made a point of inviting Group Health officials to this and every subsequent meeting of the new cooperative.

The Board, now headed by Eleanor Brand, was initially cool to launching a new medical center nearly 70 miles south of its central facilities to serve 150 current members in the area. It told the Olympia group that it wanted to open a center in Tacoma first, but Carson and his cadre were persistent suitors. A formal liaison committee was organized and by July 1970, Group Health found itself committed to opening an Olympia facility within two years.

George Bolotin, the Board's longtime "architect in residence," stepped down in order to supervise the design and construction of the new center, which was sited near St. Peter Hospital, while Dr. Ward Miles agreed to head up the center staff. "They asked me," Miles remembered, "because nobody else wanted to go. This is the way I got into several good things."

Dr. Miles had earned a reputation as a maverick among mavericks on the medical staff. A Quaker and conscientious objector during World War II, Miles developed an interest in both psychology and medicine during his wartime service as orderly in the mental ward of the Pennsylvania State Hospital. He joined Group Health's staff in 1954 and became one of its leading advocates of family practice and integrated approaches to physical and mental health. (Miles was also elected to the Board following his retirement in 1984.)

When Group Health entered Olympia, Miles had just returned from a stint in the Peace Corps. He expected to take charge of mental health services, but "the thought of having a family practitioner be chief of mental health was too much for anybody to bear." Miles saw Olympia as the opportunity to escape the

Cooperative's internal politics and "to start a different model" of family care.[7]

Group Health immediately encountered an old problem: Restrictive language in the Thurston County Medical Bureau's charter enjoined its members from assisting "closed panel" doctors or their patients. According to one press report, Group Health attorney John Riley "heatedly charged the Medical Bureau with being 30 to 50 years behind the times." Thurston County's medical establishment got the point and grudgingly amended the Bureau charter in January 1972. The Olympia cooperative dissolved itself on May 23, and precisely two months later more than 1,000 area citizens and new Group Health members attended the formal opening of the Olympia Medical Center.[8]

At the same time, Group Health launched one of its most important medical initiatives: the establishment of a full-time emergency care team. This was a new concept, since emergency rooms were traditionally staffed by physicians and nurses rotated in from other duties. Dr. Robert McAlister, a family practitioner with extensive experience in the ER, recognized that emergency care was becoming a specialty in its own right.

He and Dr. Richard Tinker took charge of assembling a team of five emergency care physicians while Mary Gruenwald recruited a comparable squad of nurses. One of the team's first hires was Dr. Howard Kirz, who had participated in a similar effort with Kaiser Permanente in California and was a charter member of the American College of Emergency Physicians in 1971.

"In those early years, Group Health invented half a dozen strategies which are now standard emergency pracitices," Dr. Kirz later explained. One example is the telephone consulting nurse program. Begun in 1970, it was greatly expanded with the reorganization of emergency services and became one of the Cooperative's most popular—and cost-effective—programs. Group Health also pioneered the use of emergency department observation wards, now called "rapid care units," in which specially trained physicians and nurses treat and monitor patients for up to 12 hours as an alternative to conventional hospitalization. Kirz cites these as examples of Group Health's intrinsic impulse as a prepaid program "to wring maximum health out of every dollar" instead of maximum dollars out of every illness.[9]

The other major development in 1972 involved the reorganization of Group Health's research and patients' rights committees into a single body. The Cooperative had finally obtained federal certification as a charitable institution the previous year, which made it eligible for a broader range of grants. To rationalize both the solicitation and donation of grants, research director Dr. Richard Handschin proposed establishment of a "Group Health Foundation," but this was not realized for several more years. Instead, the Board restructured its existing charitable trust.

Group Health expanded its own public service activities in 1972 by lending aid to the new "Country Doctor" community clinic on Capitol Hill. At the same time, it attracted funds for a major long-term study to test the effectiveness of breast cancer screening and early detection.[10]

General inflation climbed during 1972, propelled by the cost of the Vietnam War and the fiscal echo of the Great Society. Medical costs rose twice as fast and the federal government saw its expenditures on health programs increase from less than 5 percent of all outlays to more than 10 percent.

Group Health was not immune to these forces, and members began to complain about several years of annual double-digit dues increases. The Board held a major round of district meetings in October 1972 that attracted some 600 members. Some felt the Board was "softening them up" for another hike in dues, but the temporary lag between enrollment growth and opening of new facilities actually allowed the Board to forego raising dues in 1973. It became academic when President Nixon imposed wage and price controls to rein in runaway inflation throughout the national economy.[11]

Medical cost increases intensified pressure for reform on the national scene, and emboldened activists within Group Health. Roger Leed, an attorney famed for leading local fights against freeways and for environmental protection, challenged the Board to restructure itself. He proposed term limits for the Board and a rule mandating one trustee per 10,000 members. Aubrey Davis replied that Leed's ideas would deprive the Board of experienced leadership and diminish its ability to oversee management. Leed's representation formula would also add scores of new trustees, turning a policy board into a miniature legislature.[12]

Coincidentally, Davis had already decided to leave the Board in 1973 after 20 years of service. He was now mayor of Mercer Island and chair of the committee responsible for the newly formed Metro Transit system. (He couldn't stay away forever, and returned to the Board nine years later.)

In planning for the 1973 annual meeting, the Board had some reforms of its own to present to members. The absorption of Olympia had prompted creation of a "structure committee" to review Group Health's governance. Members Aubrey Davis, Lyle Mercer, Louis Stewart, and Jean Yourkowski proposed that the eight member districts be reorganized to focus their jurisdictions and activities on the medical centers. It also recommended allowing group enrollees to join in district advisory activities, including the nomination of candidates for the Board. As Lyle Mercer later explained, 55 percent of Group Health enrollees had no franchise at the time, while "less than 1 percent of our membership participates in Co-op activities."

While the structure committee supported granting full voting privileges to group members in principle, they agreed with Davis that the status quo should be preserved "at least for a while longer." At the April 1973 annual meeting, the membership approved allowing advisory participation by group members, but the voting franchise would not be broadened for another two decades.[13]

The annual meeting was dominated by another fractious debate over contraception and abortion that went so long the session had to be recessed until September 22. The April meeting also marked the debut of a new movement at Group Health: women's liberation.

Unease with Group Health's treatment of women had been growing for some time, but social convention tended to squelch complaints. It is a measure of the sea change in attitudes to come that when Hilde Birnbaum rose during a 1969 meeting to question the departure of Group Health's sole female obstetrician, her remarks shocked both women and men in attendance. There were audible whispers, "How can Mrs. Birnbaum be so tactless to bring this issue up? That's nothing to be discussed."

Women, at least, were less demure by 1973. Early in the year, Birnbaum recalled, a "woman called me and asked me what they could do about getting a room to meet [in]. They said they couldn't get a room at Group Health." She arranged for the space and decided to attend the gathering on March 21.

She and most of the 100 or so other participants wore jeans and casual clothing. This made two "well dressed women" who were taking notes impossible to miss, and Birnbaum recognized them as Group Health's personnel director and her secretary. They were recording the names of those in attendance, a fourth of whom worked for Group Health. "They didn't want the revolution," she remembered, and they were astonished when she objected to their intelligence mission.

A week later, Birnbaum briefed trustees on the meeting and reported, "There is one thread through it: a certain amount of dissatisfaction with family planning, aspects of pregnancy, abortion," and other services. At that Board meeting, she convinced her fellow trustees to edit out sexist—that is, masculine—pronouns from the bylaws.[14]

The new Women's Caucus failed in its first mission at the annual meeting when its Board nominee, Emma Beezy, lost to Ralph Bremer, but it pressed on under the leadership of Caroline MacColl. As assistant director of the Puget Sound Health Planning Council, a nurse with a master's degree in public health education, and the second wife of Dr. William MacColl, she knew her way around Group Health very well. She lobbied successfully to win official recognition for the Caucus, which established the precedent for sanctioned special interest groups within the Cooperative.[15]

Caucus members and their allies had their hands full when the annual meeting reconvened in September. The argument over contraception had been building for months, and Hilde

Birnbaum found herself pitted against some members of the Board and Group Health staff. In arguing the economics of contraception coverage, she felt "they made a very funny calculation" to inflate the cost of birth control by equating it with pap smears."[16]

Many of Group Health's members also opposed contraception coverage. According to Birnbaum, the "Catholic Church had them to go to the [1973 annual] meeting and vote against" birth control, producing "more tangible opposition to that than to abortion." Despite this effort, contraception was added to Group Health coverage by a vote of 214 to 171; voluntary sterilization was also approved by a similar margin. As with so many Group Health battles, this was just a warm-up.[17]

The main event followed on April 27, 1974. More than 900 members and spectators packed the annual meeting. Conservative forces failed to repeal contraception coverage by only 10 votes, but their position on abortion was rejected by a decisive margin. The same body elected Group Health's first African-American trustee, Ida Chambliss, and Louis Stewart to the Board, which later named Hilde Birnbaum president and architect James Evans vice president.[18]

In 1974, reformers came the closest yet (and possibly since) to winning a national healthcare program for all citizens. Major changes had already been implemented with the 1972 establishment of federal Professional Standards Review Organizations to monitor healthcare institutions, and passage of the HMO Assistance Act in December 1973 with the goal of seeding the creation of 1,700 such health maintenance organizations.

Liberals such as Senator Edward Kennedy were not satisfied and pressed for a Health Security Act. They found an unlikely ally on February 6, 1974, when President Nixon declared that national healthcare insurance was "an idea whose time has come in America." His budget director, Caspar Weinberger, offered a plan for universal coverage with copayments of 25 percent capped at $1,500 per year.

A compromise was clearly possible that spring, but by now

the president was foundering in the rising tide of Watergate revelations. His enemies, particularly organized labor, refused to approve a plan that might throw Richard Nixon a lifeline, and Democrats calculated that a sweep in the fall congressional elections would give them the chance to enact a stronger plan. Senator Kennedy paid another visit to Group Health on June 3 to champion his Health Security Act, and the Board joined him in urging a postponement of any health insurance program to the next Congress.[19]

"If the name on the administration's plan had not been Nixon, and had the time not been the year of Watergate," historian Paul Starr later observed, "the United States might have had national health insurance in 1974." The opportunity for reform died on August 9 with President Nixon's resignation.[20]

Liberals got their congressional majority that fall, but they did not anticipate the recession compounded by hyper-inflation that followed the lifting of wage-price controls. Hospital costs soared 18 percent above 1973 levels, and physicians' fees rose 23 percent, making 1974 what Hilde Birnbaum later called an "unprecedented year of financial crisis" for Group Health. The only financial bright spot was the fact that Group Health's annual per capita costs were still running at two-thirds the national average, $191 versus $311, thanks to its low rates of hospitalization and surgical intervention.[21]

The year also marked a number of transitions. In April, the Board restructured the administration, and gave Dr. Newman the new title of executive vice president. New posts were created for an assistant to the president and coordinator for Cooperative affairs, filled respectively by John Philbin and Anna Clark.[22]

There were other new faces at Group Health. Mike Lowry, former assistant to state senate majority leader Martin Durkan, had taken over the Cooperative's lobbying program; photographer Paul Temple was appointed editor of *View*; and Phil Nudelman succeeded Ruth Brown as head of the pharmacy in 1973 and, later, all paramedical services.

Nudelman had wearied of traveling the countryside as a

healthcare consultant. He remembered that his children returned from school one day with pictures they had drawn of their father. "Daddy had a suitcase in his hand. That was their impression of me." When Dr. Burry Pelzel offered him a full-time job, Nudelman didn't hesitate to accept, and immediately devoted himself to computerizing Group Health's pharmacy system.[23]

Rudy Molzan announced he would resign on July 1 and his position was retitled vice president for finance and administration. Dr. Newman praised Molzan as "the kind of guy that had very good instincts, and he was very easy to work with." The Cooperative found an able replacement in Donald A. Brennan, a faculty member in preventive health and administrator at the University of Colorado Medical Center.

Not long after, Art Siegal resigned from the Board to fill the new position of director of planning and construction. By now, the Board had despaired of the long battle to develop its Bellevue site, which was opposed by nearby residents. Newman later confessed, "I've never fully forgiven the political powers that be in Bellevue for what they did to us" during two and a half years of negotiations. He shifted the focus to Redmond, where "it was such a relief to work with the city fathers."[24]

Ernie Conrad returned to the Board in November 1974 to fill the balance of Siegal's term. That same month, Group Health bid farewell to one of its founding physicians as Dr. Sandy MacColl entered retirement, but he didn't cease playing a major role in the life of the Cooperative to which he had now devoted nearly 28 years.[25]

The worsening economy forced the Board to delay opening its new Federal Way Medical Center, and it put plans for West Seattle and Rainier Valley medical centers on hold. In January 1975, the Board approved a 15 percent dues hike to take effect the following July, while the operating budget rose from $39 million to $51 million in a single year.[26]

The news prompted Dr. MacColl, Carol Higgins, and Bettykay (no last name) to sponsor Resolution 1 at the April annual meeting. This mandated a study of alternative approaches to Group Health capital planning, staffing, and expenditures for such customs as mailing Christmas cards to members.[27]

The last activity entailed a lot of postage. Enrollment was approaching 196,000 individuals by April 1975, but growth had slowed dramatically. Because Group Health was losing 20,000 enrollees per year to attrition, pressure was all the greater to attract new groups. An expanding patient population, so long a source of grief, was now a requisite for survival to offset inflation, and in May the Board set a new target of serving 300,000 enrollees by 1980.

At the same meeting, Hilde Birnbaum told the Board, "There is a revolution in the delivery system of healthcare, and the question is not whether, but how fast, Group Health can adapt. Continuing inflation makes tighter management methods, greater efficiency and better utilization of manpower and capital absolutely essential." Group Health's position was complicated further by the new HMO act, lingering hopes for a comprehensive program of national health insurance, and the aftereffects of its membership cap, all of which confused consumers and made group managers hesitant to pursue new contracts.[28]

Part of the problem was that Group Health was not a "federally qualified" HMO. The Cooperative did not find the Social Security Administration's (SSA) rules for health maintenance organizations to be a very comfortable fit, so it set out to create a new, tailor-made system. Dr. Newman later explained, "If we could get the federal government to recognize what we were, and pay us in a way that we felt we could be paid, that is on a capitation basis, [it] would be a very good thing."

Group Health's goal was to win advance payments for each Medicare patient based on an average per capita cost of service, instead of billing retroactively for services already delivered. Despite an excellent track record with federal employee benefits, Dr. Newman found the SSA to be "cautious and somewhat suspicious that we would deliver what we said we could deliver."

He persisted over months of negotiations. "I just had to explain over and over again that, look, you've got a lot more controls" with prospective payments. Dr. Newman's idea was a variant on the "risk-basis" model already permitted in the law, which rewarded HMOs if their Medicare charges fell below the average per capita healthcare costs in their areas while delivering most of the savings back to the federal government. Knowing that its Medicare costs were running about 80 percent of those experienced by other providers, Group Health proposed to charge 90 percent of the average rate. This allowed Social Security to reap a 10 percent savings and freed Group Health to apply its share of savings to supplement Medicare coverage for such services as out-of-area emergencies and to reduce the portion of Medicare administrative costs subsidized by all enrollees. If Group Health miscalculated, it absorbed the loss. Thus, Group Health's plan became known as "risk-basis, savings-sharing."

In the fall of 1975, Social Security finally accepted the proposal for a two-year demonstration project commencing the following July. Dr. Newman said, "The way we won the argument was, we knew that we could provide more coverage for less money than they were getting from the fee-for-service community in general. So we were able to set up the 90 percent formula" for advance capitation payments. "It simplifies the administrative costs. I mean it's a beautiful way of operating. And you're putting the program at risk in a [way] that controls its quality, controls its utilization, and controls its costs." This study helped to pioneer the rules and standards that now apply to all HMO risk-sharing contracts with Medicare.[29]

There were other innovations in 1975. Phil Nudelman unveiled the new "Co-OpRx" computerized prescription system on July 1, giving doctors and pharmacists instant access to patients' drug histories, including allergies and potential problems with drug interactions. This system laid the base for further automation of patient records and helped make Group Health a leader in electronic information systems for healthcare. Pete Penna later built on this system to monitor patient drug use and to integrate clinical pharmacists as full members of Group Health's medical team.[30]

The Cooperative joined the national Surgical Adjuvant Breast Cancer Project later in July, and it agreed to put itself under the microscope as part of a long-term Rand Corporation study of health costs (which would lend scientific validation to Group Health's reputation nine years later). The Co-op also began planning a new centralized Support Center in Renton to supply services and materials to its growing number of medical centers.

Shortly after the opening of the Federal Way Medical Center on September 5, Dr. Newman took a long leave to study at Harvard's Advanced Management Program. Despite Dr. Newman's many accomplishments, the Board's approval of this leave was less a reward than a hint that it was looking for fresh executive leadership.[31]

Dr. Newman returned in the new year to find Group Health's reputation battered by a familiar complaint that its services might be wonderful but nobody could get at them. The difficulty that 208,000 enrollees experienced in making appointments became so notorious that KING Television News did an investigation. Reporter Don McGaffin told viewers that it took him 78 calls to arrange a visit with his Group Health physician. The Board was not amused and commissioned a consultant study of the problem.[32]

On a happier note, Group Health unveiled its new Progressive Care Facility on January 12, 1976, and Kay Kukowski began revitalizing the Cooperative's health education program. In March, the Board approved a new "Well Adult" program designed by Dr. Robert "Tommy" Thompson. This program was modeled on the Cooperative's revamped "Well Child" effort, begun the year before, and it addressed the perennial issue of annual physicals by establishing a schedule of periodic health inventories and tests. The new program also gave Dr. Thompson a base from which to launch a later series of groundbreaking studies as the medical staff's director of preventive care research.[33]

Thompson was a pediatrician who had trained at Johns Hopkins and had conducted his public health studies at the University of North Carolina at Chapel Hill in connection with a program of federally funded neighborhood health centers founded by Dr. Amos Johnson. He developed an interest in Group Health when the Centers for Disease Control assigned him to a stint at the Washington State Health Department.

Thompson returned to Seattle in 1972 to join Dr. MacColl's

staff at Northgate. He was impressed by the elder pediatrician and his style of leadership. MacColl encouraged his staff to eat lunch on the premises and assigned doctors to cook for their colleagues on a rotating schedule. "You really got to know one another much better than you otherwise would," Thompson recalled, "and a lot of the business of the clinic could be transacted on a much more informal basis." At the same time, Thompson was appalled when MacColl's turn to cook came up. "We called him 'Mr. Grease,'" for his fried lunches. There was nothing preventive about MacColl's culinary skills.

Prevention research was Thompson's driving interest from the outset: "I wanted to essentially take public health thinking and try to make it happen in day-to-day clinical practice. And the place to do something like that is in a place that's got a large defined population."

"Prior to that time you could not say that Group Health had recommendations for prevention [of] anything," Thompson says. What practice and trials there were amounted to "purely individualized cottage-industry stuff." His interest in doing more was shared by colleagues such as Drs. John Gilson, Rich Watkins, and Bob Monroe, and they asked themselves, "How could we get off the dime?" We finally decided that maybe a good way to go would be to find out what we're doing now."

Thompson credits veteran cooperators such as Hilde Birnbaum, Jack Cluck, and Eleanor Brand with launching the 1973 Prevention Task Force that allowed him to formalize his reasearch. "I don't think I would ever have had a chance of even doing this if it hadn't been for the consumer movement at Group Health." As one of the first results of his work, Thompson's new Well Child" schedule of exams proved just as effective as conventional practice with far fewer trips to the doctor.

Yet there was resistance from an unlikely quarter—more conservative physicians who adamantly opposed standardizing preventive practice. Thomson remembers that some complained, "This is a communist plot. You are interfering with the God-given relationship between doctor and patient, and you can't do this." Such unusual sentiments from Group Health doctors would be heard again.[34]

The biggest controversy at the April 1976 annual meeting centered on a resolution to mandate free copies of medical records. The issue was raised by the new interim Patients' Bill of Rights, adopted by the Board in January.

The Bill of Rights was based on "Between Us," a 12-point document of patients' rights first promulgated by the American Hospital Association two years earlier. Adapting these principles to Group Health proved harder than anticipated. The main sticking point for all sides was a patient's right to review his or her medical chart. Most of his staff objected because, as chief of staff Dr. Hartquist later explained, "there are definite times when that can be damaging to the patient" due to candid comments, information from spouses, and other data not intended for the patient's eyes.

The dispute came at a time of renewed tension between the Cooperative and its doctors. Hartquist recalled, "There was a movement on part of the group that the medical staff should incorporate separately from the organization," as had Kaiser plan physicians. This proposal, pushed chiefly by surgeons, led to "one of the big battles" in the Joint Conference Committee.

The JCC proved its worth again as a forum for compromise. The insurgent physicians were pacified by improvements in the retirement system and a compromise on patients' right of records review. "I think the ultimate procedure that came about was a good workable solution," said Dr. Hartquist. "We had a waiting period. We had the patient stand the expense of copying. The rest of the patient bill, we did change it. We also wrote some provisions of responsibility on the part of the patient."[35]

The ultimate version guaranteed that Group Health would respect each patient's personal dignity and privacy, allowed patients to review medical records subject to separate policies, affirmed the right to select a personal physician, specified standards for informed consent, allowed consultation with or referral to an outside physician at cost, and required advance notice if the patient was the subject of a research study or receiving treatment that entailed additional cost. The document also demanded that a patient provide truthful answers to medical staff questions and respect the Co-op's rules.[36]

The member resolution to mandate open access to and free copies of medical records failed at the annual meeting on April 24, 1976. The discussion lasted so long that the meeting lost its quorum after disposing of only five of a dozen resolutions. The balance of the agenda was taken up on June 30, and the membership adopted Resolution 9, sponsored by Ronald Jasperson, a scientist and member of the Olympia District Executive Commitee. Noting that full Co-op members had shrunk proportionately to a third of total enrollment, the resolution mandated "a study of the role of the Group enrollee and Group Conversion enrollee in the future of Group Health Cooperative." The Board tapped Caroline MacColl, then head of the Visiting Nurse Service of King County, to lead a new Governance Task Force, on June 8, 1976. The effort would take more than two years to run its course.[37]

The Board and its new leadership, president James Evans and vice president Ida Chambliss, should have been able to look forward to a pleasant summer celebrating the official Bicentennial of the American Revolution, during which Group Health was to be honored as an exemplar of community action. The forecast turned stormy as the Washington State Nurses Association and other unions adopted a hard line in negotiations with the Seattle Area Hospital Council and with the Cooperative.[38]

Group Health was the only "union shop" in the area, and its employees were organized into 13 distinct bargaining groups at this time. Despite the Cooperative's long record of solidarity with organized labor, communication had been difficult to maintain. Aubrey Davis explained, a union "doesn't feel represented because you have got one of their members on the Board." There were trustees with close ties to labor, such as Louis Stewart, Lyle Mercer, and Gene Lux, but said Davis, "If you haven't got the leader, you haven't got labor." Labor representation on the Board was hard to guarantee through open elections, but it may not have mattered given the growing mood of rank-and-file militancy.[39]

Employees of nonprofit hospitals had gained the right to strike under federal labor law only two years earlier. Group

Health experienced its first walkout in March 1975, when its X-ray technicians left their jobs to demand higher wages. The matter was quickly settled and they returned in 10 days, but it was a signal that Group Health could no longer rely on its historic alliance with organized labor to insulate it from tough bargaining as unions struggled to regain incomes eroded by wage controls and hyper-inflation.[40]

The talks with nurses were stalemated when Dr. Newman decided it was time for him to move on. The move was not entirely voluntary, for many on the Board, led by Ernie Conrad, had begun to doubt if Newman had the skills necessary to guide Group Health into its fourth decade. Criticism of Newman sharpened as enrollment began to fall behind projections and the Cooperative grappled with the fiscal and organizational demands imposed by expansion to the east side of Lake Washington.

Don Brennan, Group Health's vice president for administration, later commented that Dr. Newman's problems stemmed from "bad relationships, not bad decisions. The Board resented how much Group Health had taken on his personality." Dr. Hartquist watched them "chew him up" with a sinking heart. "I thought they were unkind to Frank, on an interpersonal level, the way things were said in open forum meetings. My own feeling was, why don't we get this over with."[41]

Dr. Newman tendered a long and gracious letter of resignation on July 28, 1976, which closed, "I love this organization and want only the best for it and for its membership." Newman hoped to remain at Group Health in a clinical capacity, but Kaiser quickly snapped him up as its new vice president. He later joined the federal government and became a major architect of the HMO industry that he had helped to conceive.[42]

It fell to Don Brennan, as the Cooperative's acting head, to guide the Cooperative through most of the 28-day nurses' strike, which began August 1. Group Health's nurses finally agreed to a new contract giving them cumulative raises of nearly 25 percent over three years and increasing their participation in planning and assignments.

After the settlement, Brennan cautioned the Board not to assume "that the stated demands in fact represent the true issues" of the strike or that Group Health's historic labor harmony had been permanently restored. "There are deep-seated feelings that go beyond statements of position."[43]

The same could be said of relations among Group Health's other constituencies.

Chapter 12

The Coming of the CEO

1976 ~ 1981

*Don Brennan and Dr. McAlister Take Charge ~ Caroline
MacColl and Ida Chambliss ~ Midwives, Medicare,
Governance Reform, and Consumer Criteria ~ Tacoma at
Last ~ Exit Brennan, Enter Gerry Coe ~ University of
Washington ~ The First Chief Executive Officer*

*D*on Brennan was the first nonphysician to head the Co-operative since Don Northrop's resignation in 1952. The elevation of a professional manager to Group Health's top post, combined with the proportionate decline in full Co-op membership, the nurses' strike, and the approaching completion of the new Eastside complex, prefigured deep and unsettling changes to come.[1]

That changes were necessary was made clear on September 1, 1976, when the consultant team of Drs. Robert Rushmer and Steve Yarnell delivered a report on Group Health's "Problems of Appointment Availability." It noted that the difficulties "permeated the entire organization, one which is inherently set up to bring about encounters between physicians and enrollees. Therefore appointment availability could not be regarded as a problem that could be studied in isolation."

The report observed that at the Co-op's current rate of growth and turnover, half of Group Health's current enrollment would be replaced within three years. "These people must be educated" because "there is great confusion and uncertainty as to how to use the system." At the same time, the consultants pointed out a "mismatch between what consumers desire and expect and what a health care system is prepared to deliver."

Group Health had already undertaken important improvements such as the "Well Adult" program and telephone consulting nurses. The latter were now handling 10,000 calls per month, and resolving 6,000 of these contacts without a doctor's appointment. With an average cost of 56 cents per phone consultation versus $25 per office visit, this service yielded a dramatic efficiency—and efficiency, or its absence, was the thrust of the consultants' critique.

Dr. John Gilson, Group Health's head of staff education, commented that "the real impact of the report" was to force Group Health to take an "ongoing look at how the Cooperative is delivering healthcare" and "to engage in self-examination and self-renewal from now on." Indeed, this report was the first of a series of medical, management, and consumer initiatives over the next four years that would transform Group Health's delivery system.[2]

In December 1976, the medical staff elected a new chief of staff, Dr. Robert McAlister. Nobody knew it at the time, but he would be the last chief of staff chosen by Group Health's full complement of physicians.[3]

That same month, Grant McLaughlin was appointed to fill Don Brennan's old post as vice president for finance and administration. McLaughlin had joined Group Health's staff in 1972 and made his mark by negotiating an $8 million refund for the Cooperative and its employees when Group Health temporarilly opted out of Social Security coverage.[4]

Brennan's own status was not resolved until the eve of the annual meeting. On April 20, 1977, Ida Chambliss, then chair of the Board's Special Committee on Executive Management, interrogated Brennan on a host of issues. Many of the questions were loaded: Brennan was asked to "list five positive aspects of consumer involvement" and to explain how he would use them "constructively." He was then told, "It is very clear, at least to some of the trustees, that there is a need to clarify working relationships of the Chief Executive Officer with the medical staff and Board," and asked how he proposed to address this need.

In his response, Brennan argued that the executive vice president should be the "point of interface between the Board and organizational staff" and suggested that the Board's own staff assistants should really report to him. Chambliss replied that "this raised some philosophical issues regarding the perception of the Board's responsibility by its constituency."

At the end of the session, Chambliss asked if Brennan accepted his job description. Brennan's answer was that "he does accept it although he does not like every part of it." In particular, he thought he should have greater appointment power. He told the Board he felt he could do the job it needed, but he would also cooperate with a "search if that is the Board's choice." The Board chose not to, but not every trustee was enthusiastic about the decision to make Brennan the new executive vice president.[5]

With his appointment confirmed, Brennan focused his attention on Group Health's long-awaited expansion into the burgeoning suburbs east of Lake Washington. Direct responsibility for planning the new "East Region" had been given to Phil Nudelman in late 1975, and he was named regional administrator in April 1976. Under his leadership, Group Health signed joint planning agreements with its new neighbors, Overlake and Evergreen General hospitals, which helped address community concerns over Group Health's arrival. This effort was rewarded on July 11, 1977, with the opening of the new Eastside Specialty Center in Redmond, followed on September 12 by completion of the Eastside Hospital. The latter was operating at capacity within one year.[6]

On the other end of the facilities scale, chief of staff Dr. McAlister pressed the Board in June to pursue development of "mini-clinics" to help relieve pressure on the main medical centers. He also saw these as a "creative, beneficial attempt to more closely involve communities in healthcare" (the Board approved the concept in October 1977).

In June, Group Health stepped into the world of high-technology medicine with the purchase of its first CAT scanner. The same month, it joined with the new Fred Hutchinson Cancer Research Center in the Southwest Oncology Group Project, a

national program for identifying and tracking patients participating in statistical and clinical research on new cancer thera-
pies such as bone marrow transplants. Group Health had initiated one of its most significant long-term research projects as a
partner with the Boston Collaborative Drug Surveillance Study,
which was later coordinated at Group Health by Dr. Richard
Watkins.[7]

In the fall of 1977, Dr. McAlister reported that Group Health's
delivery rooms were busier than ever, delivering more than 270
babies in August alone. This was the first rumbling of the "baby
boom echo," and it is no coincidence that the Women's Caucus
voted that same summer to endorse the use of natural childbirth
techniques and trained midwives as an alternative to traditional
obstetrical practice. The Board authorized a Midwifery Task
Force, which began work in the new year.[8]

During the year, Group Health introduced a new procedure
to implant artificial interocular lenses, and it launched an affirmative action program to raise the representation of minorities
and women on the medical staff above its current 5 percent,
which fell seriously below the community's demographic averages.[9]

The medical staff also reorganized and intensified its internal education system under its new director of medical education, emergency physician Dr. Howard Kirz. "We had begun to
recognize that our clinical practices were unique," Kirz explained,
"because they were driven by patient care outcomes rather than
conventional 'community standards.' The [professional] community standard struck us as being based more on economics,
not necessarily on the best results for the patient."

As a result of more innovative staffing and shorter hospital
stays (which reduce exposure to infection and accelerate recovery), "Group Health patients did slightly better than the average," commented former chief of staff Dr. Glenn Hartquist. He
added, "There was nothing in the community like what we were
doing." Dr. Kirz began translating Group Health experience and
related health data into an eduational program that eventually
provided more than 5,000 hours of accredited in-house medical
staff training per year.[10]

Membership growth had rebounded during 1977. In the fall, the Cornish School for the Allied Arts signed Group Health's 1,000th group contract, and newly installed Governor Dixy Lee Ray joined the Cooperative, helping to push its total enrollment to nearly 242,000 by year's end.[11]

The new year began with a classic debate between the Board and management. The issue was advertising, a familiar bone of contention pitting cooperative idealism against market realities. The leading spokesperson for the former had left the field with the resignation of Hilde Birnbaum, but Bellevue City Council member Nancy Rising proved an able and like-minded successor. Caroline MacColl, who had been elected to the Board the previous April, also joined Lyle Mercer and Ida Chambliss in waving the banner of old-time cooperative values.

At the Board meeting on January 4, 1978, Don Brennan proposed spending $92,000 in 1978 to promote "greater understanding of the concept of prepaid healthcare systems" in general and Group Health in particular. While the sum represented little more than a 10th of 1 percent of the total $88 million operating budget, it was a red flag for traditionalists. Brennan's cause wasn't helped by the fact that Group Health had been featured in an NBC television news special on "Medicine in America" the night before this meeting. Given such free publicity, Rising and MacColl persuaded their colleagues to set aside the ad campaign, and the funds were ultimately reallocated for special services.[12]

In the months leading up to the annual meeting, the Board focused chiefly on the issue of voting rights for group and group conversion enrollees. The Board crafted several bylaw amendments that would allow enrollees to vote for trustees and resolutions at the annual meeting. The Board also authorized the first use of "fractional" ballots, allowing spouses in member families to cast independent votes.

The annual meeting on April 22 featured the first Health Fair to promote better lifestyles and individual responsibility for disease prevention. It featured an on-site daycare service for the first time (Group Health later leased space for permanent daycare centers in its major buildings).

The main business at hand was supposed to be the amendment of the bylaws, but the membership had its own priorities. They adopted a resolution directing the Board to "develop a description of alternatives for future Group Health size and membership, and submit those alternatives together with arguments pro and con, and their recommendations, to the next annual meeting." The resolution cited concerns over maintaining the personal character of medical services, demands on management, and impacts on governance. The clock ran out before the bylaw amendments could be discussed and the meeting was recessed until November 18. It was just as well since much more education was clearly needed on the proposed reforms.

Three weeks following the annual meeting, the Board adopted a new policy "recognizing the inevitability of growth" beyond the current target of 300,000 enrollees. At that same session, the Board elected Ida Chambliss president, making her the first person of color to lead the Cooperative.

Chambliss was raised in Alabama, with 14 brothers and sisters, many of whom pursued careers in healthcare. She chose social work for her own profession, and took her degree from the University of Wisconsin. She had already joined Group Health by 1969, when she met Hilde Birnbaum at a health education seminar and found herself recruited to join the Birnbaum's Member Services and Hospital Committee. She began devoting more and more evening hours to its affairs, while working by day as the coordinator of a state program training daycare staff and foster parents.

As Cooperative president, Chambliss saw her role to "assure that interaction takes place" among Group Health's constituent parts, "so existing policy can be reviewed and new policy formulated as needed." Her philosophy clashed with Don Brennan's more conventional and hierarchical approach to management. "We had a love-hate relationship," Brennan later admitted, in which they often fought during Board meetings and then socialized as if nothing had happened.[13]

Don Brennan had antagonized Chambliss and other Cooperative traditionalists by describing his role as "board in residence," in dealing with medical and organizational staff between Board meetings. The arrogation of the executive vice president to a status equal to the Board also rankled some members of the medical staff, including their chief, Dr. McAlister. At the same time, the Board recognized, in trustee Gene Lux's phrase, that there is a "marked line between managing and policy setting and it causes trouble when either crosses the line. The Board must keep track of where it is in relation to the line."[14]

Accordingly, the Board faced up to its voracious appetite for administrative minutiae. In the early 1970s, for example, it devoted substantial meeting time to redesigning Group Health's logotype. The choice was between a caduceus or the staff of Aesculapius. The former is a symbol of the Greek god Hermes and features a pair of snakes entwined around a winged scepter, while the latter depicts a single snake coiled around a rod to represent the Roman god of medicine. The old logo was a hybrid with two snakes braided around a simple staff. After three years of debate, the Board voted to add wings.[15]

In a conscious effort to focus on more important issues, the Board established a policy manual system in 1978 to track major decisions and provide a framework for future deliberations. It took one of its more far-reaching steps in July 1978 by authorizing the Midwifery Project, a two-year pilot program coordinated by Cathy Carr at Eastside Hospital.[16]

In September, the Board approved a "slow growth policy" to add 10,000 enrollees during each of the next three years. It also adopted an $18 million capital plan for medical centers in Rainier Valley, Kenmore, and Factoria, expansion of the Olympia Medical Center, and new miniclinics near Northgate and in Seattle's Madrona neighborhood.

At the same meeting, the Board approved development of an "administrative center" off Capitol Hill. It also formally launched discussions of an "affiliation" with the Sound Health Association, which operated a medical center in Tacoma and a clinic in Port Orchard, on the Kitsap Peninsula. Both decisions were to have far-reaching impacts.[17]

Group Health's talks with Sound Health were aided by the law firm of Houghton Cluck, which had helped organize both organizations, but they were not entirely voluntary on Group Health's part. U.S. Senator Warren Magnuson, who was at the peak of his power as chair of the Senate Appropriations Committee, leaned heavily on the Cooperative to rescue the ailing Sound Health—which was the nation's first federally qualified health maintenance organization. As Dr. Ward Miles recalled the situation, Magnuson argued that "to have another [HMO] take it over was much better than having it fail."

Although Sound Health had experienced a remarkable success in recruiting more than 12,000 enrollees since 1974, it was facing default on $2.5 million in federal loans and falling behind in other bills. Miles blamed its ills on the fact that "the whole HMO thing was way oversold by the Nixon Administration. And those of us who were in the field despaired, because I was afraid it would kill the whole HMO movement."

Indeed, President Nixon had predicted that 1,700 HMOs would be spawned by his 1973 law; after five years there were only 300. Miles "felt the strategy of the Nixon Administration in many ways was to damn by faint financing," but Presidents Gerald Ford and Jimmy Carter did little to rectify the problem.

Group Health had watched the worsening situation in Pierce County for some time. Dr. Miles said the medical staff "wanted to let [Sound Health] go bust" and then launch a fresh program, but Senator Magnuson's voice proved more persuasive. By October 4, Group Health was negotiating a takeover. At Grant McLaughlin's urging, the Board rejected a purchase and simply agreed to assume responsibility for Sound Health's assets and liabilities.[18]

These developments were not widely known as the membership gathered to resume the postponed debate over bylaw amendments on November 18, 1978. Caroline MacColl's Governance Task Force had issued its formal reports the previous May and June and conducted a series of special forums in September. The issues were complex and not even the Board could reach consensus on how best to extend Group Health's democratic franchise. The need was clear, though: Co-op membership, which peaked in 1959 at 79 percent of total enrollment, now constituted only 29 percent of some 240,000 enrollees.

The Task Force report warned, "Because of the past decline

and anticipated continuing decline of the percentage of Cooperative (individual) members, new approaches are needed if democratic direction and control of the GHC is to be maintained." To this end, it proposed that "governance rights, including voting, should be separated from type of coverage. Thus, passing health screening would no longer be a prerequisite for eligibility to vote." The report also called for eliminating the current ban on members between the ages of 60 and 65, when they qualified for Group Health's Part B Medicare coverage.

Here the agreement ended, at least among trustees. MacColl and a majority felt that the right to vote should be earned by some action on the part of the voter. Specifically, the group enrollee should initiate an application and pay a $25 processing fee. He or she should also have three years of experience with Group Health. A minority of trustees, led by Ralph Bremer, felt that membership should be automatic and an alternative set of bylaws to this effect was prepared. Both sides did agree to limit group enrollee voting to the election of trustees and adoption of resolutions. Since the bylaws already gave group enrollees the theoretical power to dominate a district committee, the Task Force report declared that the extension of such annual meeting voting rights was not so radical a leap as it might seem. At the same time, group enrollees were denied the right to run for the Board or to vote on bylaw amendments, since these represented the "most significant power afforded to Co-op members."

Anticipating the objections of full Co-op members, most of whom had paid a $175 capital assessment upon joining Group Health, the Task Force reported that group enrollees were already paying their "fair share" of capital funds. In fact, the capital portion of a group enrollee's dues added up to $175 in nine years, compared with the 10 years over which a Co-op member could pay his or her capital assessment. The report also noted that Co-op members' hospital and service utilization rates were 22 percent to 50 percent higher than those of group enrollees.

A second part of the Governance Task Force report addressed a District Council proposal of May 1976 to expand the Board to 13 members to keep pace with expanding enrollment. The Task force found this "inadvisable" and argued that trying to achieve the ideal of perfect proportionality among nominating areas and trustees would require "frequent redistricting."

Since state law held Group Health's trustees responsible for the organization as a whole, the report offered a simpler solution: Eliminate nominating areas completely and elect an 11-member board at large. It also proposed to eliminate the Cooperative's service districts and reorganize local member participation through Medical Center Councils. The Task Force pointed out that the arithmetic was already getting pretty confusing since Group Health currently had 10 districts, 9 medical centers, and 8 nominating areas, each with its own set of boundaries.

Finally, the Governance Task Force recommended that only full Co-op members should be eligible to run for the Board, that each trustee should be limited to three consecutive terms, and that mail-in ballots should be used for all elections. This last proposal relegated the annual meeting to the status of an education and discussion forum.[19]

Such was the tangled agenda faced by members on November 18, 1978, but they swiftly cut through the Gordian knot by the direct expedient of voting down every reform except the use of mail-in ballots for trustee elections. It was a deep disappointment for trustees such as Caroline MacColl who had invested two years in the effort, but it also reinforced the old principle that democratic leaders can't get too far ahead of their constituents.[20]

There were other political gaps within the Cooperative. The Board ended 1978 by holding a "study session" with leaders of the medical staff on December 19. Although friendly, the discussion revealed deep differences over fundamental, even definitional, aspects of the Cooperative. The physicians challenged Group Health's goals to develop "the most outstanding hospitals" (they thought "more outstanding" was a better adjective) and they questioned the practical meaning of prevention and even "healthcare." One doctor argued that the staff was "trained to provide medical care, not health education or preventive care," and another suggested "medical care without frills" as a better description of Group Health's services. The Board and staff agreed to disagree on these issues, despite the obvious divergence of views on Group Health's purpose and mission.[21]

Lead responsibility for organizing Group Health's takeover of Sound Health fell on Robert Pfotenhauer, the Cooperative's director of planning, and Dr. Ward Miles. The latter had stepped down as chief of staff at Olympia to return happily to practice, and he was all but dragooned by Dr. McAlister into taking charge of the staff in the new South Region.

The problems were familiar, starting with relations with the Pierce County Medical Society, which Miles summed up as "terrible. There's such a long history of this, too," he later explained, noting that Pierce County doctors had established the state's first medical bureau half a century earlier to compete with contract physicians. Pierce County's opposition seemed particularly anachronistic since a Group Health doctor, William S. Spence, had been elected president of the King County Medical Society the previous January. Opposition to Group Health seemed to be "in the blood and the air," commented Miles.[22]

Because of this hostility and the fact that Sound Health did not have its own hospital or pharmacy, Miles had to establish new relationships. He bid out hospital services competitively, chose a single emergency room for Group Health members, and built up a Tacoma pharmacy from scratch. He also saw an opportunity in Sound Health's Port Orchard operation. "There had been a lot of talk about small clinics, and I said…let's experiment with it and see whether it will work." In these undertakings, Miles was aided by Dr. Al Truscott, an obstetrician who succeeded him as chief after four years.[23]

Although Group Health did not pay a cent for Sound Health and most of the federal debt was forgiven, the sudden assimilation of 11,000 new members (roughly 1,500 Sound Health members declined to convert) still proved expensive. The first year's annual budget for Tacoma/Port Orchard totaled $4.8 million, before Group Health committed to remodeling an old tire repair shop into a new Tacoma Specialty Center.[24]

In January 1979, the Board took up the report of the Task Force on Aging, convened 14 months earlier under the chairmanship of former trustee Dr. Charles Strother. While the report gave Group Health high marks for direct medical care delivery, it found that more could be done to address social and environmental causes of health problems. The report recommended additional preventive and support services, "particularly counselling and referral to community agencies." The exploration of the special needs of elderly did not end with this report; the Task Force continued for several years and later helped spur creation of a Senior Caucus among enrollees.[25]

Shortly before the annual meeting on April 28, the Board approved participation in a new "inter-co-op study group," which later organized the Puget Sound Cooperative Federation as a successor to the defunct Co-op League. Interest in such an association was revived in part by creation of a federal Consumers Cooperative Bank in the previous year, and by a congressional appropriation of $300 million to seed low-interest loans to co-ops. Although Group Health Dental was faltering, there was a major new group, the Puget Consumers Co-op, formed in 1971, to help lead the effort. The Federation was up and running by fall and the Board appointed Lyle Mercer as Group Health's representative.[26]

Given the previous November's debacle, the Board wisely held its peace on governance at the annual meeting. Richard Spady, owner of the Dick's Drive-In restaurant chain, had his own ideas. He proposed a series of novel notions for democratic reform and offered himself as an alternative to incumbent trustee Ralph Bremer. Spady failed on all counts, but the meeting's results represented one milestone in the evolution of Group Health's governance: For the first time, mail-in ballots outnumbered attendees.[27]

The membership debated 10 resolutions and voted to add postsurgery breast reconstruction, maternity care, and speech therapy to Group Health's basic coverage. It also gave Lyle Mercer another victory in his seesaw campaign to cancel Group Health's membership in the Chamber of Commerce. The most heated discussion turned on a resolution sponsored by the medical staff to ban Group Health statements on "extraneous" issues. This was narrowly defeated, indicating that physicians were not alone in their annoyance with political distractions.

At the annual meeting, Ida Chambliss presented the Board's first "interim report" on Group Health's growth and management in response to the previous year's resolution. She noted that 290 physicians were serving nearly 255,000 enrollees at the end of 1978. In addressing the concern of "access to care and personalization," the report cited the transition to a panel system of a "personal family physician" for each enrollee, the decentralization of appointment scheduling, and the expansion of the consulting nurse service.

The report declared that "the real question is how to grow rather than whether to grow." Based on the previous experience with an enrollment cap, the Board had concluded that "such an action could have lasting adverse consequences." Instead, it was committed "to hold growth to a net increase of 10,000 enrollees per year in King and Snohomish counties during the next two years" and to build an "adequate" enrollment in Pierce County (goals for Thurston and Kitsap Counties were not yet established).[28]

This proved an unusually accurate forecast. With the absorption of Sound Health and significant growth in every county, Group Health's enrollment increased by 23,000 during 1979. Dr. McAlister was able to keep up by hiring 53 new doctors, but the division of staff into three regions, each with its own chief of staff and executive committee, created new problems. As former chief of staff Dr. Hartquist later lamented, "We weren't one big happy family anymore."

The same could be said for Group Health's administrative staff. Group Health's new vice president for operations, Robert Shaver, shook up established lines of authority in attempting to establish his own power beginning in February 1979. The internecine warfare led East Region head Phil Nudelman to resign in July to join the Careage Corporation, but the Board lured him back with directorship of the Cooperative's Central Region. Shaver took his leave soon after.

This incident could have been interpreted as a sign that management was beginning to think and behave in ways no longer subordinate to the Board or medical staff. Yet, the Board approved leasing an interim administration center in the Elliott Bay Office Park on the northwestern edge of downtown Seattle, which physically separated Group Health's administrators from most of the staff actually delivering healthcare.

That fall, facilities began falling behind enrollment growth. Brennan predicted that the Central Hospital would be overloaded by 1983, and further expansion was all but precluded by Group Health's 1974 agreement with the Capitol Hill Community Council. New hospital space would have to be added on the Eastside or in Tacoma.

Recognizing the need for another building boom in September 1979, the Board turned to an old friend, Seafirst Bank, for a $25 million line of credit. The following month, the Board was understandably cool to Lyle Mercer's motion that Group Health join a labor boycott of Seafirst in sympathy with the bank's unionized financial employees.

With its credit secure, the Board accelerated its construction of medical centers, beginning with a groundbreaking for the long-delayed Rainier Valley Medical Center at a new site on October 29. In January 1980, it committed to opening five new centers, including the Tacoma Specialty Center, over the next 20 months, but this quickly proved overly ambitious.

During its first meeting of 1980, the Board decided to drop its application for federal HMO qualification. Group Health had operated under an administrative "determination" since 1978, which allowed it to enjoy the benefits of HMO status without regulatory intrusion into its rates and benefits.

The Board's taste for federal regulation had been soured in part by official criticism of its performance under its risk-sharing contract with the Social Security Administration. Four separate government studies accused Group Health of manipulating its Medicare enrollment to inflate the $1.3 million in "savings" it had generated to date. The reports received extensive national and local publicity, and Group Health was especially embarrassed by charges that it had deliberately excluded low-income Medicare recipients from Seattle's Central Area. All of the allegations were disproved and the risk-sharing experiment ultimately laid the foundation for future HMO regulations, but this was no comfort at the moment.[29]

By the time the Board adopted a new "controlled growth" policy in February, its assumptions had been nullified by the national economic "stagflation" that paired double-digit interest rates and double-digit inflation. Enrollment growth evaporated and construction of Factoria and Kenmore medical centers was put on hold. Rising dues were also taking their toll as the first of thousands of state employees began to opt out of Group Health during the year.[30]

A relatively calm annual meeting in April 1980 concealed the renewed tension between the Board and administration. The major event was approval of a two-year pilot program to test the concept of Medical Center Councils by allowing existing district committees to assume additional responsibilities for liaison with center staff and consumers. The membership also changed its mind on the Chamber of Commerce, and voted to reverse the previous year's decision to withdraw.[31]

This session was Ida Chambliss' last as president, and she was succeeded by Safeco Insurance attorney Ralph Bremer on April 30, 1980. Four weeks later, he accepted Don Brennan's letter of resignation. "I was burned out," Brennan later explained.

"The job took its toll," Brennan said, particularly the demands of the Board. He once chided trustees, "This is an avocation for you, but it's a vocation for me. You get to go home after the meeting; I have to go back to work." Brennan had already decided it was time for a change when he was asked to lead the Sisters of Providence hospital system in Washington state.[32]

Brennan's last meeting with the Board on June 25 featured one item of good news: Group Health had finally won a four-year argument with the state government over the constitutionality of its tax-exempt hospital bonds. The Board promptly issued bonds to refinance its $25 million loan from Seafirst. At the same meeting, the Board named Gerald Coe, Group Health's lead in-house attorney, as acting executive vice president, and launched a nationwide search for a permanent successor.[33]

Gerry Coe was no mere seat warmer, however. He imposed a hiring freeze and pared $2 million from Group Health's operating budget, which was now approaching $150 million a year. He also presided over the opening of the new Tacoma Specialty Center and Madrona Medical Center in November. At the same time, Coe guided the final stages of two projects of lasting importance to the Cooperative: the adoption of Consumer Criteria for the Assurance of the Quality of Healthcare, and negotiation of a formal affiliation agreement between Group Health and the University of Washington School of Medicine.[34]

The first had been in the works since November 1977, when the Board established a Healthcare Assessment Task Force. Based on its initial report in July 1978, the Board approved establishment of concrete measures for aspects of healthcare service delivery such as accessibility and comprehensiveness. The Healthcare Committee, chaired by Caroline MacColl, spent another year and a half working with staff and management, led by Phil Nudelman, to identify specific objectives and quantifiable criteria for monitoring Group Health's performance from the consumer's point of view.

"If management sets its own standards, we never know whom we are really pleasing," Nudelman explained when the final criteria were published in February 1981. He called the new standards "a major breakthrough because we have involved consumers directly in determining their expectations." They were also the first standards imposed by a healthcare institution on its outpatient services as well as its hospital care.[35]

The affiliation with the UW was also a breakthrough and marked the first formal alliance between a major university medical school and a health maintenance organization. It had been worked out in principle by Dr. Howard Kirz, Group Health's director of medical education since 1977, and Drs. Jack Chase and Jack Lein, respectively dean and director of continuing education at the School of Medicine.

The UW recognized the distinctive character of Group

Health's approaches, given its close collaboration on projects such as the family practice residency program. In formally affiliating,Group Health and the medical school jointly agreed to provide a number of medical student courses at the Cooperative, developed several shared clinical programs in such areas as cardiac surgery and inpatient mental health, and greatly increased opportunities for Group Health's research program. The outlines of the agreement were settled by November 1980, but it took the attorneys another year to write the fine print.[36]

The Board was also active during late 1980. It created a new district for the Port Orchard area, and wrote the rules for the first pilot Medical Center Councils. In September, faced with flagging enrollment, the Board voted at long last to lift the age limit on Group Health membership. Group Health ended the year with a net increase of only 1,040 enrollees. Given the loss of 6,000 state employees during the year, it was lucky to have registered any growth at all.

By early 1981, the Board had reviewed the résumés of scores of candidates for executive vice president, and it settled on one individual, who held the same post at the American Hospital Association. He wanted a different title, chief executive officer, and the power to hire and fire all subordinate administrators. The Board granted both requests, and at the annual meeting on April 25, 1981, introduced the Cooperative's first official CEO, Mr. Gail Warden.[37]

Chapter 13

Expanding Horizons

1981 ~ 1983

Enter Gail Warden ~ Surviving the Reagan
Revolution ~ "Elegant Bay" ~ Welcome to Everett ~
New Centers for Health Studies and Health
Promotion ~ Buying into Spokane ~ Founding a
Foundation ~ A Whiff of Censorship

*G*ail Warden was one of 200 prospects for Group Health's
chief administrator. It was a measure of Group Health's
national reputation in 1981 that many applicants were
highly qualified, and none more than Warden. He had headed
up Chicago's vast Rush-Presbyterian-St. Luke's Medical System
and directed the American Hospital Association.

But Warden was different from other candidates in one key
respect: He didn't want the job. "I had been aware of the fact
that it was one of the premier prepaid healthcare organizations
in the country," Warden later reported, but "I also knew that it
had a history of turning over CEOs fairly rapidly in the late Sev-
enties." He turned down two queries from an executive place-
ment agency. On the third call, he was lured from a conference
in Denver to meet Ralph Bremer and Caroline MacColl in Seattle.

MacColl opened the meeting by looking Warden in the eye
and declaring, "I want you to know that you're management's
[the Board leadership's] candidate for this job, not mine, and
secondly, I want you also to know that Mr. Bremer and I don't
agree on much of anything." Warden took these comments as "a
signal to me that I was getting into something I never expected

and that it was a very different kind of organization. And yet that's probably what attracted me to it because I was really interested in the whole idea of an organization that consumers really did control."[1]

Warden also got a taste of Group Health's unique culture at his first annual meeting on April 30, 1981. In their most important decision, members voted to impose a limit of three consecutive terms on trustees (they could return to the Board after a one-year absence), but most of the debate was spent on a resolution committing Group Health to the cause of nuclear disarmament because atomic weapons "represent the world's most serious threat to public health."

This resolution was spearheaded by Dr. Charles Janeway and sponsored by Dr. Robert Jaffee, Amy Koppel, and Lyle Mercer. An overwhelming majority of members rejected an attempt to table the motion and passed the resolution, which declared in part, "It is the responsibility of our generation to prevent this final epidemic." This success led later to the formation of a new Group Health special interest caucus, the Nuclear Awareness Group, which became known as NAG—all too aptly, in the opinion of some.[2]

These activists were alarmed by the bellicose stance toward the Soviet Union then being struck by President Ronald Reagan, who had taken office just four months earlier. Reagan had more than just the "evil empire" in his gun sights. One of the first casualties of the "Reagan Revolution" was the federal Plan 9 rural healthcare program, which Group Health operated in King County. Funding for some 6,000 beneficiaries was wiped out during 1981.

The Reagan administration also targeted the federal system of public health hospitals and the new National Consumer Cooperative Bank (the latter survived). Most threatening of all to Group Health, the president's advisers began to tout a new strategy to contain Medicare costs by dramatically expanding the number of HMOs under federal contract. The principle was first contained in the bipartisan Gephardt-Stockman bill of 1981 and enacted in the comprehensive Tax Equity and Fiscal Responsibility Act of 1982. In effect, the federal government was actively promoting Group Health's first head-to-head competition in the region.[3]

Gail Warden had seen it coming from his vantage point at the American Hospital Association, and he now recognized the irony that Group Health's past successes could become the cause of future problems in the healthcare market. Thanks to Group Health, he later explained, "people knew what prepaid healthcare was, what an HMO was," and this made Puget Sound "a natural place for competitors to come in, because they didn't have to sell the idea."

Warden cautioned the Board that it was "going to have to take a fairly hard line about change, and the necessity of change." In the process, he "very quickly learned that [his] role was to teach them that they were a business and they had to behave like a business." He knew that "some tough decisions had to be made about what kind of organization it was going to be."

This prediction was fulfilled in July 1981, when the Board reluctantly confronted the fact that Group Health's traditional dues structure had cost it the enrollment of 6,000 state employees when the state capped its share of their premiums. The Co-op learned the hard way that imposing a payroll deduction to meet a premium cap only forced those enrollees using fewer services (and costing less) to drop out. The Board responded with a new package incorporating a deductible, copayments for drugs and office calls, and "experience rating" to tailor premiums to the actual costs of serving the state employees group. These provisions violated Group Health's fundamental principles of complete coverage for the "first dollar" received and community rating based on the per capita costs of the entire population, but they rebuilt lost enrollment.

Trustee James Farrell argued that such an important change should be submitted to the membership, but his colleagues did not agree. The limited application of these heretical notions to a single group contract muted protests from purists within the Cooperative for the moment. This would change as the new economics of healthcare took hold throughout Group Health.[4]

Also in July, Warden introduced the Board to a new kind of

thinking, strategic planning. Unlike conventional long-range planning, which is driven by internal goal-setting, strategic planning is more sensitive to external conditions and places greater emphasis on the evaluation of organizational capabilities and resources.

"The essence of strategic planning," Warden told the Board in July 1981, "is to find out where you are; find out what is going on around you; be honest about what you have to work with; agree on what you want to accomplish; decide what is the most promising way to do it; see that something is done about it; and check back to see if your ideas worked out." The first step required an understanding of both Group Health's business environment and the organization's strengths and weaknesses, followed by the identification of "match-ups" representing new market opportunities and potential competitive threats. The ultimate aim, Warden said, is "to anticipate and influence the future."[5]

The view of the future was pretty bleak in the winter of 1981-82. The local economy was suffering from more than its fair share of the national recession. Unemployment rolls were climbing into the double digits, and newly elected conservative officeholders were slashing public payrolls, which affected half of Group Health's enrollment. At the same time, the aging of Group Health's membership was driving up utilization rates and costs, which forced a 17 percent dues increase in early 1982, on top of the 15 percent hike enacted a year earlier. This was not a good way to position the Cooperative in expectation of its first direct HMO competition.[6]

Despite these adversities, Group Health ended 1981 with 7,048 new enrollees—but this was little more than half of its goal for the year. Most of the gain came in the suburbs east of Lake Washington and in Pierce County. Board president Bremer later told the membership that Group Health had averted a net loss in enrollment only through "exceptional marketing efforts."[7]

In his first annual report to the membership in April 1982, Warden predicted more turbulence ahead due to "outside forces ranging from government cutbacks to individuals seeking more flexible benefit packages" as well as growing pressure by employers to limit health benefit costs, and competition from new HMOs and traditional providers. "The challenge will be to respond to the needs of consumers and employers without compromising our guiding principles," Warden acknowledged, but he knew this would be a hard promise to keep.[8]

The April annual meeting was Dr. Robert McAlister's last as chief of staff. He actually had a new title, acting medical director, but the first word was unplanned.

McAlister had led the medical staff through more than five years of wrenching change and expansion during which he began computerizing medical records, reinforced quality assurance criteria for hospital and outpatient care, strengthened research and medical education, and helped to negotiate new relationships with the University of Washington School of Medicine and area hospitals.

His crowning achievement was adoption of a new hierarchical structure for managing the 300-plus members of the medical staff. Physicians in each of Group Health's three regions now elected their own executive committees and chiefs of staff — initially, Dr. James Garrison at Central, Dr. James DeMaine (followed shortly by Dr. Harold Leland) at East, and Dr. Ward Miles at South. They joined three at-large appointees to form an Executive Council that managed medical staff finances, set medical staff policy, approved medical care directors, and hired the overall medical director.

McAlister had reasonably anticipated winning this position, but he encountered unexpected competition and resistance on the Executive Council. The result was a stalemate, and the Executive Council had to look outside the Cooperative for its first permanent medical director. In May 1982, the Council agreed on Dr. Turner Bledsoe, an endocrinologist, former associate dean at Johns Hopkins, vice president for health affairs at the prestigious Maine Medical Center, and, in the words of one colleague, a "doctor's doctor."[9]

Warden made changes of his own that spring. He named Phil Nudelman as senior vice president and chief operating officer and gave Grant McLaughlin the equivalent post for Group

Health finances. Carol Schlosnagle had also joined the core staff as the new vice president for communications. They were based at Group Health's new administrative center in the Elliott Bay Office Park, which the Cooperative had leased the previous November. The executive suites were a vast improvement over Group Health's cramped administrative quarters on the 6th floor of the Central Hospital, but they struck some as a little too luxurious. This inspired a nurse and doctor to pen a satirical "Ode to Elegant Bay." Not everyone found humor in the situation.[10]

Aubrey Davis, who returned to the Board in April, remembered an early visit to the new offices. He was incensed to see a sign reading "Corporate Copy Center." Davis marched into Grant McLaughlin's office and told him to "have that sign down by noon." Corporate-speak was "the wrong voice," Davis said, for a consumer cooperative to use.[11]

Group Health's new president, Caroline MacColl, no doubt agreed with Davis' sentiment, and she preferred to hold Board meetings in outlying medical centers rather than at the administrative center. But MacColl did not shrink from experimenting with new ways to achieve the Cooperative's mission and assure its survival. In the first Board meeting over which she presided, in April, trustees approved an unprecedented capitation contract with non-staff physicians to serve Group Health enrollees on Vashon and Maury Islands, lying southwest of Seattle in Puget Sound.[12]

That spring, MacColl led the Board in lowering the barrier to full Cooperative membership by dropping the requirement for a physical examination. This separated the status of voting membership from health coverage, for which an entrance physical exam was still necessary. The move was motivated by the precipitous "disenrollment" of voting members, down from 62,000 to 58,000 in just three years. The Board had already launched a Governance Task Force II to reform and reinvigorate consumer participation at the district and medical center council levels.[13]

In June, the Board took another step on the path of change by approving a "new model" medical center for Everett, a port city north of Seattle. For the first time, Group Health proposed to use nonstaff specialists on a regular basis. Former chief of staff Dr. McAlister, who had returned to full-time practice, took on the job of organizing the new center and negotiating contracts with local hospitals and specialists at the doctor-owned Everett Clinic.

Warden was wary of the latter and not overly surprised when the director of the Clinic called him late on the night of December 5, hours before the new medical center was to open. "We thought this over," the director said, "and we're not going to be able to offer specialty care to Group Health enrollees, so don't send us any patients."

Warden recognized the bait-and-switch tactic. "This was something which happened time and again all over the country," as local providers attempted to thwart the entrance of HMOs into their communities by initially agreeing to serve their patients and then pulling out at the last minute. Warden told his caller, "Let me just tell you that we're coming anyway. And we'll find a way to do it." Warden and McAlister itemized the Everett Clinic's specialists and "went out and found all their competitors." The new Everett Medical Center opened without a hitch.

After a few months, Everett Clinic administrators suggested that they wanted to reconsider their relationship with Group Health, giving Warden the satisfaction of telling them, "It's too late." (Cordial relations were later established, and the Everett Clinic's specialists are now valued members of Group Health's healthcare team.)[14]

The new year began on a sad note with the death of Jack Cluck on January 27, 1983. His dedication and formidable legal and political skills had given Group Health its original form and enabled it to triumph over a host of powerful adversaries both in court and in the state legislature. He epitomized the progressive confidence in the human ability to solve the thorniest social and economic problems through democratic means, a faith that animated and guided Group Health through its first 38 years and made it one of the finest expressions of the cooperative movement.[15]

Cluck would have been pleased with the developments at Group Health during 1983. With his management team now assembled, Gail Warden initiated a flurry of major organizational reforms that not only addressed Group Health's immediate challenges but actually strengthened its central values.

The first two initiatives were approved by the Board on January 26, 1983: the creation of a Center for Health Studies and a Center for Health Promotion.

The former institutionalized Group Health's research activities, which had been coordinated in a somewhat ad hoc fashion by the medical staff. While praising the efforts of Dr. Robert Thompson as director of preventive care research for the medical staff (and the only staff member funded by his colleagues to perform research), Warden wanted to give future studies a stronger mandate. He felt that research was being treated as a "back room kind of thing, and I thought that their activity ought to be given more visibility."

The Center for Health Studies' first director was Dr. Ed Wagner, who had been Thompson's mentor at the University of North Carolina. "What he brought in was markedly different from before," Thompson explained later. "We had coordinated external investigators [under Drs. Dick Hanschin and Rich Watkins] but now we were going to develop our own internal research capabilities." Thompson added, "Medicine is a pretty imprecise science," but thanks to the Center and other research, "We're beginning to establish the basis for what I would call evidence-based medical care." This meant actually tracking the outcomes of specific medical protocols, in what Dr. Howard Kirz called "a relentless quest for best practice."[16]

The research program was closely allied with the medical staff's internal education program, directed by Dr. Mike Stuart, and with the new Center for Health Promotion, since prevention remained the primary area of Group Health's investigations. Given Group Health's fundamental commitment to preventive care, Warden was surprised that some "physicians particularly resisted" the new Center. "They felt that spending money on health promotion was a waste of money." Medical director Dr.

Turner Bledsoe disagreed strongly with such views, and he persuaded the staff to support both Centers.

If Warden's initial enthusiasm for prevention grew out of dreams of major cost savings, Dr. Thompson probably disabused him: "I don't think you can save money through prevention. You've got to die of something sooner or later." For a system offering comprehensive care, like Group Health, this means that more costly procedures will be required at one point or another in a patient's life, "unless you see the ideal Group Health member [as] someone who pays her dues and never comes in." The real benefit of preventive care is measured in terms of the member's quality of life and the avoidance of health problems resulting from poor habits or environmental risks.

Thompson credits Warden for making "a concerted decision and effort to approve of what we were doing and researching it." Warden admits, "The Center for Health Promotion was a tough sell but...it's turned out to make Group Health a leader," beginning with its founding director, Bill Beery, Ph.D. Also early in 1983, Group Health intensified its health education efforts by sponsoring a KIRO Television special on the hazards of drunk driving and by publishing its first "Good Health Catalog," detailing resources, recipes, and strategies for healthy living.[17]

At its April 27, 1983, meeting, the Board reviewed the formal evaluation of the midwifery pilot program at the Eastside Hospital. East Region administrator Cheryl Scott noted that while some staff obstetricians were "not sympathetic," midwifery had proved itself a viable alternative form of care. The Board approved the hiring of 10 midwives on a permanent basis.

During the same session, the Board approved new priorities for its capital plan, emphasizing facilities in southwest Tacoma, Factoria, and northwest Seattle; it had earlier approved construction of the long-stalled Rainier Valley Medical Center on a new site. The Board also recognized the new Senior Caucus as a formal special interest group. Warden later hailed the effort for producing "a huge advocate for the organization" instead of "a pain in the neck."[18]

The following month, Gail Warden briefed the Board on a

dramatic new opportunity: The Insurance Companies of North America (INA) were willing to sell their existing health maintenance organization in Spokane, the largest city in eastern Washington, "for a song."

Warden had already concluded that "if we wanted to ensure our future, we needed to be a statewide organization." Late in 1982, he was approached by officials of INA Health Plan, which provided healthcare to 20,000 enrollees in the Spokane area (including communites in nearby northern Idaho). This initial contact was not pursued, Warden later explained, "because there were higher priorities with which management was occupied at that time and because more time was needed to think about the implications of going statewide."

INA renewed its queries in January of 1983 and offered to sell its Spokane operation for $1,750,000. This was not necessarily a bargain since the program had lost money for much of its existence due to high staff costs and low enrollment growth. Group Health's medical staff also questioned the priority of expanding east when the Cooperative was struggling to serve its Puget Sound enrollment.

Medical director Dr. Bledsoe and Group Health senior vice president Gerry Coe reviewed these concerns with Dr. Henry Berman, INA's Spokane general manager and medical director. They came away from this session "with a lot of enthusiasm" and reported that Spokane had turned around its finances while providing quality care with "an orientation toward family practice" similar to Group Health's. Warden believed that Group Health could "take a model that we had in Seattle, change it a little bit, and provide a different kind of healthcare to the people of Spokane than they had ever experienced." In particular, he looked to greater reliance on nurse practitioners and use of nonstaff specialists.

The real motivation behind INA's offer was its decision to retrench and focus on its home markets in California and the Sun Belt. Amid the initial negotiations, INA merged with CIGNA Healthplan, Inc., but the new parent was no less eager to sell the Spokane system.[19]

This did not reassure newly elected trustee Maryann Huhs,

an assistant director of the Seattle Engineering Department. She questioned Group Health's own "ability to manage an organization so far from our home base." Pointing out the Spokane program's lack of hospitals and specialists, Huhs worried that the purchase "would mean taking on more purchased services at a time when we are unable to control our current [costs]" and "embarking on another experimental delivery model when we have already committed ourselves" to nontraditional arrangements in Everett and on Vashon and Maury Islands.

Huhs was most troubled by the rush to approve the acquisition "without consulting with the consumers." Aubrey Davis joined her in this last opinion, but he recognized the urgency and the fact that Trustees were elected to "use their best judgment in these kinds of circumstances." In the end, only Huhs voted against a resolution instructing management on the purchase, but she fully "committed herself to ensuring its success."[20]

The Spokane purchase was in fact reviewed with members at the April 30, 1983, annual meeting, but it was not put to a vote. Members occupied themselve with a long list of other important issues. In the end, they approved a study of "comparable worth" criteria to equalize salaries for women and men performing equivalent jobs, expansion of Group Health into north Kitsap County, elimination of smoking in Group Health facilities, endorsement of a handgun ban, and support for the Nuclear Freeze campaign to halt the production of new or additional atomic weapons.[21]

Spokane came back into the foreground shortly after the annual meeting when members learned that the operation would not be organized as a consumer cooperative. Instead, the new "Group Health of Spokane" was to be an "affiliate" nonprofit corporation entirely owned by Group Health Cooperative of Puget Sound.

This decision had not been reached lightly, but the Board agreed with Caroline MacColl that "Spokane enrollees need some facilitating help to decide the type of consumer involvement which would best fit their needs." To this end, Group Health of Spokane's founding board was filled with dedicated cooperators, such as Ernie Conrad, Eleanor Brand, and Aubrey Davis, and chaired by Dr. Charles Strother. They assumed their new duties effective July 1, 1983, and Dr. Berman was retained to direct the new corporation.[22]

The Co-op retained ownership of the Spokane operation in order to ensure statewide consistency in programs and policies. However, the Spokane board took the opportunity to experiment with consumer governance, and it built a system to involve all consumers—not just a select member electorate—in decision making. Dr. Strother later noted that Group Health Spokane (and its successor, Group Health Northwest), innovated a new "model for the addition of consumer participation in governance to conventional administration/staff systems," unlike the Cooperative.

Serving scattered eastern Washington communities also engaged Group Health in the development of a managed-care system for rural areas for the first time. Reliance on a network of semi-independent clinics was a major departure from the parent Cooperative's more centralized system, and some Group Health physicians considered it "subversive of the closed staff structure in Seattle," Strother remembered.[23]

Nursing was undergoing major changes at this time, some planned, some not. Gail Warden created a new vice presidency for nursing, which was filled by Sarah Detmer, building on a Nursing Steering Committee process begun late in 1981 under the leadership of Karen Rossman. On May 18, 1983, Group Health's 1,200 nurses took matters into their own hands and voted to replace the Washington State Nurses Association with a new bargaining agent, District 1199 Northwest of the National Union of Hospital and Healthcare Employees. In August, the new union and Group Health peacefully negotiated a new contract with a 5 percent pay increase later that year, but 1199 leader Diane Sosne signaled that Group Health nurses would be taking a more assertive stance on financial and workplace issues in the future.[24]

In June, Group Health reorganized its programs for "unsponsored" and "uncompensated" care (respectively, the care of individuals without formal health coverage and the care of indigents unable to pay), and the Board created a new matching fund to aid local community health clinics. The Board also voted to cosponsor "Target Seattle," a community education project scheduled for that November to address the risks of nuclear war with the Soviet Union.

The September 1983 edition of *View* magazine sounded its first alarm on a different kind of menace, a horrible new disease dubbed Acquired Immunodeficiency Syndrome, or AIDS for short. It reported that as of early August, six cases of AIDS had been diagnosed in Washington State (none yet at Group Health) out of 1,972 cases nationwide. The disease appeared to be spreading quickly among very specific populations, particularly homosexual males, hemophiliacs, and intravenous drug users.

As yet, scientists did not understood why, but they knew that a diagnosis of AIDS was a death sentence: Nearly half of the known victims in 1983 had already died. Within three years, the Board formally recognized AIDS as "one of the foremost public health issues of the 1980s" and committed Group Health to an "active and expanded role" in research, prevention, and treatment.[25]

On September 28, the Board acted on another of Warden's major reforms by incorporating the Foundation of Group Health Cooperative. This idea had first been raised a decade earlier by Dr. Richard Handschin, and it was resurrected in Group Health's 1982 strategic plan. Warden looked to the Foundation not only to generate funds for research and special programs, but to engage the community's larger circle of civic and philanthropic leaders in the work of Group Health and, thereby, to elevate its public profile. This mission was carried out for more than a decade by the Foundation's president, Barbara Lardy.[26]

On the same day the Foundation was incorporated, news arrived that former Cooperative president Ida Chambliss had suffered a fatal heart attack in Zimbabwe while performing humanitarian work for Africare. A month and a day after Chambliss' passing, Group Health dedicated the new Rainier Valley Medical Center, which she had worked so hard to establish during her years on the Board.

The Cooperative later organized the Ida Chambliss Memorial Health Team to carry on her work of aiding the poor in other nations. In a similar effort, "Partners for Health," Group Health physicians and nurses also volunteered to assist the residents of Nicaragua, whose leftist government was besieged by U.S.-backed Contra guerrillas.[27]

The American Smelting and Refining Company's towering smokestack in Tacoma cast a long shadow over Group Health that winter when a planned article in *View* magazine on the health risks created by the giant smelter's operation was suppressed just as the November issue was about to go to press. Caroline MacColl found the article's discussion of ASARCO's arsenic emissions, which wafted over Vashon and Maury Islands, "too inflammatory." Gail Warden agreed, and he felt that after earlier reports on the perils of nuclear holocaust, home health hazards, and disease-ridden daycare centers, "*View* readers needed a break from these kinds of intense articles."

Word of the article's cancellation spread immediately, and many interpreted it as blatant censorship. *View* editor Paul Temple told the *Seattle Post-Intelligencer* that Group Health managers feared the article "might be in conflict with its marketing policy" (the Co-op had a group contract to cover ASARCO employees). John Dolstad, chair of Group Health's Vashon Island consumer group, was reportedly "incensed," and he later chided management for making "an error in judgment." A revised version of the article was scheduled for the January 1984 edition, but its freelance author, Barnett Kalikow, complained that since this would follow federal hearings on the ASARCO issue, "it really loses its public health value."

View feature editor Nick Gallo quit over the matter, and Paul Temple also left within six months (he was succeeded by Wendy Noritake). The real effect of the ASARCO controversy, Warden observed, was to create a "credibility gap between consumers and Group Health's leadership."

Amid the controversy, Lyle Mercer, who ardently defended the article and the role of *View* as social and political forum, announced that he would resign from the Board in 1984 in order to fight "Orwellian world trends."[28]

Chapter 14

On the Beaches

1984 ~ 1987

Meeting the Competition ~ The Rand Study ~
Arguing Abortion in the Tacoma Dome ~ Age-Rating
and Copayments ~ A Nuclear Freeze Heats up in
Hanford ~ Losing Enrollment ~ Transplanting
Organs ~ Slashing Budgets ~ Warden Departs

*G*eorge Orwell's dystopian vision was not realized in 1984, but the year did witness more deep, sometimes wrenching, changes for Group Health as management and the Board tried to prepare the Cooperative for the brave new world of competitive healthcare.

Reforms and innovations were pursued on a dizzying variety of fronts. In January, Group Health intitiated discussions with its old allies, Minnesota-based Group Health, Inc., Health Insurance Plan of New York, and the Harvard Community Health Plan, about organizing a national "network" of HMOs. Closer to home, a site was purchased for a new medical center in Kenmore at the north end of Lake Washington. Group Health began negotiating capitation agreements with a private clinic in Winslow, on Bainbridge Island.

Planning also started for a "primary care network" using physicians in Bellingham to serve Whatcom County consumers. This entailed the creation of a "synthetic group practice" of non–Group Health physicians led by Drs. Bertha Safford and Gary Snyder. The experience gave Group Health a different and less capital-intensive staffing model by which to meet growing demands from employee groups for statewide service. [1]

Services also grew and diversified. The Cooperative began implementing a major new program to screen members for breast cancer; hired its first plastic surgeon, Dr. David Zehring; and named Dr. Iris del Toro to manage ADAPT, a program for treating alcohol dependencies. The Co-op entered into an alliance with the Safeguard plan to offer dental care benefits to state employees (the dental co-op had by now collapsed), and opened a retail HEAR Center to sell hearing aids on Capitol Hill. This was the first of several health business enterprises for marketing medical devices and supplies, and it was followed by HEAR and new SEE centers on the Eastside by year's end.[2]

More changes were under way. On March 28, the Board reviewed the findings of its task force on flexible benefits, as directed by a membership resolution passed in 1982. Task force chair Aubrey Davis emphasized the necessity of change "because GHC is beginning to experience serious adverse selection" as its promise of comprehensive care attracted "older and less healthy" enrollees. At the same time, younger individuals and families were opting for lower-cost plans offering deductibles and copayments. Age-rating would adjust dues to fairly reflect utilization rates, Davis declared, but this would also be "one of the most fundamental changes we...can consider" and required "extensive discussion throughout the Cooperative."[3]

Caroline MacColl listed Group Health's numerous challenges at the 1984 annual meeting, her last as Cooperative president. "We now see growth as 'multi-faceted,'" she explained. It was no longer merely a matter of enrollment or geographical coverage. Now, growth also meant the "development of related businesses, establishment of affiliations and networks, acquisition of existing healthcare systems and development of new healthcare systems."

Group Health would have to find answers to some hard questions, she told members. "What are the implications of the aging of the population" for Group Health costs? What will regionalization of management and services mean for Group Health's consumer democracy? "How can we make Cooperative membership more attractive" and what should be done "to make the organization more responsive and the service delivery system more personal and accessible?" Finally, Group Health would have to decide "how much...we want to compromise the concepts of first-dollar coverage and community rating" in competing with health insurance plans and other HMOs.[4]

Despite this preview, age-rating and similar issues did not dominate the proceedings of the annual meeting. Most of the membership's energy was spent defeating an attempt to repeal the previous year's endorsement of the Nuclear Freeze and debating (and finally tabling) a mandate for equal pay for equal work by men and women. Complaints were also sounded against Group Health's latest 14 percent general dues increase by the Cooperative Members Action Group, which had been granted official status by the Board in February.

Action on six other resolutions had to be postponed. The meeting ended with the election of three new trustees, Susan Doerr, future state Representative Sylvia Skratek, and Lois Price Spratlen, the second African-American to serve. The Board later elected Aubrey Davis president, and Ken Cameron, a state planner for senior citizen services, became vice president.[5]

Community recognition of Group Health grew during 1984. Dr. Ward Miles was appointed to the state Health Coordinating Council, and Judith Rae Miller became the first health educator to take a seat on the State Board of Health. However, the Cooperative was stung on May 20, 1984, when *The Seattle Times* printed Daniel Barash's harrowing account of his own treatment at Group Health for amyotropic lateral sclerosis (ALS), better known as Lou Gehrig's disease.[6]

A longtime Group Health member, Dan Barash suffered the first symptoms of this progressive paralysis in 1980. His family physician at Group Health quickly referred him to a neurologist who diagnosed the always-fatal disease. At this point the system broke down: Barash was denied coverage for additional tests and not informed about community resources. Although he retained his Group Health membership and received extensive home healthcare, Barash bitterly complained that his doctors' attitude seemed to be, "Our responsibility is at an end, nice knowing you, go home and kick off."

Ironically, such failures in coordinating primary and specialty care were key issues for the medical staff as it prepared its first strategic plan that summer. With hiring again lagging behind enrollment growth and rising pressures to control costs, medical director Dr. Turner Bledsoe focused his energies on developing Group Health's specialties and assigned much of the responsibility for improving the medical staff's planning and management expertise to Dr. Howard Kirz, who was named Senior Associate Medical Director.[7]

The public cloud created by Dan Barash's article was dispelled within a few weeks by release of the first results of the Rand Corporation's federally funded, eight-year comparative study of Group Health and other delivery systems. The report, titled "A Controlled Trial of the Effect of a Prepaid Group Practice on Use of Services," appeared in the June 7, 1984, edition of the *New England Journal of Medicine*.

The study was designed to answer the question, "Does a prepaid group practice deliver less care than the fee-for-service system when both serve comparable populations with comparable benefits?" The study monitored four major samples. The first group enjoyed service at no charge from physicians of their own choosing. The second group also used private physicians but it was subdivided into those who had to pay a portion of their bills (up to an annual cap of $1,000 unless low-income) or were subject to a $150 annual deductible ($450 for families) for outpatient services.

The third experimental group was offered free enrollment in Group Health with no strings or copayments. The final "control" group was made up of a random selection of ordinary Group Health members. The participants in each sample were carefully screened to equalize health risks and, thereby, address the oft-repeated suspicion that the costs of prepaid group practices were lower only because they deliberately enrolled healthier individuals.

Even the most enthusiastic backers of prepaid group practice were pleasantly surprised by the results. Research leader Willard Manning, Ph.D, and his team found that the Group Health experimental group generated "imputed" (annualized per capita) healthcare expenditures *28 percent lower* than the group using free private physicians. The control group of Cooperative members similarly generated imputed expenditures 23 percent lower than the group enjoying free care from traditional fee-for-service doctors.

Only the subgroup paying a high deductible generated lower costs than Group Health participants, but its participants also paid fewer visits to the doctor. This fact was significant because the free fee-for-service group and the Group Health enrollees were almost identical in their office calls and use of outpatient services. The key variable was the rate of hospitalization: Both the experimental Group Health sample and control group registered *40 percent fewer* admissions and days in the hospital.

"We conclude that GHC physicians were simply practicing a different style of medicine from that of fee-for-service physicians," declared the researchers. They could not comment definitively on the relative quality of care delivered under different models of service delivery, but they argued that after decades of experience and research, "it seems unlikely that there can be large deleterious health effects" associated with prepaid group practice. (Later findings confirmed that "lower hospitalization rates were not reflected in lower levels of health status"; special problems were initially identified in Group Health's outcomes for low-income enrollees but subsequent findings revealed "no additional differences to indicate an adverse effect of HMO enrollment on the health of persons of low income at elevated risk.")

In short, the level and quality of care delivered by Group Health did not appear to be any lower than fee-for-service providers, but its cost was thanks to its control of hospitalization. The clear implication for healthcare reform was that a "less 'hospital-intensive' style of medicine than that practiced by the average physician is possible." In the same issue of the *New England Journal of Medicine*, economist and longtime HMO advo-

cate Alain Enthoven, Ph.D., hailed the Rand study as "a landmark on the journey toward a cost-effective health-care system."[8]

Of course, Group Health had recognized these advantages
from the very beginning. Now its program was front-page news
around the country, and for a cooperative dreading the immi-
nent arrival of competing HMOs, this was not entirely good
publicity.

In the November 1984 issue of *View*, staff writer (later editor)
Joan DeClaire reported that for-profit HMOs such as Americare,
HealthAmerica, and Personal Care of Puget Sound were expected
to set up shop in the region early in 1985. Other new competitors included Pacific Medical Center, a community corporation
that had salvaged the old Public Health Hospital on Seattle's
Beacon Hill, and the new "doc-in-a-box" CHEC Medical Centers. Also, DeClaire reported, "five area health insurance companies are expected to start marketing prepaid plans in the coming months."

In the same issue, *View* writer David Suffia documented the
pressures that had been building for containment of medical
costs. He pointed out that new "diagnosis related groups" had
been established in 1980 to standardize and cap Medicare reimbursements for treatments of sets of comparable illnesses. Major
local employers such as Boeing, Weyerhaeuser, PACCAR, the
City of Seattle, and Tacoma Public Schools had also formed a
Healthcare Purchasers' Association in 1982 to apply leverage on
the healthcare system by limiting the growth of fringe benefits
and encouraging competition.[9]

Group Health sympathized with such efforts, but the emerg-
ing marketplace put it at a special disadvantage. As Gail Warden explained, "Because we've been efficient all along, our ability to cut costs further by limiting the length of hospital stays is
fairly limited." At the same time, Jane Crigler, vice president for
planning, predicted that some new HMOs and prepaid insurance plans would lure "young healthies" away from Group
Health with low premiums and high copayments, as they had
done to Group Health of Minnesota. This scenario created a potential squeeze play in which an aging, more service-intensive

enrollment could force Group Health's costs upward with no relief available through significant new efficiencies or the recruitment of healthier enrollees. Something would have to give.

Caroline MacColl observed that the market for prepaid healthcare had sparked an "amazing and frightening trend in the enormous expansion of the for-profit ownership of medical institutions." Leo Greenawalt, head of the Washington State Hospital Association, also worried that "if incentives for quality don't balance the desire for lower costs, we could see cuts that hurt people in terms of quality of care."[10]

Warden vowed "to meet the competition on the beaches." To this end, Group Health undertook a serious round of budget cuts and continued reinventing itself through the fall and winter of 1984. It opened a new Take Care store on Capitol Hill to market health products. In October, the Board established three regional councils to adapt its consumer governance structure to its expanding empire. The following month, Group Health opened its new medical center in Silverdale, on the Kitsap Peninsula. This was the site for a new experiment in physician-nurse teams in health promotion, case management, and care in cases of acute illness.

As a new wing of the Eastside Hospital was nearing completion for its January 27, 1985, opening, the Board also began negotiating to establish a medical center in Ballard to serve Seattle's northwest neighborhoods, but this plan was later abandoned.

On December 11, the Foundation kicked off its first major fund-raising campaign by hosting the world premiere of *Dune*, a science fiction film based on a popular novel by Group Health member Frank Herbert. Back on Earth, Group Health ended 1984 with a total enrollment of more than 332,000, but adult Co-op membership had fallen below 50,000 for the first time in 20 years.[11]

Worries over Group Health's ability to compete were already being confirmed when trustees convened their first meeting of 1985. Gail Warden reported, "The pricing stategies of Group Health competitors are becoming more aggressive." In order to respond, the Board approved a relatively lean operating budget of $327 million, reflecting Group Health's first single-digit dues increase—8 percent—in many years. It would still be too high for the market to bear, but no one knew this yet.[12]

President Davis tried to prepare the membership for Group Health's next major adjustment, implementation of age-rating in the form of a new Plan 1 Cooperative dues structure favoring younger members and group enrollees. In his annual report, Davis warned, "The young adult can now buy healthcare on an age-rated basis from our competitors at a much lower price than our community rate." He added, "Obviously our original plan no longer works."[13]

This issue should have dominated the April annual meeting, but Group Health members had their own priorities, as usual. Both sides of the abortion debate had been noisily rallying their forces for another confrontation over the issue, and the Board expected a record turnout.

Jim Diers (later director of the Seattle Department of Neighborhoods) had the task of finding a suitable arena. He picked the new convention center at the Tacoma Dome.

More than 2,000 members (representing 1,525 voting contracts, not counting absentee ballots for trustees) gathered in Tacoma for Group Health's first membership meeting outside Seattle. They were met by busloads of picketers and counter-picketers, who harangued members to support or oppose a resolution to repeal Group Health's performance of abortions. The long lines and clash of protestors—including some who passed out little plastic replicas of human fetuses—delayed the meeting's start by an hour.

Aubrey Davis brought the session to order at 10:35 a.m. It took another hour to dispense with the rules and reports and get to the first major agenda item, a proposed bylaw amendment to provide for mail-in ballots on all future amendments and resolutions. This drew sharp opposition from former trustee Eleanor Brand, who felt that the amendment would nullify the annual meeting as a forum. Such a meeting, she declared, "is the only time the membership has the authority to control the Cooperative. Mail balloting destroys this authority." UW professor

Alex Gottfried also objected and argued that attendance at annual meetings would dwindle and voting would become more "amenable to special interest" manipulation. The membership was unpersuaded and passed the amendment.

Following a lunch break, the membership took up a second bylaw amendment proposed by the Board. This one replaced Group Health's old district structure with the medical center councils (MCCs), although it retained the old District Council, and added MCC representatives to the process for nominating trustees by area. Eleanor Brand suggested a substitute that went further by eliminating the District Council in favor of a Medical Center Council Assembly and by mandating that the new MCCs meet four times a year. This time Brand prevailed.

Next, the membership elected trustees: Hilde Birnbaum's daughter Ann won election (she had been appointed in 1984) as did John Sweeney, who ran under the banner of the Co-op Members Action Group. Ken Cameron was re-elected over Bob Kirk, and Aubrey Davis ran unopposed.

The first resolution of the day cited a 78 percent increase in Group Health's total administrative costs since 1982 and demanded a "stringent cutback" in the future, with annual reports on management's progress. This failed, but a more broadly worded resolution was passed to direct the Board to "reassess the commitment to 'growth'" in its strategic plan.

Resolution 3 was the main event. Moved and championed by Tom Wingard-Phillips, it simply banned any further abortions at Group Health facilities. A passionate but civil discussion ensued, and the only real fireworks came over a motion for a secret ballot. Former State Senator George Hurley, a longtime leader in progressive causes, fought this back, presumably fearing that anonymity might inflate the votes for the resolution. He needn't have worried: It was crushed under 1,146.5 ballots to 293. Amazingly, this would still not be the last word in the great abortion debate.

Three remaining resolutions passed quickly: To study addition of orthopedic devices to Group Health's basic coverage, to support national research into the health effects of radiation as a food preservative, and to support labeling of any irradiated food products. A 5:21 p.m., Aubrey Davis brought down his gavel to adjourn what most agreed was "a most successful annual meeting."[14]

The glow didn't last long. By summer it was clear that something was seriously wrong as enrollment growth fell further and futher behind projections. Management and the Board went back to their "ABCs," that is, alternative benefit concepts, and began offering employer groups the option of copayments to secure dramatically lower premiums. Observers such as Nick Gallo, then reporting for *The Seattle Weekly*, called it a "bold move" and quoted one competitor as wondering aloud, "I can't understand how they're doing it."[15]

In reality, Group Health had no choice. Management had already begun a concerted campaign to slash its budget. Hirings and new facilities were postponed, and the decision was made to sell advertising in *View* magazine commencing that fall. More than $3 million in savings were identified by midyear, but it still wouldn't be enough as major corporate layoffs began to peel off hundreds of enrollees.[16]

While facing the defection of younger enrollees, managers and trustees were delighted when more than 3,000 senior citizens showed up for a Long-Term Care Insurance Forum held at Seattle Center on July 18, 1985. Cosponsored by the Senior Caucus, the forum was part of the Cooperative's new Senior Initiative to improve services to older people. The issue of long-term care "obviously touched a nerve," said Gail Warden, and he recognized a new market when he saw one. The high level of interest reflected the anxiety of many seniors facing longer life expectancies without the traditional support of large families able to care for aging parents. Group Health responded by accelerating development of its own long-term care package.[17]

A week after the senior forum, the Board finalized principles to guide the introduction of age-rating into its Co-op membership coverage, which was losing some 500 members a month. Anticipating howls from older members, the Board voted to phase in age-rating over two years and offset dues increases with "tenure credits" rewarding longtime membership. It also approved the concept of offering Co-op members the option of copayments, paired with lower dues, for the first time.[18]

Despite an enrollment now 14,000 shy of its goal, and advance warning that its Medicare revenues would be cut by $4 million in 1986, the Board approved the purchase of medical center sites in West Seattle and north Everett. Buoyed by the success of the Co-op's Spokane affiliate, the Board also voted on July 24 to incorporate Group Health of Washington to provide healthcare in Yakima and the Tri-Cities, an area in the south-central part of the state that included the huge Hanford nuclear complex. This set up an inevitable collision with the Nuclear Awareness Group, to which the Board had granted official recognition the previous January.[19]

The bad enrollment news continued into the late fall, and the Board approved a new drive to retain Co-op memberships, which had fallen by more than 2,200. Such losses did not deter the Board from incorporating yet another new affiliate, Group Health Enterprises to pursue noncare business opportunities such as health-product retailing.[20]

When the 1985 books were closed, Group Health registered its first net enrollment loss in 38 years. Although the decline constituted less than 1 percent of all persons covered, Group Health required $12 million in budget cuts to eke out a positive balance of $1.9 million. Gail Warden told the Board, "It was not a good year."[21]

Joe Gardiner might have disagreed. On November 18, 1985, a team of University of Washington surgeons saved his life by performing the Northwest's first heart transplantation—and Gardiner's Group Health membership paid the entire cost, upward of $75,000.

The last thing Group Health needed at this point was to take on an expensive new medical procedure, and "it was another time when I came close to getting fired," Warden later remembered. He was not entirely unprepared for the contingency of approving a transplant operation. The medical staff had established a Bioethics Steering Commitee in March 1984, and it was already drawing up plans for an Ethics Council and membership forums on the issue of transplants and other expensive medical procedures and technologies.

Shortly before Gardiner's operation, Dr. Simeon Rubenstein, cardiologist and chief of staff for the Central Region, advised Warden that a Group Health member was a prime candidate for a new heart if one became available. He asked if the Cooperative would cover the bill. Warden replied, "It's going to cost a lot of money [but] if it's proven, I think that it ought to be available" to Group Health members. He and medical director Dr. Bledsoe made the final decision to proceed in the middle of the night when the death of a young man in a car accident made a heart available for Gardiner.[22]

Some members questioned the coverage, given Group Health's financial situation. The Board and medical staff responded by establishing the new Ethics Council and a staff Technology Implementation Committee, and conducted forums and surveys to test membership opinion. These later revealed that most enrollees, particularly young adults, rated the availability of high-technology medical care and Group Health's emphasis on preventive care as the Cooperative's most important benefits. Ironically, they valued member-initiated services such as mental health the least.[23]

Meanwhile, on January 8, 1986, the Board approved the new age-rated dues structure for Plan 1 individual and family Co-op memberships, which took effect April 1. Additionally, the Board established specific group ratings for the four main sectors of Group Health enrollment: Plan 1 Co-op members, group enrollees, group conversion enrollees, and High-Option Medicare enrollees. The new calculation limited average increases in Co-op dues to less than 4 percent, and actually lowered dues for members between the ages of 21 and 34. Most group enrollees' dues increases also averaged about 4 percent.

Group conversion enrollees, who took over responsibility for their dues when they left an employee group contract, were not so lucky. A 20 percent hike in their dues reflected the costs of serving their historically high rates of utilization. High-Option

Medicare enrollee dues also rose by 20 percent, but this was the result of the federal government's retroactive cuts in reimbursements, not the new age-rating system.[24]

Also in January, the Board established its second major affiliation, this time with Children's Hospital. This led later to a joint venture for an adolescent health center on the Eastside, which was co-founded by Dr. Jeffrey Lindenbaum, who remains its medical director today.[25]

The issues of age-rating and Group Health's financial struggles were major topics at the annual meeting in April 1986. Aptly, the assembly heard an address by Dr. Michael Garland, architect of Oregon's new system for "rationing" healthcare under its Medicaid system.

Following this, a resolution to "sunset" age-rating was amended merely to require a study of its effects. The members also endorsed amendments to increase terminal patients' rights to limit the artificial prolongation of their lives under the state Natural Death Act, originally passed in 1979.

Several important changes in Group Health's bylaws were also approved by attendees. The first created a standing trustee nominating committee to recommend candidates for five at-large seats and for two seats assigned to each of Group Health's three regions. Adoption of this new formula for Board representation marked the end of Group Health's old system of districts and nominating areas, which had evolved since 1949.

A second amendment also changed the titles of Group Health's leadership to conform to a more corporate model: the "president" became the "chair" of the Cooperative, and the chief executive officer became the "president/CEO." The third amendment extended membership on the Medical Center Council Assembly to representatives of the new Advisory Councils, which were formed for consumer participation at non-GHC-staffed medical centers. This brought enrollees served by contract clinics and primary care network facilities inside the tent of Group Health governance.

Members passed a related resolution urging the Board to consult with MCCs in planning future alterations to Group

Health's democratic structure. However, they rejected a proposal to mandate consumer-elected boards for Group Health's affiliated corporations.

Once again, abortion generated the most heat. Anti-abortion activists gambled that the new mail ballot system might yield a better result than they had secured at past annual meetings, so they sponsored a new resolution to ban the procedure.

It failed two to one. None of these results were known when the annual meeting ended at the Seattle Center; the votes of attendees were purely advisory. The final say belonged to the holders of 6,201 Co-op memberships (out of 36,719 eligible "contracts" including both individual and family memberships) who mailed in their ballots.[26]

Group Health followed the annual meeting by sponsoring a major conference on "Community Health Promotion: The Next Steps," on May 28. The Cooperative's leadership in preventive care and advocacy of healthy lifestyles also garnered major honors in 1986 from the W.K. Kellogg Foundation and the Centers for Disease Control.[27]

On July 23, the Board returned to the issue of coverage for transplant operations. The meeting was packed with members and media curious about how the trustees would vote. Any suspense was settled when Joe Gardiner stood up and introduced himself.

"It's good to see you here, Joe," said Aubrey Davis by way of greeting. "You were just a name to us until tonight."

Gardiner told the Board, "I'm a living example that [heart transplants] work. The technology is now. It's permanent. And I think you'll lose your number-one position if you don't cover it."

Seven of the nine trustees present concurred, but Ann Birnbaum and Nancy Ellison still feared the financial consequences. These anxieties were soon addressed, and Group Health pursued a very generous policy in covering the transplantation of many other organs and tissues.[28]

During the summer, Gail Warden reorganized his management team and created a new executive vice presidency for administration, which he filled with a former colleague, Robert Flanagan. Phil Nudelman was appointed to a parallel position for operations.[29]

Warden and the Board also restructured Group Health's eastern Washington affiliates by creating a new corporation, Group Health Northwest. This superseded Group Health of Spokane and later absorbed the operations of Group Health of Washington. (The latter corporation was retained as a legal "shell" for future Co-op ventures; as yet, it has not been reactivated.) Dr. Berman became the CEO of Group Health Northwest, and he was also named to a senior vice presidency at the Co-op. In December, the Board voted to offer a low-option individual plan and dropped the fee for maternity care. It also began exploring a possible partnership with Metropolitan Life to offer a long-term care insurance package later dubbed Security Care.[30]

Total enrollment for 1986 sank by another 12,000 individuals to 316,622, although age-rating helped to boost Co-op membership back up to 68,317. The Board ended the year by signing a lease to move its administrative offices from "Elegant Bay" to the former headquarters and printing plant of the *Seattle Post-Intelligencer,* located at 6th Avenue and Wall Street in the Denny Regrade area north of the downtown Seattle business district. The remodeling would take about a year before Group Health could move in.[31]

Group Health's administration began 1987 in turmoil. The Board's finance committee had rejected Gail Warden's proposed operating budget for 1987 as overly optimistic, and he was "livid," in the word of one coworker. A new budget required renegotiation of the contract with the medical staff, which in turn undermined medical director Dr. Bledsoe's credibility.[32]

"The rapid pace of change within GHC and the negative effects of our newly competitive market have been significantly disturbing," Dr. Bledsoe wrote in his annual report. Despite declining enrollment, hiring freezes had exacerbated physician-patient ratios, particularly in the fast-growing South and East regions. The shift to regional capitation had ignited parochial rivalries over budgets and staff, and Gail Warden's new executive management team structure only added to the "chronic disharmony between Medical Staff and Management," according to Bledsoe.[33]

Many blamed a lack of leadership on the Medical Director's part for the resulting disorder—although many of these forces were beyond his control—and it became clear that the medical staff's Executive Council would not renew Dr. Bledsoe's contract beyond its expiration on January 22, 1987. Another stalemate resulted when members of the Executive Council, some of whom sought the position, could not agree on a new medical director. Bledsoe encouraged his senior associate, Dr. Howard Kirz, to take the post on an acting basis, but Kirz was not an eager recruit. "Howard, the reins are dragging in the dust," Bledsoe told him, "and it's ugly." Persuaded that there was no other option, Kirz took over as acting medical director in January and he was formally confirmed as permanent director three months later.[34]

April's calm annual meeting—which lacked the ritual warfare over abortion—offered a stark contrast to these mounting tensions. Advisory votes at the meeting and later mail ballots defeated a resolution for coverage of naturopathic care and formally incorporated the new regional councils into the bylaws. Members elected retired banker Robert Humphrey to the Board, along with federal health administrator Dorothy Mann, who became the third African-American to serve as a Group Health trustee. After the meeting, Aubrey Davis turned the chair's gavel over to Susan Doerr, a health and human services consultant, and the Board elected accounting professor Allen Vautier vice-chair.[35]

Also in April 1987, the Board married its marketing and health promotion goals by approving Healthy Lifestyle discounts for enrollees and members who, for example, did not smoke tobacco. Group Health joined with the University of Washington to win a $2.9 million grant for health promotion. It also expanded its affiliation with the UW to establish a joint medical center and cooperate in delivering mental health services, which Dr. Lafe Myers (and later Mike Quirk) reorganized to improve integration with primary care.[36]

The following month, Group Health celebrated the passage

of Washington State's Healthcare Access Act of 1987. This legislation had been first advocated by State Senator Dr. Jim McDermott in 1985, and its adoption on May 17 was the climax of his career as a state legislator. (McDermott, a child psychiatrist, left for government service in Africa but returned in 1988 to win election to Congress from Seattle.) Gail Warden and other Group Health leaders had been key advisers in writing the law, which established the Basic Health Plan to subsidize enrollment of 30,000 low-income beneficiaries in HMOs. Group Health pledged to take 10 percent of the initial enrollment in 1989, and this in turn helped to address its chronic problem of financing uncompensated care for indigents, which was costing the Co-op more than $6 million annually.[37]

Later in May, the Board discussed its growing concerns with the impact of "certain elements" of the Nuclear Awareness Group's program on Group Health Northwest's marketing in the vicinity of the Hanford nuclear reservation. As an official special interest, NAG exercised its right to place literature endorsing the Nuclear Freeze on weapons development in all Group Health facilities, including offices serving Hanford.

The distinction between NAG's views and those of Group Health proper was lost on outraged Hanford workers and their families, who depended on nuclear weapons research and production for their livelihoods. Gail Warden later complained that NAG was "using Group Health as a forum on the whole nuclear awareness issue and in doing so used up [an] unbelievable amount of resources and time and also compromised us at a time when we were just about to introduce our plan in the Tri-Cities area."

Aubrey Davis initiated a dialogue with NAG co-chair Frank Kirk over NAG's activities. The Board turned up the heat with a temporary suspension of NAG's special interest group privileges on July 22.[38]

While both sides sought a solution, the Board met on September 30 to explore introduction of a Multiple Options Product (now called point-of-service plans), which would allow enrollees to choose either Group Health services or private physicians.

Peter Brumleve, vice president for marketing, explained that Group Health was now facing "22 competing managed care plans, 15 of which are preferred provider organizations," networks of allied fee-for-service doctors and private hospitals.

Management hoped for a decision at the October 7 Board meeting, but trustees were reticent. Ann Birnbaum questioned how Group Health could "assure quality of care by the hundreds of additional providers envisioned to be necessary." Speaking for the medical staff, Dr. Al Truscott expressed "special concern" that reimbursing fee-for-service doctors raised the "potential of increasing services to maximize income." Multiple Options was, in short, a proposal that seemed to contradict Group Health's core principles of conservative medicine and group practice. It took another three years to approve a final point-of-service plan, Options, via a new for-profit subidiary, Options Healthcare, Inc.[39]

The final exchange over NAG took place on October 7. It was a virtual membership meeting, which pitted many of the Cooperative's most liberal and loyal activists, including Lyle Mercer, Dr. Rick Rapport, and Diana Brower, against the Board and management. Alex Gottfried argued that withdrawing NAG's recognition would "be a purely economic act, without ethical rationale." To the suggestion that nuclear issues were incidental to Group Health's mission, former assistant director Dr. Burry Pelzel replied that Group Health's support for the Equal Rights Amendment was no less "inappropriate." Frank Kirk feared that Group Health "was trapped by its strategic business plan…which does not take into consideration the Co-op's history of social responsibility."

In the end, 8 of the 11 trustees voted to nullify NAG, but they weren't happy that the pressures of Group Health's expansion and marketing needs had put them at cross purposes with their own social ideals.[40]

The NAG debate was the final trauma in a bruising year. Although enrollment ultimately recovered the ground lost in 1986, competition and slow growth forced painful adjstments. Medical director Dr. Howard Kirz later wrote that after a "blush of red ink, things went steadily down hill. Budget frenzy ruled.

Old styles of management and older still conflicts prevailed. In-tra-organizational finger-pointing broke out." There was a "dra-matic sense of the Co-op's lack of commitment to quality healthcare in favor of short-term budget objectives; a crisis of confidence in the Board and HMO management; in short...the crazies."[41]

On October 28, 1987, Gail Warden announced that he would step down as president/CEO to take over as head of the Henry Ford Health System in Detroit, Michigan.[42]

Over the course of nearly seven years at Group Health, War-den had introduced a staggering variety of innovations into an organization that, despite its radical origins, had become quite resistant to change. Warden challenged this complacency in or-der to adapt Group Health to a new market in which it no longer held a monopoly on managed care. To meet and often beat the competition "on the beaches," he took the Co-op's services state-wide, introduced health product retailing, established networks with private physicians and hospitals, established the Group Health Foundation, Center for Health Studies, and Center for Health Promotion, and diversified its array of coverage plans. Foremost, Warden guided the emergence of a professional man-agement culture and raised it to the status of a third institutional force equal to Group Health's medical staff and consumer de-mocracy.

It was an extraordinary record of invention and reform, but it exacted a high cost in terms of Group Health's morale and sense of its own ethos. The Cooperative needed some time to reconcile all the new internal and external forces it now faced with the collective traditions and spiritual impulses at the heart of its being.

At this juncture, there was no better person to help Group Health find its bearings than Aubrey Davis.

Chapter 15

A Regency

1988 ~ 1990

*Corporation or Cooperative? ~ An Evolving
Constitution ~ Nurses Strike Again ~ Total
Quality ~ Goodwill Games ~ Davis Gives
Notice*

B y February 8, 1988, when Aubrey Davis formally assumed
his duties as president and CEO, staff had already settled
into Group Health's newly renovated Administration and
Conference Center. The facility occupies the former headquarters of the *Seattle Post-Intelligencer*, and its interior is dominated
by a skylit, three-story atrium where roaring printing presses
once churned out morning editions, extras, and bulldogs.

The spacious, cheerful offices did not prevent Davis from
recognizing that "the organization clearly had an internal morale problem that was pretty acute." Some of this was inevitable
for an organization now numbering nearly 9,000 staff and 325,000
enrollees. "It was partly just a problem of bigness and the impersonality that that generates," Davis later observed. He credited Warden for making "an enormous contribution" in adapting Group Health to the realities of modern healthcare. "He
shaped the organization up a lot," but many of the changes Warden wrought were "threatening to the historical culture" of the
Cooperative.

Warden didn't focus on the problem, Davis said, because he
"had his eyes on the outside scene" of a dynamic and dangerous
healthcare market, "more than the inside scene." As the founder

of a successful building products business, Gaco Western, and most recently head of the Northwest regional office of the federal Urban Mass Transit Administration, Davis recognized that "symbolic management" was just as important as the nuts and bolts of strategic plans and financial audits.

So in his first days as president/CEO, Davis asked aloud what was on everyone's mind: "Are we an insurance company instead of a healthcare organization? What's our mission? Why are we here after all? Are we here to make money for, God knows who, for anybody, or are we here to take care of the patients?"

He answered his own question: "I didn't come here to work for an insurance company." He added, "Insurance is what we use, it's not what we do." Davis remembers that staff members came up to him almost in tears to thank him for reasserting Group Health's true purpose.

Aubrey Davis also bristled at the new habit of referring to the administrative center as *corporate* headquarters. When he moved in, he placed a jar on his desk and announced, "Anybody who calls this 'corporate' headquarters in this office has to put a dollar in that jar. The spelling is C-O-O-P-E-R-A-T-I-V-E. It's *Cooperative* headquarters."[1]

Davis and Group Health were blessed with a relatively calm year in which to digest the changes of the past and plan the next round of improvements. Enrollment surged, reaching 332,000 by March, some 13,000 contracts over projections. The medical staff also grew, topping 600 physicians by April, despite a bare-bones operating budget of $350 million.[2]

At the annual meeting in April 1988, the Board announced that it would introduce copayments to help control the costs of Plan 1 Co-op memberships and that Group Health was joining a major national study on AIDS. The only action at the meeting came when Caroline MacColl made a bid to return to the Board. Her nomination by petition pitted her against Art Siegal, another former trustee and Group Health's one-time director of facilities. She prevailed, as did a resolution adding drugs for mental health treatment to the basic coverage; a resolution endorsing an "environmental awareness" caucus failed, however, suggesting a narrowing of the membership's focus on social issues.[3]

Susan Doerr was re-elected as chair but resigned shortly afterward to take a position with Sisters of Providence. Allen Vautier was elected in her place, and Nancy Ellison remained vice-chair.

In July, Group Health was tapped to conduct a study of preventive care for Medicare patients. The Co-op's own plan for long-term care was sidetracked the same month when the state insurance commissioner ruled that its new Security Care insurance plan could not exclude applicants on the basis of pre-existing conditions. Metropolitan Life dropped out as Group Health's partner. Aetna Insurance was later recruited to take Met's place. Group Health extended its commitment to senior citizen services, which were now directed by Mark Stensager, when the Board approved a study sponsored by the Senior Caucus for a senior cooperative housing project. (Silver Glen, an independent cooperative, was eventually built in Bellevue without Group Health funds.)[4]

Enrollment topped 350,000 (and Group Health Northwest passed 45,000) by year's end. In contrast to a scant $263,000 operating surplus in 1987, Group Health closed its 1988 books $3 million in the black. But this was still a very narrow margin, representing less than one percent of annual revenues.[5]

On February 20, 1989, Group Health mourned the death of one of its best-loved founders, Dr. Sandy MacColl. His idealism and vision had made Group Health possible back in 1946 by helping to unite the struggling Cooperative with the Medical Security Clinic, and his persistence and persuasion had guided it through the dark days of the early 1950s when conflicts between the Board and medical staff nearly led to a divorce. Dr. MacColl pioneered the development of Group Health's first successful medical center at Northgate, and his enthusiastic advocacy of group practice and family medicine inspired generations of young physicians and made him a national leader in healthcare reform.

Group Health honors Dr. MacColl today with a Center for Healthcare Innovation and annual lectures in his name. His real monument is the legion of Group Health members who still remember him fondly as their family pediatrician.

Dr. Sidney Wolfe, who founded the Public Citizen Health Research Group with consumer activist Ralph Nader, addressed the annual meeting on April 15, 1989. President/CEO Davis reported on the previous year's accomplishments, including the opening of new West Olympia and Factoria Medical Centers, purchase of a new site for an expanded Northgate Medical Center, inauguration of a new Teen Health Center on the Eastside as a joint venture with Children's Hospital, and the start of a $57 million rehabilitation and expansion of the Central campus.

Chair Allen Vautier disclosed that an additional $40 million capital program was being planned for new facilities in South Tacoma, Silverdale and Port Orchard. The financial good news was that Group Health had saved $8 million in interest by refinancing previous debt, but this did not prevent an average 20 percent dues increase.[6]

The chief item of business before the membership was a Board proposal to eliminate the $175 capital assessment levied on Co-op members, effectively reducing the cost of a voting membership to a one-time $25 service charge. This idea offended Rochdale adherents, who believed that a substantial capital contribution ensured that new members were truly committed to the purposes and welfare of the Cooperative.

Art Skaret commented, "If I am just throwing in a few bucks to join, I am not a real owner in the Cooperative." Susan Doerr rebutted that the high fee was "an artifact of past practice" and "a psychological barrier to participation." Since Co-op membership had again shrunk by 10,000 during the previous year, the numbers seemed to be on her side. The attendees at the annual meeting agreed with the Board, as did a majority of mail ballots—but just barely. The final vote was 1,433 to 1,416.5.[7]

With this decision, Group Health completed another important phase in the decades-long process of reforming its internal democracy, and it is appropriate to reflect on the evolution of the Cooperative's governance. The original community of dedicated cooperators contributing energy and capital to build an

In 1976, Don Brennan (top) became the first non-physician to direct Group Health Cooperative since 1952. Dr. Jack Brown (lower left) joined the staff as the first full-time psychiatrist in 1966. Gerry Coe served as acting executive vice president in 1980-81.

Ida Chambliss, shown jogging along Lake Washington, was the first African-American elected to chair the Cooperative. Dr. Ward Miles organized the South Region medical staff in Olympia and Tacoma.

During his 1971 tour of the new Family Health Center, Sen. Edward Kennedy pauses with executive director Dr. Newman (far left) and trustees Hilde Birnbaum, Gene Lux, and Lyle Mercer.

Gertrude Dawson joined Group Health's staff as its first African-American nurse, and later helped to design and direct the Family Health Center.

Cooperative chair Eleanor Brand (below) spent much of her time in the early 1980s lobbying state and federal officials in the cause of healthcare reform. Opposite, Governor Dixy Lee Ray (left), County Council member and future governor Mike Lowry, and Cooperative Chair Ida Chambliss drive a bulldozer at the 1979 ground breaking for the Rainier Valley Medical Center.

*The 1982 Board of Trustees included James Farrell
(left), Aubrey Davis, Bruce Hulce, Eleanor Brand,
Lyle Mercer, Arthur Rolfe, Ken Cameron, Allen
Vautier, and Caroline MacColl.*

A Group Health member expresses her views on abortion while waiting to enter the Tacoma Dome for the 1985 annual meeting. Members reaffirmed reproductive rights at the following year's annual meeting.

Midwife Chris Convery examines Bobbie Garner at the Olympia Medical Center.

Mary Gruenwald (left) helped to organize Group Health's innovative consulting nurse service (photo: Kim Zumwalt), and Sherry Shamansky serves as both Group Health's vice president of nursing and an assistant dean at the University of Washington School of Nursing.

*Dr. Turner Bledsoe, a "doctor's doctor,"
became Group Health's first full-time
medical director in 1982. Decades of
planning culminated in the opening of the
Eastside Hospital and Specialty Center in
1977. Pediatrician and peace activist Dr.
Benjamin Spock (opposite) addressed the
Nuclear Awareness Group in 1985.*

Opposite: Administrative staffers demonstrate their gymnastic skills on the lawn of "Elegant Bay," while Group Health Cooperative promoted both world peace and itself as the medical service for the 1990 Goodwill Games.

Steve Turnipseed (upper left) was the first African-American trained by the Medex program at Group Health. Dr. Henry Berman (below) guided his Spokane-based health system in merging with Group Health in 1983 and now leads Group Health Northwest. Chief financial officer Grant McLaughlin helped write the rules that now govern all risk-sharing Medicare HMOs.

Dr. James Garrison, Group Health's first African-American physician and Central Region chief of staff, chats with president/CEO Gail Warden and Dr. Jack Chase, dean of the University of Washington School of Medicine. Chief of staff Dr. Robert McAlister (left) and future medical director Dr. Howard Kirz introduced major improvements in emergency medicine.

Cooperative chair Caroline MacColl and president/CEO Gail Warden struggled to adapt democratic values to a new, highly competitive healthcare market in the 1980s.

Ken Cameron (front row, center), here pictured in 1980, chaired the
Cooperative as it negotiated its alliance with Virginia Mason
Medical Center in 1993. Executive vice president Cheryl Scott
initiated the first talks with members of Virginia Mason's staff,
headed by president/CEO Dr. Roger Lindeman.

After striking more serious poses for an advertising photo in 1988, members of the medical staff revealed their Groucho-Marxist leanings.

Medical Director Dr. Al Truscott (left), president/CEO Phil Nudelman, president emeritus Aubrey Davis, and Cooperative chair Dorothy Mann have led Group Health for much of the 1990s (photo: Kathleen King).

alternative healthcare system based on principles of mutual aid had faded with time, and, in large part, as a result of the success of many of Group Health's own principles, particularly its evangelical expansionism. The growth of its enrollment produced a new, more diffuse base, which the membership reforms finally enfranchised as a broad electorate of consumers for whom the right to vote was an option separate from their healthcare coverage.

Similarly, the old district system—more akin to legislative representation—had been refocused on consumer participation in actual service delivery via the Medical Center Councils. The new Regional Councils provided a measure of geographical representation and a new elective layer just below the Board, while the trustees strove to operate on a higher, more detached level as solons using their independent judgment to discern and serve the common good rather than particular localities or special interest groups.

The latter did have entree into the system through the organization of official caucuses, although the fate of NAG demonstrated that there were tacit limits on how far they could press their advocacy. While special care had once been taken to ensure the presence of key constituencies such as organized labor and the farm granges on the Board, the new trustee nominating process now prized professional expertise and the ability to grasp the big picture most of all.

Similarly, the annual meeting's role as a periodic "town hall" of the Cooperative had been diminished by explicit reforms such as the mail ballot and by the apathy that inevitably accompanies general approval of an elected leadership's actions. Dissent, not consent, drives participation. In this respect, the annual meeting remained a culturally important forum for the presentation of new and divergent views, and offered an opportunity for the "governed" to express grievances. Instances when the assembly has actually overturned the Board are rare; much more common are cases when the trustees, although not legally bound to, have faithfully acted on membership resolutions.

The changes in Group Health's governance were not the outcome of a nefarious plot to "corporatize" the Cooperative, but a function of the fact that consumers and their elected Board are part of a larger power-sharing alliance. At first, it was a partnership with the medical staff; then the development of a professional administration created a three-way arrangement. In this troika, the Board *is* the consumer-owner, representing the collective interests of members with a single voice whenever possible vis-à-vis its two internal partners.

Tensions between professional, administrative, and consumer sectors have destabilized many other cooperatives. The fact that the Board has remained the "most equal" of Group Health's three institutional estates suggested that there was a practical wisdom behind its approach.

It did not mean that the system was perfect or that the governance debate was now closed. The Board would pursue further reforms to institutionalize its Platonic style of cooperative republicanism—and it would also encounter stiff resistance from the Cooperative's loyal opposition.

Reform was not limited to governance. In the late 1980s, Group Health leaders began exploring the concept of Total Quality Management. Developed first by W. Edwards Deming and Joseph Juran, two management consultants working first in Japan, TQM was introduced into American industry beginning in the late 1970s. The philosophy held that true quality was to be found in "consistently meeting or exceeding customer needs." Attaining this goal required continuous improvement and measurement of all work processes in an organization, and it was best carried out by empowered, cross-disciplinary teams.

The application of TQM to healthcare was first nationally espoused by Dr. Don Berwick, a physician at the Harvard Community Health Plan. TQM was first introduced into the medical staff by Dr. Kirz in 1986, and he found a modified form of the approach to be effective in helping physicians to think strategically about their practices and management activities.

Aubrey Davis remembered that he and other Board members were not initally impressed. "Oh, here we go again," he thought, "Another fad of the month. We'll just ignore it for a while and it will go away like the rest of them." But Davis and other trustees were won over when they recognized that the TQM style of management actually fit nicely with Group Health's history and culture.

Phil Nudelman also became an early and enthusiastic convert. "I thought the text book approach to training was too rigid," but he was intrigued by the idea of "continuous improvement through personal responsibility for quality." Nudelman saw in this an approach that refocused Group Health on a definition of quality as "meeting the needs and requirements of the consumer—and doing it right the first time." At the same time, he recognized that this could not be achieved through traditional hierarchical management.

Davis, Nudelman, Kirz, and other Group Health executives also believed that quality would be a major point of differentiation in the marketplace—and that it was the right thing to do. They announced their commitment and their desire to lead the medical staff and management in adopting TQM techniques, though Davis knew that converting the organization to TQM belonged to the next chief executive officer and medical director. (Dr. Bruce Perry later became the first organization-wide director for TQM.)[8]

Of Group Health's founding constituencies, organized labor's role had become the most ambiguous and conflicted within the organization. While Group Health never engaged in the sinister union-busting of the Reagan era and maintained generally positive labor-management relations, the forces of competition and consumer demand for lower costs inevitably created strains between the Cooperative and some of its unions.

Nowhere was this more evident than in the case of nursing. Group Health was not oblivious to the problem. It instituted an annual Nursing Congress to expand the role of its 1,300 nurses in upgrading their professional status. The simultaneous appointment of Sherry Shamansky as Group Health's vice president for nursing and as the assistant dean for residency and practice at the University of Washington's School of Nursing in the summer of 1988 helped to elevate the esteem accorded nursing within the Cooperative and forged creative linkages between nurses' education and employment in HMO settings.

But in the spring of 1989 the entire profession was trapped in the economic paradox of an acute nursing shortage coupled with stagnant salaries at most institutions. The alarm had been sounded the previous December by a national Commission on Nursing, which reported that there were no trained nurses to fill 165,000 vacancies, and that the shortage would get worse.

Part of the problem was the impact of the post-baby boom "birth dearth," which translated into fewer students and graduates in many fields. The shortage of new recruits for nursing was exacerbated by already low average salaries across the nation, which, when adjusted for inflation, had actually shrunk between 1977 and 1987. While nurses started at relatively high rates of pay, most "maxed out" their incomes within six years. Unlike other professions, there were few advancement opportunities for senior nurses within their own field.

Nursing, therefore, tended to attract only the most dedicated care-givers, and there were too few of them to meet current demand—even at Group Health's salaries, which were far higher than the national or community averages. In the March issue of *View*, Cheryl Scott, then Group Health vice president for human resources, reported that 10 percent of the Cooperative's nursing slots were vacant (typically night shifts and in critical care). This forced the Co-op to spend $3 million annually on high-priced temporary nurses hired from agencies. "It'll get worse before it gets better," Scott predicted accurately.

The high demand was itself paradoxical. The shift to HMO delivery systems was already reducing hospital stays across the nation, but those patients who were hospitalized tended to be more seriously ill and required more intensive care by better-trained nurses, actually reducing the use of licensed practical nurses and nursing aides. According to the market logic of supply and demand, the growing need for trained nurses and their limited supply should have translated into higher salaries. It didn't, because the same shift to HMO care had intensified competition and pressure to keep consumer costs low. Nurses were trapped in an economic Catch-22.

Phil Nudelman, Group Health's chief operating officer, observed that low nursing salaries were "a societal problem that demanded a societal solution." Group Health nurse Eileen Cody, who was also treasurer of District 1199 Northwest representing Group Health's nurses, agreed that "Group Health isn't going to be able to solve the shortage by itself, because it's a global problem."[9]

Thinking globally did not preclude acting locally when Group Health and 1199 Northwest sat down at the bargaining table in April 1989 to negotiate a new nurses' contract. Despite the conciliatory tones of early spring, negotiators could not close the gap between the union's demand for a 24 percent salary increase over two years and Group Health's offer of 17.5 percent.

On July 12, Group Health submitted a final offer that met many of the union's demands on working conditions, including union representation in an expanded nursing governance structure, but the two sides could not agree on the economics. The next day, Group Health's nurses walked (although nearly one in seven quit the union and crossed the picket lines to return to their duties).

Heated charges and counter-charges were aired in the press. Simultaneous negotiations against other Seattle-area hospitals, led by the Washington State Nurses Association, and the appearance of a third nurses' union in the community turned up the rhetorical thermostat on all sides. A federal mediator was called in to bridge the gap between Group Health and 1199; meanwhile the WSNA accepted an average 16 percent pay hike, below Group Health's initial offer to 1199.[10]

This cleared the way for a settlement, perhaps because 1199 was determined to drive a better bargain than its rival union. On August 18, Group Health and union leaders agreed to a tentative settlement providing for a 19 percent salary increase and an additional pay step for nurses with 20 years' experience. The increments were phased in such a way that Group Health's actual out-of-pocket expense was nearly the same as its earlier offer. Member nurses ratified the contract two days later by a vote of 601 to 5, and both sides declared victory. It was costly: Group Health spent an extra $3 million on temporary agency nurses during the strike, and the acrimony damaged the Cooperative's original spirit of solidarity with its nurses' union.[11]

That same summer, state insurance commissioner Richard Marquardt delivered the coup de grace to Group Health's struggling Security Care plan for long-term care when he reversed his previous approval of Aetna's participation. Group Health took over responsibility for serving the plan's initial 800 members and closed enrollment.[12]

The new national experiment in Catastrophic Care Insurance didn't fare much better. Passed with great fanfare in 1988, the plan became a political pariah thanks to protests over its premiums led by the American Association of Retired Persons. The program was repealed on November 22, but a new federal budget law required Medicare risk-sharing HMOs to absorb the cost of its coverage.[13]

November produced another political disappoinment when Washington voters rejected the Children's Initiative. Group Health campaigned heavily for this comprehensive effort to pump some $720 million into the state's education, welfare and healthcare programs.[14]

It wasn't all gloom: The Basic Health Plan, the state-sponsored health insurance program for the working poor passed two years earlier, started operation in mid-1989. Group Health, an advocate and architect of expanded public access to healthcare, was chosen as the Plan's first provider in 1989, and it pledged to enroll 10 percent of the Plan's potential 30,000 enrollees. This target was exceeded during the coming year, and some 7,000 Basic Health Plan members in King and Spokane counties joined Group Health.[15]

Thus, the outlook was much brighter by the end of 1989. Overall enrollment had registered a 40 percent increase during the past three years to reach 373,000. Group Health Northwest numbered more than 70,000 enrollees and was planning to enter the Ellensburg area in eastern Washington in the new year.[16]

In January 1990 the Board passed a financial milestone by approving a $555 million operating budget that was directly linked to the Cooperative's comprehensive strategic plan for the first time. Aubrey Davis decided this was a good moment to begin a new transition and gave a year's notice that he would retire as president/CEO. Not long after, Dr. Howard Kirz also announced that he would step down as medical director at the end of his current contract in August.[17]

In February 1990, Group Health expanded the network of its affiliations to include a new registered nurse baccalaureate program at Seattle Pacific University, and it opened its new University Medical Center in partnership with the University of Washington. The Board also revisited the old issue of whether or not to allow member access to non-Group Health physicians.

With some trepidation, the Board incorporated Options Health Care as a for-profit affiliate to "test several assumptions inherent in the plan design, its marketing, pricing and rating," and approved an initial capitalization of $750,000. Options was the region's first such point-of-service plan, and although it broke with Group Health's traditional mode of coverage, it met the public's demand for choice and proved to be a major addition to the Cooperative's "product line."[18]

A peaceful annual meeting in April attracted 400 or so attendees. They were addressed by Dr. Arnold S. Relman, editor of the *New England Journal of Medicine*, who denounced the American healthcare system as a failure and prescribed "many more Group Health Cooperatives" as part of the cure. The members voted to encourage the Board to add inpatient mental health treatment to all of its coverage plans, an idea that Mike Quirk, Group Health's mental health director, was already working on. Following the meeting, the Board elected Dorothy Mann and Nancy Ellison as chair and vice chair respectively.[19]

The big event of 1990 for both Group Health and Seattle was the Goodwill Games. The competition was conceived by broadcaster Ted Turner following the United States and Soviet Union's boycotts of the 1980 and 1984 Olympics amid the tensions following the Soviet entry into the Afghanistan civil war. The first Games were held in Moscow in 1986, and Seattle was selected to host the second series, in part, because of its long, liberal tradition of people-to-people interchange with the Soviets.

Group Health, in turn, was selected to provide medical care to some 2,500 athletes from 50 nations, as well as 200 staff members, and 1,500 journalists. It also organized medical staffing at 14 sports sites to handle any emergencies that might arise among an anticipated 1 million spectators attending the Games between July 20 and August 5. Administrative responsibility for these services was shouldered by Elaine VonRosenstiel while Dr. Roy Farrell directed the 350-member volunteer medical team. Even with thousands of donated hours, the effort cost Group Health $400,000, judged a small price for advancing international peace—and garnering national publicity.

No one knew at the time, of course, that the Soviet Union would cease to exist in a year's time.[20]

Shortly after the conclusion of the Goodwill Games, Dr. Al Truscott, former South Region chief of staff, was appointed as Group Health's new medical director. The Group Health Foundation sponsored a unique athletic event of its own on September 9: a mile-long fun run through the newly completed downtown Seattle transit tunnel.[21]

On October 8, 1990, the search committee for a new president/CEO reached its conclusion. Cooperative chair Dorothy Mann told the membership that Aubrey Davis would continue in a new post, president emeritus. As to the next president/CEO, after interviewing candidates from around the nation for 10 months, the Board decided "the best person for the job is already here." He was Group Health's executive vice president for operations, Phil Nudelman.[22]

Chapter 16

Full Circle

1991 ~ 1995

*Nudelman's Vision ~ Healthcare Reform Leaps
and Stumbles ~ The Alliance with Virginia
Mason ~ A Brief but Bitter Strike ~ An
Information Transformation ~ Concerned
Consumers Rally ~ Deja Vu 1946*

*P*hil Nudelman had now spent 18 years, half of his professional career, at Group Health. In that span he had computerized its pharmacy, reorganized its nonphysician professional services, coauthored its first Consumer Criteria for Quality of Healthcare, helped to plan and launch the Eastside Hospital, managed the South Region, administered the Central Region and hospital complex on Capitol Hill, and directed operational elements of the entire Group Health system.

He had contributed in countless ways to the Cooperative's development from diversifying its service plans to installing park benches—which were bolted together by his children at Eastside Hospital. After serving under five chief executives, it was his turn to lead.

While still chief operating officer, Nudelman had formulated a vision statement describing the ideal state of the Cooperative in the year 2000. Its five points are deceptively simple: Group Health would be the "best managed-healthcare organization in the nation"; it would have "the most-satisfied customers"; its "unique consumer governance structure would be a national model for the collaborative delivery of cost-effective, quality healthcare"; it would be the "most-desirable healthcare system in which to work in the Northwest"; and it would "deliver quality healthcare to all segments" of the population.[1]

Nudelman saw "Vision 2000" as more than a managerial mantra handed down from on high. "I wanted everyone to share these goals," he said, and he organized task groups to enable each sector of the organization to interpret and apply them to their own work. This effort was linked to the new management philosophy of Total Quality Management.

As later articulated in Group Health's 1992-96 Strategic Plan, TQM offered a "vehicle for giving our employees and staff the tools and authority they need to do their jobs well" via "empowered teams." These principles were manifested in the Medical Staff's "Primary Care Vision for the 1990s," which affirmed consumer satisfaction as its highest criterion for success in assisting "enrollees in maintaining or improving their health" and decentralized delivery into a system of "healthcare teams."[2]

Nudelman was blessed with a period of relative peace during 1991 in which to begin to implement such ideas. The new Options point-of-service plan was introduced under the directorship of Eileen Duncan, and it helped fuel a surge in enrollment. Group Health also expanded its reciprocity agreements with Kaiser and other members of The HMO Group.[3]

Group Health introduced a number of innovations over the course of the year: It developed a skilled nursing facility at Kelsey Creek, near Bellevue, in partnership with the Careage Corporation. The popular Zoo Walkers exercise program for senior citizens was begun at Seattle's Woodland Park Zoo. A $5 "bounty" for defective children's car restraints led to the collection of 2,000 faulty seats, which were squashed by a steamroller in a highly publicized press event. And Dr. Michael Madwed and Joni Hardcastle established a special Teen Pregnancy and Parenting Clinic at the Central Hospital to help address what was being recognized as a major social and healthcare issue.[4]

Former South Region chief of staff Dr. Ward Miles was elected to the Board at an uneventful annual meeting in April, and members also returned Caroline MacColl. In July, the Board approved a new set of Community Service Principles, which reaffirmed its leadership as a "socially responsible institution...in working towards the provision of appropriate healthcare to persons in need, regardless of their ability to pay." A survey of members reported that 74 percent endorsed "universal access" as the proper objective of healthcare reform, but the issue was eclipsed during 1991 by higher profile debates in the larger community over abortion and the right of terminally ill patients to request medical assistance in ending their lives.[5]

The abortion battle that year centered on Initiative 120, which was sponsored by women's groups and "pro-choice" organizations to write the principles of Roe v. Wade into state law (the 1970 initiative statute had effectively been superseded by the 1973 U.S. Supreme Court decision) and thereby foreclose any dilution of abortion rights under the new, more conservative Supreme Court. Group Health's Board backed the effort enthusiastically, and donated $20,000 to the ultimately successful campaign.

Initiative 119 was another matter. Group Health's members and staff had strongly supported the right of terminally ill patients to a "natural death" without extraordinary medical intervention for more than two decades, but they were divided over the ethical implications of a physician actively abetting death at a patient's request. The Board decided to remain neutral, and the initiative was rejected by a narrow majority of voters in November.[6]

On January 2, 1992, Group Health opened its new Tacoma Specialty Center. This was part of a $367 million capital program that included construction of a new Everett Medical Center, expansion of the Olympia medical campus, and completion of the Central Medical Center South building to house specialists on Capitol Hill.[7]

That spring, Group Health broadened its coverage to include virtually all nonexperimental organ transplantation procedures, as well as prosthetic breasts for mastectomies, while increasing dues by an average of 10 percent (on top of a 13 percent hike the year before). This did not slow enrollment growth, but the addition of $5 copayments for office visits in a new Medicare low-option package drew protests from senior members. (Two years later, Group Health closed its high- option plan because the coverage of drugs was creating a severe problem with adverse selection; a new plan without drug coverage was then introduced.)[8]

Healthcare reform re-emerged as a major political topic in 1992. State Senator Phil Talmadge led a strong effort to adopt a state reform package that foundered in the Legislature at the last minute. State Representative Dennis Braddock decided to take the matter directly to the people in the form of Initiative 141, but his plan's heavy dose of government intervention made Group Health trustees pause. The Board approved Group Health's own alternative set of reform principles, dubbed "Fair Care," which emphasized "pluralism in the financing and delivery of care."[9]

Fittingly, healthcare economist Alain Enthoven, a nationally prominent advocate of such a "managed competition" style of reform, was selected to address the April annual meeting, but a different kind of reform drew the most debate. The Board submitted a bylaw amendment ending regional nomination of trustees. Instead, it proposed the election of all trustees from a single at-large slate on the basis of simple pluralities: the highest vote-getters win, the rest don't.

This proposed final break with Group Health's tradition of at least partial geographical representation did not sit well with the meeting's 700 attendees or with mail-in voters. It failed by 1,628 ballots to 950.5, and the Board later went back to the drawing board by forming a Governance Action Team (GAT) to draft new reforms.[10]

Unfortunately, the November opening of the new $55 million Central South Specialty Center coincided with the announcement that Group Health would lay off 100 nurses in the new year. This not only dampened the celebration, it almost ended a three-year truce with District 1199 Northwest, now affiliated with the Service Employees International Union (the first union, by the way, to represent Group Health nurses back in 1947).

The union and Group Health had peacefully renegotiated the nurses contract in 1991, but the prospects for repeating this feat in 1994 dimmed amid a flurry of critical press reports. Some, including a *Seattle Times* reporter, made a direct connection between the layoffs and the Cooperative's ambitious capital program and its hiring of new "patient care technicians" to perform some routine nursing duties such as transporting patients. The allegation drew an angry response from Sherry Shamansky, Group Health's vice president for nursing.

Shamansky defended both the construction of facilities for in-house specialists and the nurse layoffs as essential strategies "to keep healthcare affordable for our consumer-owners" at a time when "technological advances and good management have reduced the number of patients in our hospitals." She scolded the *Times* for delaying its report on such changes at Group Health "until you could insinuate that it was somehow bad news."[11]

Seniors were also angry when their Medicare copayments were doubled to $10 for the new year, but Group Health was powerless against the federal pressure to cut Medicare costs. At least labor tensions were relieved when the Cooperative and its 11 unions united for a cycle of collaborative bargaining.[12]

Group Health executive staff spent the last weeks of 1992 preparing a massive application for the Civilian Health and Medical Program of the Uniformed Services, or CHAMPUS, which served military dependents, retirees, and retiree dependents. Chief financial officer Grant McLaughlin remembered that he and financial analyst Jim Truess only paused on Christmas Day to spend a few hours with their families, and then returned to work to finish the application by January 1, 1993.

The final product was a stack of documents that stood taller than the office doorway. The prize was equally substantial: a share of more than 250,000 potential enrollees. Group Health created a new corporate entity, Northwest Healthcare Systems, Inc., to operate the program, but its enthusiasm quickly waned as the Department of Defense kept changing the ground rules. Group Health ultimately withdrew its application, but the winner, California-based Foundation Health, invited the Co-op to join a "Tricare" consortium as a subcontractor for the program's HMO component. It has since added thousands of consumers to Group Health's rolls.[13]

The cause of healthcare reform received a tremendous boost

in November 1992 with the election of a new U.S. president and Washington State governor. Both Bill Clinton and Mike Lowry, a former Group Health lobbyist and five-term member of Congress, had put the goal of universal access to affordable healthcare at the top of their campaign platforms. Substantial Democratic majorities were also sent to both Congress and the state legislature, giving hope that 1993 would be the year when healthcare reformers finally grabbed the brass ring.

In campaigning for governor, Mike Lowry had asked his supporters not to support Initiative 141, "Health For All," which he feared would create a backlash by major employers who opposed its mandatory healthcare coverages and costs. Instead, he asked friends of reform to give him a chance to work out a compromise. They did, and Lowry delivered on his promise in the first session of the legislature.

The Health Services Act of 1993 passed on April 23, just six days after Governor Lowry told the annual meeting assembly that Group Health "is a model for where we're going." This was not accidental since Cooperative leaders such as Phil Nudelman, Aubrey Davis, and Dorothy Mann had consulted closely with the governor and legislators in constructing the new law based on the principle of "managed competition."

The core concept was simple: Organize all consumers into large purchasing cooperatives to maximize their buying power, and organize all providers into large service alliances to maximize their efficiency. Then let managed care givers compete on the basis both of cost and quality, as measured by state "report cards."

As elegant as the principle might be, the actual legislation mandated an intricate system of new public and private institutions and complex rules. Key components included the establishment of a Health Services Commission that would draw up a uniform benefits package and corresponding schedule of fees and insurance premiums. This package would constitute a mandatory minimum level of coverage to which all citizens would have to subscribe, either as individuals or through their employers. The latter would be required to pay at least 50 percent of their employees' healthcare premiums by 1999.

A variety of mechanisms were built into the plan to help contain costs and soften the financial impact on consumers and businesses. First, employers would be required to offer a choice of three plans, but their cost obligation would be capped at the full premium of the cheapest plan. Thus employees choosing higher-priced coverage would have to absorb part of the cost of their decision.

Individuals and businesses would have to join one of four proposed Health Insurance Purchasing Cooperatives (HIPCs) to maximize their purchasing power. At the same time, insurers and providers were expected to form alliances to achieve greater efficiency and keep their costs competitive.

The new law also expanded the Basic Health Plan, turning it into an HIPC for individuals, small businesses, and state employees as well as low-income beneficiaries. Subsidies were dramatically expanded by raising taxes on tobacco products and alcohol, and new taxes on hospital services and healthcare premiums were intended to finance administration of the new system.

All of this was intended to slow the inflation of medical costs for both consumers and employers, guarantee universal access, shield families from catastrophic bills, and establish uniform standards for measuring and managing the quality of care. Additionally, the Health Services Act mandated "community rating" for all coverage plans and prohibited the exclusion of anyone on the basis of pre-existing conditions.[14]

The Health Services Act was a double-edged sword for Group Health. It created new opportunities for diversification and expansion for enterprises such as the Northwest Center for Medical Leadership, organized by the Group Health medical staff and headed by former medical director Dr. Howard Kirz. In July, he told the Board, "the community has decided to be in a managed care world and GHC has special expertise to share" in preparing physicians for it.[15]

The prospect of comprehensive reform also intensified market pressure to slow the steady increase of Group Health's rising dues. Phil Nudelman pledged to cut the cost of healthcare delivery by 9 percent, and this inevitably translated into more layoffs. Fortunately, Group Health was able to negotiate a process with the Unions United coalition representing nearly two-thirds of its unionized workers to balance the loss of 200 administrative and healthcare positions with a $3 million package of severance benefits, including tuition for retraining programs.[16]

Washington's new system heavily influenced the Clinton administration's thinking as it prepared its own plan for national healthcare reform, and Phil Nudelman was invited to serve on the White House Task Force drawing up the president's proposal. Group Health found itself sharing the spotlight during 1993 as *U.S. News and World Report* and *Money* magazine praised it as one of the nation's best HMOs. Group Health Northwest also became the first HMO in the state to be certified by the new National Committee for Quality Assurance (and its parent Cooperative became the second).

Aubrey Davis and medical director Dr. Al Truscott were summoned to advise Congress and administration strategists, and Group Health and the Mayo Clinic were the only models cited in the final White House plan. When President Clinton unveiled his proposal for "Health Security" in a speech to Congress on September 22, Nudelman and Group Health chair Ken Cameron attended as the president's guests.[17]

The initial euphoria of reformers was followed by a lot of head-scratching over the details for both Washington's new plan and President Clinton's proposal. Critics on the left distrusted any reliance on private insurers and preferred a single-payer system in which the government collected healthcare taxes and dictated the cost of care. Critics on the right mounted a slick national media campaign exploiting confusion over the plan's intricacies while, ironically, reviving the old bogey man of "socialized medicine."

In Washington State, conservatives mounted their counterattack in the form of Initiative 602, which proposed to repeal all new taxes adopted by the 1993 legislature but really targeted the higher tobacco and alcohol taxes needed to finance the state's healthcare reforms. The companion Initiative 601, which capped the growth of state spending at a rate equal to population growth, also weakened the financial base for implementing healthcare reform. Group Health took a strong stand against both, and formally expressed its "displeasure" when the Greater Seattle Chamber of Commerce endorsed 602. Despite the Chamber's support, the initiative failed on November 2. Although 601 eked out a narrow victory, the state's healthcare reform was safe for the moment.[18]

One week after the election, Group Health CEO Phil Nudelman and his counterpart at Virginia Mason Medical Center, Dr. Roger Lindeman, held a press conference to announce a new "strategic alliance" between their organizations. While the prospect of implementation of the state's new healthcare system helped to speed the final decision, Group Health had been seeking a major partner for some time.[19]

Cheryl Scott, Group Health's executive vice president and chief operating officer, explained that the state reforms created "new imperatives for provider organization's size, scope, and level of choice in order to compete." Since no one institution was large enough, "everybody was talking to everybody. I gained 10 pounds going to lunches and dinners" with executives from other healthcare groups.

Scott compared the initial flurry of talks to a "high school mixer, where you dance and then the boys go back to their side of the room, and the girls go back to theirs." One dance partner stood out from the rest: Mike Rona, Virginia Mason's executive administrator, and Scott's old college classmate. They began serious, although informal, talks in November 1992.[20]

The June 1993 update of Group Health's five-year strategic plan identified a new mandate: "Develop partnerships with other healthcare systems/providers as a broadbased strategy to increase GHC's capacity, gain access to potential enrollees, and improve public perception of physician choice at GHC." The following month, staff reviewed Group Health's partnership options in a memorandum that asked, "Why can't we go it alone?"

There were three answers. First, reaching Group Health's desired market share of 20-25 percent (up from about 15 percent at the time) would require a tremendous expansion of staff and facilities at a time when the market demanded that costs be cut. Second, Group Health needed to associate with a respected provider to address "the community's lingering perception" that the quality of its care was inferior to other providers, a myth that no amount of empirical evidence seemed able to dispell. Finally, a partnership "with another healthcare system with common goals and complementary strengths" offered a potential synergy to "accomplish what neither party can accomplish alone."

The memo noted that Group Health already had ample experience with a diverse set of healthcare partners, including the University of Washington, Children's Hospital, and Tacoma's MultiCare, which provided hospital care to Group Health members in the South Region. None of these existing relationships provided all of the necessary ingredients, however, for achieving Group Health's goals. The relationship with the UW was the strongest, but the state constitution posed serious obstacles to its ability to function as a "shared risk" business partner.

Of these current and possible new partners, Group Health analysts concluded that Virginia Mason offered the best fit by far. It operated a 336-bed hospital, a central clinic with 300 physicians, 13 neighborhood medical centers, a skilled nursing facility for AIDs patients, and a pre-paid plan with 41,000 subscribers. It was also universally esteemed as one of the region's most advanced practitioners in most medical specialties.

As "a non-profit, integrated delivery system, built around a multi-specialty group practice...committed to pre-paid managed care," Virgina Mason was a virtual first cousin of Group Health. The differences—Virginia Mason's emphasis on tertiary care and relative inexperience in health maintenance—were viewed as inducements, not impediments, to collaboration. Whatever peril there might be in an alliance, the memo concluded, was offset by two inescapable facts: "The turbulence of the environment will demand that we change to improve, and we will be taking risks no matter what we do, even if we do nothing."[21]

Beyond this matchmaker's checklist of compatibilities, what made Virginia Mason the most attractive was its willingness to join its fate with Group Health's. Cheryl Scott noted that Virginia Mason offered a "synergy we couldn't get elsewhere. Neither of us was in the business of just running hospitals. We were both more focused on the whole continuum of patient care." Phil Nudelman saw a unique opportunity "to share scarce resources, raise quality, and introduce new products with expanded physician choice."[22]

The Group Health medical staff took some convincing, but after meeting with his Virgina Mason colleagues, medical director Dr. Al Truscott reported, "We discovered we shared uninformed prejudices about each other" which "literally evaporated once we began talking to each other." Alan Blackman, Group Health's former planning director and a healthcare consultant, played the role of a skeptical chaperone for Group Health and Virginia Mason's initial courtship. The early "dates" were held at the Battelle Institute in Seattle.[23]

The engagement was sealed at a private party of the two organization's chief executives in the Columbia Tower Club high above downtown Seattle. Just to make sure that everyone understood the nature of the commitment they were about to make, Phil Nudelman declared, "There is no point in forming this alliance if we can't envison a single organization down the road." All those in attendance nodded "I do," but the Cooperative's voting members would still have to bless the union.[24]

The initial reaction to the November 9, 1993, announcement of the alliance was mixed. The medical and business communities greeted the idea with enthusiasm and the competition was gratifyingly alarmed, but many inside Group Health wondered what the alliance would mean for their organization and their positions within it.

There were few hard answers for the inevitable questions. In the January 1994 issue of *View*, Phil Nudelman outlined some of the anticipated areas of shared activity: a "new insurance product" to "allow consumers to select providers" from both Group Health and Virgina Mason; referrals of Group Health patients to

Virginia Mason for specialty services such as kidney transplants; opening hospitals to both organizations' staff, particularly on the Eastside where Virginia Mason had no hospital; and collaborative research and evaluations.

The last was implemented in December with the establishment of a joint Institute for Healthcare Excellence. The next step came in April when Group Health's Eastside Hospital treated its first patient referred by Virginia Mason (Virginia Mason reciprocated in May by performing heart surgery on its first Group Health referral).[25]

There was more to come. Virgina Mason president/CEO Dr. Lindeman cited an example of mutual benefit. "Instead of each organization buying the newest MRI [Magnetic Resonance Imager, an advanced form of X-ray device], we need to look into sharing facilities, sharing staff as a way to reduce costs." This seemingly benign notion sent shivers up the spines of physicians, nurses, and support staff in both groups: would their jobs be sacrificed to achieve such "economies of scale"? Patients similarly wondered if they would be forced to change doctors, and Cooperative members asked how member-governance would be preserved in the new arrangement.

Officials of both organizations quickly assured all listeners that no fundamental changes were in the works beyond the exploration of "complementary differences." Group Health chair Ken Cameron said he liked "the idea of bringing these talented folks into the family. Creative sparks fly...." Unfortunately, these sparks would eventually ignite the tinder of suspicion.

Given the pace and scale of the changes represented by the alliance and the scale of the publicity, the topic received surprisingly little attention at the annual meeting on April 16, 1994. Instead, the Cooperative's vocal left wing vented most of its energy defending Congressman Jim McDermott's single-payer proposal as an alternative to President Clinton's managed competition model for healthcare reform. A special membership forum was subsequently arranged for July 14 to allow all sides to be heard.

The annual meeting also debated a resolution recognizing

violence as a public health issue. Dr. TommyThompson, director of preventive care reaearch, explained that "violence has a
clear and measurable impact on the physical and mental health
of all our citizens [and] on our clinics, our hospital emergency
rooms, and all our healthcare facilities." Some objected that
Group Health was again veering off on a political tangent, but
the majority agreed that Group Health should pursue an aggressive campaign to combat violence.

One of the first results of passage of this resolution was the
adoption of a policy banning weapons at all Group Health facilities. The assembly and later mail ballots also approved a bylaw amendment allowing the Board to shift the date of future
annual meetings to better conform to its planning and budget
cycles. The next meeting was later set for October 1995.[26]

In May, Group Health chair Ken Cameron unveiled the pre-
liminary findings of the Governance Action Team. GAT proposed
to scrap Group Health's superstructure of committees, Medical
Center Councils, and Regional Councils in favor of a "broader
definition of member involvement" ranging from individual interactions to participation in focus groups and consumer forums.

The plan drew heavy fire from veteran volunteers such as
Mike Koppa, a member of the Tacoma Medical Center Council,
who saw a "shifting of power away from the grassroots and into
a small, centralized Board of Trustees." Selina Chow, chair of the
Central Regional Council, asked, "What if consumer participation doesn't happen? What is there to ensure that there's an effort to make it happen?" The Board decided this was not a good
time to overhaul Group Health's governance structure.[27]

On July 7, a week after Group Health's union contract with
1,400 registered nurses and 100 social workers had expired, District 1199 Northwest took its bargaining issues public with ral-
lies at the Central and Eastside Hospitals. Union officer Karen
Zytniak told *The Seattle Times*, "We feel absolutely betrayed" by
Group Health's initial proposal for wage and benefit concessions
to moderate layoffs. The two sides returned to the table, but there
was little progress in the coming months.[28]

Phil Nudelman later told the Board, "Despite our difficult

situation with 1199 NW, the remainder of our 10 labor union relationships are excellent." This was critical since 5,700 of Group Health's 9,100 employees worked under collective barganing contracts. Group Health put into place a number of reforms during 1994 to improve workplace conditions and cooperation, including a 26-member Labor/Management Council representing all unions. "It's a way for all involved to pull together," Nudelman said, and to "identify areas of disagreement, and strive for ways of resolving issues." Group Health also implemented its Economic Security Fund to provide voluntary severance alternatives and cushion the impact of layoffs, established a Crisis Outreach and Relief program to aid employees during periods of financial or family stress, and became one of the first major private employers to extend medical fringe benefits to workers' "domestic partners" as well as their spouses.[29]

Also in July, the Boards of Group Health and Virginia Mason incorporated their first joint subsidiary, Virginia Mason-Group Health Alliance, to market a family of insurance plans providing access to both systems. The first of these, Alliant Plus and Alliant Select (a point-of-service plan allowing use of doctors outside of either alliance member) were unveiled in September. That same month, Virginia Mason physicians began using Group Health's Eastside Hospital.[30]

In October, Group Health passed a milestone when total enrollment passed 500,000. This included 115,000 enrollees served by Group Health Northwest and another 30,000 covered by Options Health Care, Inc. The Cooperative ended 1994 having collected $1 billion in annual revenues for the first time in its history, and it earned a record $35.7 million net margin .[31]

Hopes for healthcare reform suffered a concussion in the Republican landslide of 1994. Among the casualties was Congressman Mike Kreidler, a former Group Health optometrist who had represented much of southern Puget Sound for one term.

President Clinton's American Health Security Act had already passed into a deep coma in Congress thanks to confusion over its details and a multimillion-dollar propaganda campaign funded by insurance companies. Conservative Republican majorities in both the U.S. House of Representatives and U.S. Senate promptly took the whole issue of reform off life support when Congress met in January 1995.

Republicans also won control of the lower house of Washington's legislature, but Democrats hung on to the Senate. This gave Governor Lowry just enough leverage to work with both moderate Republicans and Democrats to salvage the expanded Basic Health Plan in the 1995 session, while conservatives killed most of the Health Services Access Act's other reforms. At the same time, the Legislature mandated coverage of forms of "alternative care" such as naturopathy by health plans; the state insurance commissioner's later interpretations of this law led to disputes with Group Health and other insurers.

As discouraging as these setbacks were for Group Health, they did not slow the momentum of its internal "business process re-engineering" or the deepening of the alliance with Virginia Mason. Although these efforts had been partly shaped by anticipation of managed competition reforms, they were no less important in meeting the challenges of unmanaged competition in the healthcare market. Indeed, the arguments for diversifying products and services, cutting costs, and sharing resources were now stronger than ever.

Group Health launched its Alliant line in 1995 with great success and offered a new, less expensive Plan A Co-op membership package incorporating the Basic Health Plan's threshold level of services. It joined an Aetna preferred-provider network, the first time it ever made its physicians and facilities available through an outside insurance program. At the same time, Group Health intensified its own marketing and won inclusion of its plans in benefit options offered by major employer groups such as the Association of Washington Cities and Washington Restaurant Association.

Internally, the Cooperative developed ARPA, an automated appointment, registration, and patient accounting system that went on line in July of 1995. This system was intended to solve the daunting problem of serving hundreds of thousands of consumers with different types of coverage. When fully implemented, it will enable staff to make appointments, register patients when they arrive, check benefit and co-pay status, and bill for any uncovered services, all within a single tracking system. ARPA will also give Group Health the ability to administer different plans, such as Tricare, and administer the joint neighborhood healthcare centers with Virginia Mason.[32]

Group Health also linked most of its employees via computer networks, ventured into cyberspace on the Internet and World Wide Web, and established an "ideal process flow" to coordinate and synchronize planning and budgeting within and among its many divisions. This massive investment in information systems, approaching $100 million and entailing the installation and interconnection of 3,000 desktop computers, reflected what Phil Nudelman called the evolution "from bricks to bytes."

Information techonologies also had direct consequences for the quality of healthcare, particularly in advancing Group Health's quest for a more rigorously empirical medicine. "Evidence-based care asks, How can we best organize the information about the risks and benefits of treatment so that providers and patients can make reasonable decisions about the best care for that patient?" explained Matt Handley, family practice doctor. Finding the answer demands the management of huge quantities of data to evaluate how patients respond to particular treatments, as well as an ongoing review and analysis of the reams of articles and reports published in medical literature. This information must then be translated into "clinical pathways" to guide staff in delivering care that has been scientifically proven effective.

The idea of basing treatments on known results may sound like common sense, but much of medical science and practice remains "squishy," according to Dr. Tommy Thompson, Group Health's director of preventive care research. Group Health's new information systems have given its physicians powerful tools in firming up clinical knowledge and in establishing the Cooperative's national reputation for the development of evidence-based protocols.[33]

A direct outcome of this effort is the development of "clinical roadmaps" for major chronic diseases such as diabetes and heart disease. Phil Nudelman compares these to a flight plan (he was a commercial airline pilot before entering healthcare), "a data-driven 'best' route which, coupled with the specifics of a patient and the judgment of the provider, results in the most appropriate outcome." Systematizing clinical approaches also allows the Co-op to focus resources on key illnesses. For example, diabetics constitute only 3 percent of Group Health patients, but they consume 12 percent of its total costs.

These information systems have had another benefit. Efficient data management and speedy internal communications have helped Group Health keep its "medical-loss ratio" for administrative costs to a minimum while delivering a record 91.5 cents in service for every dollar received—compared to 70 cents achieved by most for-profit HMOs.

Negotiations of a new nurses' contract with 1199 NW dissolved into bitter recriminations, and the union announced a one-day walkout for March 22, 1995. Union president Diane Sosne called it a "measure of last resort. We've tried going to the table. We've extended the olive branch by agreeing to work without a contract for nearly a year."

The issue was less about paychecks—Group Health still paid the highest salaries in the market—than job security. The nurses shortage of six years earlier had evaporated with dramatic reductions in the rate and length of hospitalization and greater reliance on out-patient care. The union had already made what it considered to be major concessions by accepting a three-year wage freeze, benefit cuts, and a 10 percent across-the-board reduction in staffing.

The union's key demand was to limit future layoffs to those with the least seniority. Group Health executive vice president Cheryl Scott replied that "the difficulty is that those nurses aren't necessarily in positions which needed to be done away with." For the union, it was a classic conflict between principles of worker security and management discretion; for Group Health, it was a question of survival in a market filled with lower-cost competitors.[34]

Group Health told the union and its members not to show up for the entire week bracketing the Wednesday walkout, because it was legally obligated to plan for a strike of indeterminate length. Even with a one-day walkout, it would take a week to shift hospital patients out of Group Health facilities and then move them back. The union charged Group Health with staging a "lockout" to punish nurses, and filed complaints with the National Labor Relations Board (which were later rejected).

The strike not only devastated staff morale, it cost the Cooperative nearly $5 million for patient relocation and interim staff, forced the delay of other organizational reforms, and contributed to an operating loss for the year. Nor did the rancor abate when nurses returned to work. District 1199 had published ads questioning the level of care at Group Health and it gave its nurses buttons with a slash through the word "quality" to wear while on duty. Phil Nudelman angrily denounced such "distorted and slanderous statements" at an all-staff leadership conference in May. "Most of our union leaders," he added, "understand the tumultuous healthcare environment that we are in" and realize that unless Group Health adapts, "there will be no jobs—for anyone."[35]

Group Health did return to the bargaining table with 1199, with a federal mediator sitting in. A new contract wasn't hammered out until August 30. Group Health later reached agreement on an overall package with Unions United, which was finally approved by their memberships early in 1996.[36]

Much of the vehemence of 1199's bargaining tactics stemmed from the suspicion that Group Health's alliance with Virginia Mason—which *The Seattle Weekly* called "staunchly non-union"—would lead not only to massive layoffs through a consolidation of staffs and facilities but to decertification of existing labor representation. The union's worst fears seemed to be realized when the boards of both organizations voted on June 14, 1995, to pursue "closer ties." These took the form of proposals to establish a jointly owned operating company to manage most of their respective assets and develop new enterprises, and to reorganize Group Health's Central Hospital to handle maternity care and out-patient surgery while all overnight acute care was transferred to Virginia Mason's First Hill campus.[37]

Not only did the alliance look to some like a sneaky way to take Group Health nonunion, it appeared to open a back door by which managers could quietly supersede Cooperative governance. Such, at least, was the view of Concerned Group Health Cooperative Consumers, whose leaders announced in April 1995 that they had to oppose the alliance "to keep Group Health true to its soul." Soon after, Concerned Consumers prepared a bylaw amendment that would require membership approval of the alliance or any comparable change in "the Cooperative's existing health services, providers, facilities, or scope of consumer governance." Left-wing lions such as Alex Gottfried and Lyle Mercer joined new activists such as Al Selby and Charles Cooper in leading the charge for Concerned Consumers.[38]

The Board responded with its own bylaw amendment providing for notice and discussion of major changes, but reserving the final decision for the trustees. It argued that the Concerned Consumer proposal was "too ambiguous" and would hamstring the Board in making many routine decisions.

Both sides let loose a barrage of leaflets and mailings, while Group Health staged a series of member forums to debate the issue. Amid the battle, Group Health chair Ken Cameron was forced to resign by the "potential appearance" of a conflict of interest between his Cooperative duties and his employment by the state's Department of Social and Health Services, which handled Medicaid funds. Jean Donohue, a career counselor, took over as chair of the Co-op, and Aubrey Davis, who had recently resigned as president emeritus, was later appointed to serve out Cameron's term as trustee.[39]

Late in the campaign, management sent a flyer to members in which national consumer activist Ralph Nader declared, "If there is too much member voice and rights...the cooperative becomes subordinated, anemic and paralyzed." The quotation was accurate but it was taken from a 1992 book about a consumer co-op in Berkeley, California. Nader denounced the quote's use as "grossly misleading and reprehensible" and endorsed Concerned Consumers' position on the Alliance.[40]

Despite the public wrangling, the Board carried on behind-the-scenes talks to try to find a compromise with Concerned Consumers. This effort ended on October 11, when the Board refused to put the alliance to a direct membership vote, explaining that the relationship was still too vaguely defined to offer a clear up-or-down choice. This set the stage for the final confrontation on Saturday, October 14, in the Husky Union Building ballroom on the University of Washington campus.[41]

More than 700 members crowded into the room to show their support for Concerned Consumers or the Board. Dorothy Mann, former (and future) Group Health chair, kept order as the assembled members tried to follow some confusing parliamentary maneuvers beginning with the Board's proposal to amend its bylaw amendment to strengthen its notice provisions.

Wayne Everton pleaded with members not to "cast a vote of no confidence" in the trustees, and declared that "you can't drive into the 21st century in a 1947 Ford." Concerned Consumers leader Al Selby cautioned the assembly "[not to] repeat the errors of the past" by giving the Board too much power.

The amendment to the amendment passed by a large majority, setting up the debate on the main motion. Alex Gottfried warned members to "listen with your inner voice when they [trustees] say 'trust us,'" and Selby declared that "two opposing spirits, control and democracy" were at stake. The Board's majority held on a vote of 398 to 231 for passage of its bylaw amendment.

The battle was not done. Concerned Consumers argued that their own proposed amendment augmented, rather than replaced, the Board, but first they had to explain substitute language for their original amendment. This added the qualifier "fundamentally" to soften the impact of its bylaw language on the Board's ability to make changes in the normal course of business.

Board supporters such as Mark Johnson, an administrator with the UW School of Law, argued that the new words were not enough to prevent future litigation and that there are "500 fledgling lawyers who would love a shot at this language." Lyle Mercer replied that it was clear that only a "fundamental restructuring" came within the purview of the amendment.

The most eloquent speakers against Concerned Consumers' amendment were Hilde Birnbaum and Caroline MacColl, who had each invested decades in nurturing Group Health's development and whose own credentials as cooperators were beyond question. MacColl challenged the Board's critics: "Major authority entails major responsibility—are you ready?"

Birnbaum spoke to the economic reality. "Eight-hundred-pound gorillas have entered our service area, and they want to swallow us." It was this simple, she said: "Group Health must survive as a business in order to survive as a cooperative, not the other way."

The membership agreed: The amendment failed by 360 to 241.5. Concerned Consumers later filed a lawsuit to block the formal mail vote, but it went ahead. The Board's own tally committee declined to certify the results, but it later became official (and the suit was settled out of court). The final official vote defeated the alternative bylaw amendment by 7,075 to 3,641.5. The Board later backed away from its original plan for a joint operating company with Virginia Mason, while pursuing closer cooperation on hospital and healthplan management.[42]

But this was not the real issue anyway. It was a test of the Cooperative's ability to apply democratic values in evaluating economic conditions and options, a question of political trust and informed consent in making a fundamental choice. Whatever the flaws of Group Health's constitution and processes, the issues were clearly identified and thoroughly debated within and among the Board, medical staff, labor, management, and the membership. Everyone understood the stakes.

Group Health's members weighed the pros and the cons and made their decision, and like their vote 49 years earlier—almost to the day—in approving the purchase of the Medical Security Clinic, they chose to follow their elected trustees on a journey into an uncertain future.

Epilogue

*W*hat difference does it make that Group Health Cooperative exists 50 years after it started?

What in our organization's past will make a difference in the future?

The Cooperative's contributions to healthcare are many—from its emphasis on prevention and patient involvement in decisions, to its consulting nurse service and coordination of care. That these were accomplished within the swirl of political turmoil and economic stresses is a testament to the strength of Group Health—its staff and consumer members.

The future will surely bring us continued stress, both internal and external. In fact, Group Health will face the same tough challenges to its core values that the pioneers faced 50 years ago, as they struggled to define their preferred future. Understanding what the Co-op is up against, and deciding what to save and what to discard in order to thrive must be our primary focus as we start our second 50 years.

We can learn from our history that all of our people must be involved in the discussions necessary to define our own preferred future. The dialogue must include consumer members, professional providers and managers. Each brings information, experience and values that must be shared in give-and-take exchanges in order for us to move in a common direction. It has been one of our unique strengths— that a diversity of interests can result in a common purpose. Our pioneers did not find this an easy task, but they persevered and built the foundation upon which Group Health Cooperative stands today.

What rises next upon this base is up to us.

History Committee
Group Health Cooperative

Chronology

Milestones in Cooperative Healthcare and Group Health History

1911

Washington passed a pioneering workman's compensation law.

1916

Drs. Yokum and Curran established the Western Clinic in Tacoma (progenitor of Seattle's Medical Security Clinic).

1917

Washington's Medical Aid law promoted "contract medicine" via "bureaus" of physicians.

1929

Dr. Michael Shadid founded the Farmers' Union Cooperative Hospital Association in Elk City, Oklahoma.

America's first "Blue Cross" surgical insurance plan was established in Texas.

1932

The independent national Committee on Costs of Medical Care endorsed group practice and prepaid health insurance.

1933

King County Medical Association (KCMA) established its own Medical Bureau to allow members to compete with contract physicians for industrial clients.

Mid-1930s

The Kaiser Health Plan grew out of a medical bureau serving Grand Coulee Dam workers under the leadership of Dr. Sidney Garfield; coverage was later extended to defense workers during World War II under the Northern Permanente Foundation.

1938

Leslie Pendergast purchased the Medical Security Clinic in Seattle.

The first medical society–run Blue Shield plan for physician services plan was launched in California. The AMA formally approved prepaid medical plans as "ethical."

1939

November 9: Inspired by Dr. Michael Shadid's book, *A Doctor for the People*, Lily Taylor led a "discussion and report on cooperative medicine" at the Newcastle, Washington, Grange No. 11.

1940

The King County Pomona Grange adopted a resolution endorsing creation of a medical cooperative.

1941

Addison Shoudy and Robert Mitchell attended a cooperative meeting in Portland, Oregon, where they were inspired by a pamphlet by James Peter Warbasse on "cooperative medicine."

1943

The U.S. Supreme Court ordered the American Medical Association to stop "harassing" the Group Health Association of Washington, D.C., a cooperative formed by federal workers.

1945

August 14: Dr. Shadid's lecture at the Roosevelt Hotel inspired the formation of a Seattle Hospital Committee by Grange, union, and co-op leaders.

September 27: Six staff physicians (Drs. George W. Beeler, Lester L. Long, Rod Janson, Charles E. Maas, E. Janson, and Edgar N. Layton) purchased the Medical Security Clinic.

October 29: The founders of Group Health Cooperative (GHC) met for their first recorded meeting in the International Association of Machinists (IAM) Union Hall in Seattle.

November 2: The founding Board of GHC "subscribers" met officially, including Thomas G. Bevan, president; Ella Williams, secretary; and Addison Shoudy, Stanley J. Erickson, and Victor G. Vieg, trustees. The meeting record was notarized by Jack Cluck.

November 20: The Board approved GHC articles of incorporation and elected Addison Shoudy treasurer.

December 11: The Board adopted GHC's first family dues: $30 for the first person, $20 for the second, $15 for the third, and $7 for the fourth.

December 22: GHC articles of incorporation were officially filed by the State of Washington.

1946

January 7: The GHC Board met for the first time in the new GHC offices in the Arcade Building in downtown Seattle.

January 11: The Board offered the federal government $125,000 for its surplus Renton Hospital. The offer was ultimately rejected.

January 15: The Board named John Nordmark executive secretary and manager of corporation.

January 17: Dr. Shadid met Grange leaders during his second Northwest lecture tour.

March 14: Jack Cluck met Dr. William MacColl at a healthcare forum in Kirkland, and initiated discussions for GHC's purchase of the Medical Security Clinic (MSC).

September 4: GHC's bylaws were adopted at its first membership meeting, held in the King County commissioners' chambers.

October 2: The University of Washington School of Medicine opened.

October 7: The Board voted to join the newly formed Cooperative Health Federation of America (which later became the Group Health Association of America).

October 17: GHC members approved the purchase of the Medical Security Clinic during a stormy session in the auditorium of the Broadway High School (now Seattle Central Community College).

October 24: GHC members formally elected the Co-op's Board: Tom Bevan, president; Frank Stewart, vice president; Ella Williams, secretary; Addison Shoudy, treasurer; D. M. Johnson, Sidney G. Shaudies, Robert C. Scott, Robert Wells, and Nettie Jean Ross.

November 8: The Board approved purchase of the Medical Security Clinic and St. Luke's Hospital for $199,995.54 (which was reduced to $100,000 in October 1947).

November 15: Trygve Erickson became the first baby born at St. Luke's under de facto GHC management.

1947

January 1: GHC formally took ownership of the Medical Security Clinic and St. Luke's Hospital. Co-op membership stood at 383 families. Dr. Beeler served as GHC's general manager, with Dr. John O. McNeel as chief of staff.

March 27: The GHC Ladies Auxiliary held its first meeting.

April 25: GHC held its first semiannual membership meeting. The session was carried over to May 21, when members approved a $75 maternity fee, elimination of coverage of pre-existing conditions for charter members, and an age limit of 65 years for membership, to control a mounting deficit.

August 16: The Northwest Group Health Federation was founded.

October 20: GHC launched its Pioneer Bonds drive to raise $80,000 to pay off MSC purchase.

December 16: Renton voters approved creation of a public hospital district to purchase and operate Renton Hospital.

December 31: GHC membership stood at 1,024, plus approximately 8,500 group enrollees.

1948

March 22: The Board named Don A. Northrop general manager.

May 27: GHC allowed striking Boeing machinists to postpone dues payments.

July 6: GHC's Renton Clinic opened under direction of Dr. McNeel.

July 22: The Board approved construction of a 30-bed addition to the GHC Hospital.

August 6: Former Congressman and co-op pioneer Jerry Voorhis spoke in Seattle and praised GHC as "the most hopeful sign in the whole country for the solution of the health problem in this country."

December 14: The Cascade Co-op League chapter was organized.

December 6: GHC employees incorporated the independent Group Health Credit Union and elected C. Parker Paul president.

December 31: Co-op membership stood at 2,811 families.

1949

June: The American Medical Association adopted the Twenty Points criteria for prepaid healthcare plans.

June 23: GHC members voted to amend bylaws to provide for election of five trustees nominated by district and four nominated at-large.

November 25: GHC et al. filed suit against the King County Medical Society (KCMS) et al. for "monopolistic practices."

December 31: GHC enrollment stood at 9,090 GHC members and 7,497 group enrollees.

1950

July 14: King County Superior Court Judge Findley dismissed GHC's suit against KCMS; GHC appealed to the State Supreme Court.

August 9-11: An open house was held for the new hospital wing, and GHC hosted the national convention of the Cooperative Health Federation of America.

1951

March 24: The Board voted to reject the membership application of Communist Party member William J. Pennock.

March 25: The GHC medical staff dismissed chief surgeon Dr. Allan Sachs, precipitating a fight with the Board, which reinstated Sachs and allowed him to resign.

April 9: GHC purchased the Costa Vista Apartments for its new central clinic.

April: Dr. John Quinn became chief of staff.

November 15: The State Supreme Court ruled unanimously in favor of GHC and ordered KCMS to cease "monopolistic" practices.

November 17: Aubrey Davis, Jr., was elected to the Board at the annual meeting.

1952

June: The Board and medical staff formed the Joint Conference Committee to resolve conflicts.

June 16: The new Central Clinic opened.

July: The KCMS admitted all qualified GHC staff as members.

July 12: Don Northrop resigned as executive director.

October: Dr. Charles Strother joined the Board and Aubrey Davis was elected president.

November 25: The Board named Dr. William MacColl acting executive director, and Dr. Alfred Magar became chief of staff.

December 30: The GHC Board incorporated Group Health Dental Cooperative as an independent organization.

December 31: Enrollment stood at 22,440 GHC members and 9,761 group enrollees.

1953

January 15: Kathleen Q. Sumption became GHC hospital director.

April 25: Members elected new trustees Ernie Conrad, Hilde Birnbaum, and William Cowan.

June 20: *The Saturday Evening Post* profiled GHC in an article titled "Supermarket Medicine."

July 15: The Dental Co-op began operation with dentist Dr. Harry Kraft.

December 31: Enrollment stood at 25,230 GHC members and 10,594 group enrollees.

1954

April: The Board elected Charles Strother president.

June: GH Credit Union assets topped $500,000.

October: GHC launched a $250,000 bond drive to finance a new Renton Clinic.

1955

February: GHC organized a letter and petition campaign to compel the City of Seattle to add GHC to its employees' health plan.

March 16: The GHC Auxiliary was formally established, and Harla Fox was elected its first president.

April 7: Members at annual meeting approved an expanded Board of 11, reflecting two new districts (eight trustees were nominated by district, three at large). The Board later elected Hilde Birnbaum president.

April: Puget Sound Power and Light offered employees GHC enrollment.

May: GHC decided to hold off on Salk vaccine immunizations due to "instability" of early batches.

June 11: The new Renton Clinic opened.

July 5: GHC Hospital received its first full accreditation.

August: Dr. John A. Kahl assumed his duties as GHC executive director, Dr. MacColl happily returned to his duties as a GHC pediatrician.

November: The Board approved a plan for GHC to grow to 100,000 enrollees over the next decade.

November 29: Members approved construction of a new central hospital to be funded through capital dues of $175 per member.

December 31: Enrollment stood at 28,903 GHC members and 10,404 group enrollees.

1956

January: GHC announced that it would conduct its first health study in conjunction with the University of Washington. The study, coordinated by K. Warner Shaie, would monitor the health histories of 800 GHC members.

April 11: At the annual meeting, Dr. Kahl proposed the assignment of a "personal physician" to each member and elimination of annual physical exams.

April 20: GHC purchased Lou Anne Apartments on Capitol Hill.

August 13: The Seattle City Council approved the vacation of John Street between 15th and 16th Avenues for expansion of GHC's hospital, but Mayor Gordon Clinton vetoed the ordinance.

October 1: GHC was approved as an "alternative" provider for City of Seattle employees.

October 22: Public Health Service approved GHC as eligible for Hill-Burton grants.

December: The first car windshield decals were mailed to members.

December 31: Total enrollment stood at 41,840.

1957

January 23: The Board approved a new Members' Agreement lowering eligible age limit to 60.

April 6: The 10th annual meeting was held in the Olympic Hotel ballroom. The Board later elected Ken McCaffree president.

May 6: The City Council approved an

amended street vacation for the new GHC Hospital, and Mayor Clinton signed the ordinance on May 8.

1958

March 17: The Northgate Clinic opened under the directorship of Dr. MacColl.

Fall: First edition of *View* was published under editorship of John Donnelly.

October: GHC launched $1 million bond drive for new 173-bed Central Hospital.

Also in 1958: GHC launched a cancer screening program, including free Pap smears.

1959

February: A $1 million hospital bond drive was fully subscribed four months after it began.

Spring: GHC's "All-girl pharmacy" (directed by Ruth Brown since 1943) dispensed its one-millionth prescription.

April: The Board elected Myron Ernst president.

June 1: Ground was broken for new Central Hospital.

December 31: Total enrollment stood at 54,202.

1960

April 9: Jerry Voorhis returned to Seattle to address the 13th annual meeting. The Board later elected George Bolotin president.

Summer: Vice President Richard Nixon unveiled the first plan for Medicare.

July 1: Federal employees gained health benefits (GHC federal employee enrollment jumped from 3,000 to 7,000 in 1960).

October 8: New Central Hospital was dedicated.

December 31: Total enrollment stood at 60,154.

1961

April: The Board elected Arthur Siegal president.

1962

Spring: Cardiologist Dr. Daniel B. Arst was elected chief of Sstaff.

April: The Board elected Aubrey Davis president.

November: In a poll of members, 74 percent preferred a dues increase to maintain comprehensive care over a lower-cost plan with reduced benefits.

1964

March: *View* published the first letter from a member, Mrs. Millard Petersky, asking for no smoking in GHC waiting areas.

April 11: The new Burien Clinic opened.

December: GHC enrollment passed 75,000. Also, Arthur L. Schultz was elected the new chief of staff, and the Puget Sound Cooperative League was established.

1965

March: Dr. Frank Newman succeeded the ailing Dr. Kahl as executive director.

April 3: New Central Clinic opened.

July 18: Dr. Kahl died.

July 30: President Lyndon Johnson signed the Medicare Act, to take effect July 1, 1966.

December 31: Total enrollment grew by 12 percent during the year to reach 85,166.

1966

July 1: Medicare became available. GHC offered Medicare recipients full memberships for $6 per month.

September: Jack R. Brown was hired to set up GHC Mental Health Service.

December 31: Total enrollment stood at 91,819.

1967

February 19: Expanded Northgate Medical Center opened.

April 1: Adult dues increase of $1 per month took effect.

April 22: The 20th anniversary annual meeting coincided with the Group Health Association of America convention, which the GHC hosted in Seattle. The Board later elected Dr. Charles Strother president.

December 31: Total enrollment stood at 100,769.

1968

January 14: Renton Medical Center opened.

April: The Board elected Aubrey Davis president.

1969

January 1: GHC offered its first mental health outpatient coverage.

June 29: The Downtown Medical Center opened in the Medical-Dental Building.

July 1: The medical staff now numbered 107.

September 1: GHC began providing service to 500 low-income families under contract to Washington State Department of Public Assistance.

Fall: *View* reported that 180 U.S. medical co-ops now served 7 million enroll-ees. GHC launched a program of family practice residencies with the University of Washington, and the Medex program to retrain former military medics as paramedical aides.

December 31: Total enrollment stood at 121,716.

1970

April: The Board elected Eleanor Brand president. Gene Lux was later appointed to fill a vacancy on the Board.

November 3: Voters approved Referendum 20, which liberalized abortion law and had been endorsed by GHC.

December 31: Group enrollment of 71,466 passed the number of GHC members, 64,259, for the first time since 1949. Total enrollment grew by 10 percent during the year despite the "Boeing Bust" aerospace recession.

Also in 1970: Marian Gillespie, GHC Hospital supervisor since 1956, retired.

1971

January 25: Staff began moving into the new Central East Wing.

February: GHC's Seattle Model City Plan 9 began enrolling low-income Central Area residents.

March 1: The new Family Health Center opened on Capitol Hill.

April 24: The annual meeting featured the first of several stormy debates over abortion. Anti-abortion forces lost on a vote of 141 to 113.

May: President Nixon endorsed Health Maintenance Organizations (HMOs) in a white paper, "Health Policy for the 1970s."

June: Senator Edward Kennedy visited GHC and praised it as a "model for reform."

November 15: The Lynnwood Medical Center opened.

December 18: *The New Republic* published a profile of GHC.

December 31: Total enrollment stood at 168,640.

1972

February 23: The Board decided to allow nonvoting group members to participate in Co-op discussions.

April 29: GHC celebrated its 25th anniversary with an open house at the Central Hospital. The Board later elected Arthur Siegal president.

July 1: The Olympia Medical Center opened.

December 31: Total membership posted its greatest annual increase, 16 percent, to stand at 173,004. The Board voted to close group enrollment so the Co-op could catch up.

1973

March 28: One hundred attended founding meeting of the GHC Women's Caucus.

April: GHC reached an accord with Capitol Hill Community Council to address neighborhood complaints about hospital expansion.

April 14: The annual meeting featured debates over bylaw amendments to allow participation of all covered adult "consumers" in district meetings, and coverage for birth control procedures. The meeting was carried over to September 22 due to the length of discussion.

September 22: Second annual meeting was held. Contraceptive coverage passed 214 to 171, sterilization coverage passed by 215 to 167, and the bylaw amendments passed by 101 to 9.

The Board later elected Arthur Siegal president.

December: Congress passed legislation to promote HMOs.

December 31: Total enrollment grew to 189,050 despite the cap on new group contracts.

1974

April 27: Nine hundred members attended the annual meeting, where an attempt to repeal abortion policies was defeated by a large margin and coverage for contraception survived by 305 votes to 295. The Board later elected Hilde Birnbaum president.

June 30: Business manager Rudy Molzan retired after 30 years of service, and was succeeded by Donald Brennan.

November 30: Dr. MacColl retired.

December 31: Total enrollment grew to 194,973.

1975

March: GHC X-ray technicians staged a 10-day walkout.

Spring: Phil Nudelman unveiled a computerized prescription system, "Co-opRX," at the pharmacy.

September 7: Federal Way Medical Center was dedicated.

December: The Board adopted the first Patients' Bill of Rights.

December 31: Total enrollment stood at 208,082.

1976

January 12: Progressive Care Facility opened on Capitol Hill.

April: The Board elected James W. Evans president.

Spring: Distribution of vaccine to combat an anticipated swine flu epidemic began.

July 1: Medicare reforms took effect mandating provision of "high and low option" plans.

July 4: GHC was honored by the American Revolution Bicentennial "Horizons on Display" program highlighting community achievements.

August 1: Members of the Washington State Nurses Association (WSNA) went on strike at GHC.

August 10: Executive director Newman resigned and was replaced by Don Brennan.

August 28: The GHC nurses strike ended.

1977

January: Dr. Robert McAlister was elected chief of staff.

July 11: Eastside Specialty Center opened in Redmond.

September 12: Eastside Hospital opened.

Fall: Cornish School for the Arts signed GHC's 1,000th group contract, and Governor Dixy Lee Ray joined GHC.

December 31: Total enrollment stood at 241,811.

Also in 1977: A central Distribution and Support Services Facility was built in Renton.

1978

January: Dr. William Spence of GHC was elected president of the KCMS.

April 22: The annual meeting featured GHC's first Health Fair. The Board later elected its first African-American president, Ida Chambliss.

August 20: President Carter signed the bill establishing the National Con-

sumer Cooperative Bank, which was allocated $300 million for loans.

November 18: Attendees at the Special Issues Meeting defeated proposals to extend voting rights to group members and to expand the Board, but approved use of absentee ballots for trustee elections.

December 31: Total enrollment stood at 254,983.

1979

January 1: GHC purchased Tacoma's Sound Health Association and absorbed its 11,000 enrollees.

December 31: Total enrollment reached 277,920.

1980

October: The Board approved full memberships for persons between the ages of 60 and 64.

November 20: Tacoma Specialty Center opened.

November: Madrona Medical Center opened.

December 31: Enrollment grew to only 278,470, due to the loss of 6,000 state government enrollees.

1981

January: The Board adopted Consumer Criteria for the Quality of Health Care.

February: The Board approved optional Medical Center Councils to augment consumer participation.

April 25: Gail L. Warden was introduced at the annual meeting as GHC's new "chief executive officer. Members amended the bylaws to limit trustees to three consecutive three-year terms, and adopted a resolution endorsing a Nuclear Freeze on atomic weapons production.

Late Summer: President Reagan's proposed budget cuts threatened GHC's Rural Plan 9 family service program for 6,000 persons. Domestic violence was being discussed as a public health issue.

November 1: GHC opened its new administrative offices in the Elliott Bay Office Park building.

November 23: GHC and the University of Washington signed the first affiliation agreement between a university medical school and an HMO.

December 31: Total enrollment grew to 285,518.

1982

January 12: Under a new state law, GHC became the first HMO to offer tax-exempt bonds; $26 million in bonds sold in days.

April 28: The Board elected Caroline MacColl president, and approved GHC's first capitation agreement with non-GHC physicians to provide services on Vashon and Maury Islands.

Early Summer: The Board voted to eliminate medical examinations for applicants to full GHC membership. Dr. Turner Bledsoe succeeded Dr. McAlister as GHC's first full-time Medical Director.

December 6: The Everett Medical Center opened.

1983

January 26: The Board approved creation of the Center for Health Studies and the Center for Health Promotion.

January 27: Jack Cluck died.

May 18: GHC nurses voted to select the National Union of Hospital and Health Care Employees ("1199 Northwest") as their new bargaining agent

July 1: Group Health of Spokane was established as a nonprofit subsidiary of GHC. Dr. Charles Strother was elected its first chairman; Dr. Henry Berman was named CEO and medical irector.

August 15: A small medical center opened in Bothell.

September: *View* published its first report on AIDS.

September 28: Former GHC president Ida Chambliss died of a heart attack while working with Africare in Zimbabwe. On the same day, the Board voted to establish the Group Health Foundation.

October 29: New Rainier Valley Medical Center opened.

December 31: Total enrollment stood at 315,769.

1984

January: *View* published a controversial story on the environmental hazards associated with Tacoma's ASARCO smelter.

April 1: GHC facilities went "smoke-free."

April 28: At the annual meeting, the new Cooperative Members Action Group protested rate hikes. The Board later elected Aubrey Davis president.

April: Dental coverage was added to group plans via the Safeguard Health Plan.

June 7: The Rand Corporation published a major study finding that GHC was significantly more efficient than private "fee-for-service" care.

Fall: The Board created three new Regional Councils.

November 5: The Silverdale Medical Center opened and GHC contracted with the Winslow Clinic to serve Kitsap County members.

December 11: The premiere of the film *Dune* benefited the GH Foundation.

December 21: The first mail-in ballots for trustee elections were sent to members.

Also in 1984: First "SEE" and "HEAR" centers opened.

December 31: Total enrollment stood at 332,309.

1985

January 27: The new wing of the Eastside Hospital opened.

April 27: The annual meeting was held in the Tacoma Dome, the first outside of Seattle. Members rejected a ban on abortions by 1,146 to 293, and amended the bylaws to elect trustees by mail ballots.

June 1: Contracted physicians in Bellingham began treating GHC members.

July 18: Three thousand senior citizens attended the GHC Long-Term Care Insurance Forum. The event was part of a new Senior Initiative to enhance services.

July 24: GHC incorporated Group Health of Washington "affiliate" to serve the Tri-Cities.

September 30: The South Tacoma Medical Center opened.

November 1: *View* began accepting paid advertisements.

November 18: GHC member Joe Gardiner received the Northwest's first heart transplant at the University of Washington.

December 31: Total enrollment shrank for the first time in GHC history, to 328,994, and Co-op memberships dwindled to 47,597.

1986

April 1: A new Co-op dues structure took effect reflecting "age-rating."

April 26: At the annual meeting and in subsequent mail ballots, members amended the bylaws to create the position of president and CEO, to rename the head of the Board as chair, and to elect five at-large trustees and six trustees by region. They also defeated another attempt to ban abortions.

May 28: GHC sponsored conference on "Community Health Promotion: The Next Steps."

July 23: The Board voted to cover heart transplants.

October: GH of Spokane was renamed GH Northwest, and absorbed the operations of GH of Washington in 1987.

November 5: The Board approved GHC's first long-term care package, which was later dubbed Security Care. This program was abandoned in 1990.

December 3: The Board approved a new "low-option" package with co-payments, and added maternity care to general coverage.

Also in 1986: GHC was honored by the W. K. Kellogg Foundation and National Centers for Disease Control for innovations in preventive medicine.

December 31: Co-op memberships rebounded to 68,315, while total enrollment continued to shrink to 316,622.

1987

January 30: Actor-comedian Bill Cosby headlined a benefit concert for the Group Health Foundation.

February 2: Bainbridge Island Medical Center opened.

April 25: Members amended the by-laws to formalize Regional Councils. The Board later elected Susan Doerr chair, and Dr. Howard Kirz became medical director.

May 17: The state legislature approved the Basic Health Plan to enroll 30,000 low-income families in private insurance plans; GHC agreed to take 10 percent of applicants.

June 16: Ambulatory Care Center opened at GHC Central.

October 7: The Board canceled the special interest group charter of the Nuclear Action Group.

October: Staff began moving into the new GHC Administration and Conference Center in the former Seattle Post-Intelligencer building.

December 31: Total enrollment began to recover, reaching 325,910.

1988

January 1: New Medicare Catastrophic Care law took effect (it was repealed the following year).

January 11: Factoria Medical Center opened.

February 1: Aubrey Davis succeeded Gail Warden as president/CEO.

Summer: Susan Doerr resigned as Board chair and was succeeded by Allen Vautier. Sherry Shamansky was simultaneously appointed GHC Vice President for Nursing and UW School of Nursing Assistant Clinical Dean for Residency and Practice. The Board adopted a formal policy against sexual harassment in the workplace.

July 6: Temporary GHC-UW clinic opened.

December 31: Total enrollment reached 351,132.

1989

February 20: Dr. MacColl died.

Spring: GHC and Children's Hospital opened an adolescent health center on the Eastside. GHC agreed to provide medical services for the 1990 Goodwill Games.

July 13: GHC nurses went on strike until August 18.

October 1: By vote of members, GHC capital dues were eliminated, reducing the initial cost from $200 to $25.

1990

February: University Medical Center opened.

February 7: GHC incorporated Options Health Care as a for-profit subsidiary to permit member use of non-GHC family physicians.

April 21: At the annual meeting, officials reported that GHC enrollment had risen 40 percent in the past 3 years to 373,000. GH NW now had 70,000 enrollees in eastern Washington and would expand into Ellensburg in 1990. Later, the Board elected Dorothy Mann chair.

May 12: Family Beginnings maternity center was dedicated at GHC Central.

June 21: First Zoo Walkers program held at the Woodland Park Zoo.

August 9: Dr. Al Truscott succeeded Dr. Kirz as medical director.

September 9: GHC hosted a "Tunnel Run" benefit in the new Metro Transit Tunnel.

October 8: The Board selected Phil Nudelman as GHC's new president/

CEO and named Aubrey Davis president emeritus, effective February 1, 1991.

1991

May 2: *The New York Times* profiled GHC.

July: The Board adopted Community Service Principles, and approved a plan to build a skilled nursing facility in Bellevue.

September: The Board endorsed the Initiative 120 campaign for abortion rights, but remained neutral on Initiative 119, which allowed medically assisted suicide for terminally ill patients.

December 31: Total enrollment reached 471,995.

Also in 1991: GHC Child Car Seat Bounty Program paid $5 each for substandard child restraints, and the Teen Pregnancy and Parenting Clinic opened at GHC Central.

1992

January 2: New Tacoma Specialty Center opened.

April 1: Coverage added for breast prostheses and major organ transplantations.

April 24: At the annual meeting and in subsequent mail ballots, members rejected a bylaw amendment to elect all trustees at-large.

June: The Board established the Sandy MacColl Center for Healthcare Innovation as part of the Center for Health Studies.

Fall: Central Medical Center South opened after a three-year, $55 million construction program.

November 3: Former GHC lobbyist Mike Lowry was elected governor of Washington, and Bill Clinton was elected president of the United States. Both ran on platforms supporting comprehensive healthcare reform.

1993

April 23: The state legislature enacted the Health Access Act, a sweeping healthcare reform package including cost controls, guaranteed universal acces, mandated employee coverage, and expansion of the Basic Health Plan. The Board later elected Ken Cameron chair.

July: *Money* magazine rated GHC the 7th-best HMO in the U.S.

Fall: Board voted to oppose Initiatives 601/602 which would endanger healthcare reform. GHC launched a Top Quality management reform campaign.

September 22: President Clinton unveiled his healthcare reform plan in a speech to Congress. GHC president/CEO Phil Nudelman and chair Ken Cameron were among 200 guests invited by President Clinton, and medical director Truscott also attended a special White House briefing on the president's plan.

October: GHC announced that it would trim administrative and medical staff by at least 200.

November 9: GHC and Virginia Mason announced agreement on a "strategic alliance." They formed a joint subsidiary, Virginia Mason–Group Health Alliance

December 28: Addison Shoudy died.

Also in 1993: *US News and World Report* profiled GHC as one of four "top flight" HMOs in the nation.

1994

January 1: GHC closed High-Option Medicare enrollment.

Spring: Seattle Public School District selected GHC to run its new Franklin High School teen clinic.

July 11: Everett Medical Center opened.

July 14: GHC sponsored a special forum on healthcare reform.

Summer: GHC members approved a resolution opposing violence. They also aproved bylaw amendments mandating bylaw reviews every three years and shifting the annual meeting to October.

September 19: Virginia Mason physicians began sharing GHC's Eastside Hospital and VM and GHC prepared to offer Alliant Plus and Alliant Select insurance policies.

October: GHC enrollment passed 500,000. Also during 1994, Options Health Care, Inc., enrollment passed 30,000, and GH Northwest enrollment passed 115,000.

1995

January 1: GHC-VM alliance began marketing its Choice Care plan. GHC extended services to Oak Harbor, Friday Harbor, and Centralia via "designated primary care providers." Patient census revealed a 22 percent decline in hospitalization since January 1994. *View* magazine renamed *Northwest Health*.

March: New Olympia Medical Center opened.

March 22: GHC nurses struck for one day.

Spring: State Legislature repealed most of the 1993 healthcare reforms. Puyallup Medical Center opened.

GHC and Aetna agreed to team up to establish "preferred provider organization" status for GHC. The Board adopted a plan to promote diversity in employment and service.

July 21: GHC's eight unions agreed to discuss concessions in "collaborative bargaining" to help GHC meet competition.

August 30: GHC and 1199 NW announced agreement on draft nurses contract.

October 14: The annual meeting and subsequent mail ballots rejected a bylaw amendment intended to put the Virginia Mason alliance to a vote of the membership.

December 31: Total enrollment reached 557,852.

Group Health
Cooperative of Puget Sound
Board of Trustees
1947~1995

The Articles of Incorporation for Group Health Cooperative of Puget Sound were signed October 29, 1945, by Stanley J. Erickson, Addison Shoudy, Thomas G. Bevan, Victor G. Vieg, and Mrs. R. E. Williams.
Members elected the 1947 Board on October 24, 1946. Subsequent elections were held in April until 1995, when the annual meeting returned to October.

1980

Ralph M. Bremer, *President*
Caroline S. MacColl, *Vice President*
Eleanor A. Brand
Ida B. Chambliss*
Mark T. Clevenger
James Farrell
Bruce T. Hulse
Marion L. Lee
Eugene V. Lux
Lyle F. Mercer
Arthur Rolfe
*Resigned 11/3/80.

1981

Ralph M. Bremer, *President*
Eugene V. Lux, *Vice President*
Eleanor A. Brand
Mark T. Clevenger
James Farrell
Bruce T. Hulse
Marion L. Lee
Caroline S. MacColl
Lyle F. Mercer
Arthur Rolfe
John Sweeney

1982

Caroline S. MacColl, *President*
Aubrey Davis, *Vice President*
Eleanor A. Brand
Ken Cameron
James Farrell
Bruce T. Hulse
Maryann Huhs
Lyle F. Mercer
Arthur Rolfe
John Sweeney
Allen Vautier

1983

Caroline S. MacColl, *President*
Aubrey Davis, *Vice President*
Ken Cameron
James Farrell
Bruce T. Hulse
Maryann Huhs
Lyle F. Mercer
Arthur Rolfe
John Sweeney
Gail Toraason
Allen Vautier

1984

Aubrey Davis, *President*
Ken Cameron, *Vice President*
Susan J. Doerr
Maryann Huhs*
Bruce T. Hulse
Caroline S. MacColl
Arthur Rolfe
Sylvia Skratek
Lois Price Spratlen
Gail Toraason
Allen Vautier
*Resigned 7/25/84; replaced by Ann Birnbaum.

1985

Aubrey Davis, *President*
Ken Cameron, *Vice President**
Ann Birnbaum
Susan J. Doerr
Bruce T. Hulse
Caroline S. MacColl
Arthur Rolfe
Sylvia Skratek
Lois Price Spratlen
John Sweeney**
Gail Toraason***
*Resigned as *Vice President* 11/6/85; replaced by Susan Doerr.
**Resigned 9/9/85;

replaced by Allen Vautier.
***Resigned 12/4/85; replaced by Eleanor Brand.

1986

Aubrey Davis, *Chair*
Susan J. Doerr, *Vice Chair*
Ann Birnbaum
Ken Cameron
Nancy Ellison
James Farrell
Thomas G. Johnson
Lois Price Spratlen*
Arthur Rolfe
Sylvia Skratek
Allen Vautier
*Resigned 7/1/86; replaced by Helen I. Marieskind.

1987

Susan J. Doerr, *Chair*
Allen Vautier, *Vice Chair*
Ann Birnbaum
Ken Cameron
Aubrey Davis
Nancy Ellison
James Farrell
Robert M. Humphrey
Thomas G. Johnson
Dorothy H. Mann
Helen I. Marieskind

1988

Susan J. Doerr, *Chair**
Allen Vautier, *Vice Chair*
Ken Cameron
Jean A. Donohue
Nancy Ellison
James Farrell
Robert M. Humphrey
Thomas G. Johnson
Caroline S. MacColl
Dorothy H. Mann
Helen I. Marieskind
*Resigned 7/13/88; replaced by Linda Steinmann.
Allen Vautier became *Chair* and Nancy Ellison became *Vice Chair*.

1989

Allen Vautier, *Chair*
Dorothy H. Mann, *Vice Chair*
Tom Brewer
Ken Cameron
Howard Connor
Jean A. Donohue
James Farrell
Thomas G. Johnson
Caroline S. MacColl
Helen I. Marieskind
Linda Steinmann

1990

Dorothy H. Mann, *Chair*
Nancy Ellison, *Vice Chair*
Tom Brewer
Ken Cameron
William Conn
Jean A. Donohue
James Farrell
Thomas G. Johnson
Caroline S. MacColl
Linda Steinmann
Allen Vautier

1991

Dorothy H. Mann, *Chair*
Nancy Ellison, *Vice Chair*
Tom Brewer
William Conn
Jean A. Donohue
James Farrell
Thomas G. Johnson
Caroline S. MacColl
Ward C. Miles
Linda Steinmann
Allen Vautier

1992

Dorothy H. Mann, *Chair*
William Conn, *Vice Chair* *
Jean A. Donohue
Nancy Ellison
James Farrell
Thomas G. Johnson
Caroline S. MacColl
Ward C. Miles
Janeen Smith
Linda Steinmann**
Allen Vautier
* William Conn resigned 8/92; replaced by Jonathan Fine 9/92.
**Linda Steinmann resigned 8/92; replaced by Ken Cameron 8/92.

1993

Ken Cameron, *Chair*
Jean A. Donohue, *Vice Chair*
James Farrell
Thomas G. Johnson*
Jeanne M. Large
Caroline S. MacColl
Dorothy H. Mann
Martin Mendelson
Ward C. Miles
Janeen Smith
Allen Vautier
*Resigned 10/93 and was not replaced.

1994

Ken Cameron, *Chair**
Jean A. Donohue, *Vice Chair*
James Farrell
Jeanne M. Large
Caroline S. MacColl
Dorothy H. Mann
Martin Mendelson
Ward C. Miles
Janeen Smith
Allen Vautier
Debbie Ward
*Resigned 8/95; replaced by Aubrey Davis. Jean Donohue became *Chair* and Dorothy H. Mann became *Vice Chair*.

1995

Dorothy H. Mann, *Chair*
Jeanne M. Large, *Vice Chair*
Ronald E. Bell
Aubrey Davis
Jean A. Donohue
Mark A. Johnson
Caroline S. MacColl
Martin Mendelson
Ward C. Miles
Janeen Smith
Debbie Ward

Group Health
Cooperative of Puget Sound
Administration

George Beeler, MD, *General Manager*, 1947

Rudy Molzan *General Manager*, 1947

Don Northrop *General Manager*, March 1948 - November 1952

William A. "Sandy" MacColl, MD, *Executive Director*, January 1953 - June 1955

John A. Kahl, MD, *Executive Director*, August 1955 - March 1965

H. Frank Newman, MD *Executive Director*, March 1965 - July 1976

Don Brennan, *Executive Director*, July 1976 - June 1980

Gerald Coe, *Acting Executive Vice President*, June 1980 - April 1981

Gail Warden, *President and Chief Executive Officer*, April 1981 - October 1987

Aubrey Davis, *President and Chief Executive Officer*, February 1988 - January 1991

Phillip M. Nudelman, PhD, *President and Chief Executive Officer*, February 1991 - present

------

Group Health
Cooperative of Puget Sound
Medical Staff

Chiefs of Staff

John O. McNeel, MD,
August 1946 - April 1951

John J. Quinn, MD, April
1951 - September 1952

William A. MacColl, MD,
October 1952 - December
1952

John H. Millhouse, MD,
December 1952

Gustav Bansmer, MD,
January 1953 - September
1953

Alfred Magar, MD,
September 1953 -
December 1961

Daniel B. Arst, MD,
January 1962 - December
1964

Arthur L. Schultz, MD,
January 1965 - December
1970

Glenn A. Hartquist, MD,
January 1971 - December
1976

Robert M. McAlister, MD,
January 1977 - May 1982

Medical Directors

Turner Bledsoe, MD, May
1982 - January 1987

Howard L. Kirz, MD,
January 1987 - September
1990

Al M. Truscott, MD,
October 1990 - present

Central Region Chiefs

James M. Garrison, MD,
July 1981 - December 1982

Simeon Rubenstein, MD,
January 1983 - December
1991

Jerome Beekman, MD,
January 1992 - present

East Region Chiefs

Harold Leland, MD, July
1981 - December 1986

Don Stromberg, MD,
January 1987 - December
1991

Edwin J. Carlson, MD,
January 1993 - present

South Region Chiefs

Ward Miles, MD, July
1979 - December 1984

Al Truscott, MD, January
1985 - August 1990

Gary Feldbau, MD,
September 1990 - present

Notes

Chapter 1

[1]Shadid description quoted from frontispiece to his *Co-op Hospital Catechism* (Walla Walla: Pacific Supply Cooperative, 1945). Meeting description is constructed from transcript of Addison Shoudy's 1981 oral history interview and related sources.

[2]This biography is condensed from Dr. Michael Shadid, *Crusading Doctor* (Boston: The Meador Press, 1956).

[3]Rochdale history based chiefly on an essay by Stuart Chase, excerpted in *View*, Fall 1972, and an essay by Richard Margolis in *New Leader*, April 17, 1972.

[4]Carlos Schwantes, *Radical Heritage* (Seattle: University of Washington Press, 1979); and Harriet Ann Crawford, *The Washington State Grange* (Portland, Oreg.: Binfords & Mort, 1940).

[5]Schwantes, op. cit.; Seattle Market: Crawford, op. cit.; M. C. Puhr, *Farmer Cooperatives in Washington* (Spokane: Spokane Bank for Cooperatives, 1941); Paul Temple, "The Cooperative Way" (*View*, November 1981).

[6]Margolis, op. cit.

[7]Joseph G. Knapp et al., *Great American Cooperators* (Washington, D.C.: American Institute of Cooperation, 1967), pp. 520-523.

[8]Emblem legend: Puget Sound Cooperative League *Cooperator*, September 1966.

[9]The discussion of CBI and WCF is condensed from Albert A. Acenas, *The Washington Commonwealth Federation: Reform Politics and the Popular Front* (Ph.D. dissertation, University of Washington, 1975).

[10]Letter from C. R. Coe to Byron Fish, May 10, 1972; Nieder is described by

Hilde Birnbaum in a letter to B. Fish, July 12, 1972.

[11]Shoudy, 1983 oral history interview and 1987 correspondence.

[12]Ibid.; Temple, op. cit; PSCL *Cooperator*; and Shoudy, 1981 oral history interview and correspondence. Shoudy's aid to REI is noted by Harvey Manning, *REI: 50 Years of Climbing Together* (Seattle: REI, 1988), p. 5.

[13]Acenas, op. cit.

[14]Shoudy, op. cit., 1981 and 1987 correspondence.

[15]Early Grange activities are detailed in a letter from R. Jean Yourkowski to Byron Fish, April 12, 1972, and in a 1981 oral history interview of Ida Taylor, Lily's daughter.

[16]John Phillip Holden, *Group Health Cooperative of Puget Sound, an Institutional Study of a Unique Medical Service Organization* (M.A. thesis, University of Washington, 1951), p. 36, based on an interview of A. Shoudy. There are slight discrepancies concerning this and other events among Shoudy's various interviews and recollections.

[17]Shoudy, op. cit. 1981.

[18]Ibid., and Shadid.

[19]Shoudy, op cit. The *Grange News*, July 6, 1946, reported that the federation was actually formed on June 25, 1946.

[20]Ibid., and Holden, op. cit.

[21]Jonathan Rae Tompkins, *Consumer Participation in the Delivery of Health Care Services: An Organizational Study of Group Health Cooperative of Puget Sound* (Ph.D. dissertation, University of Washington, 1981), pp. 34 and 35, and William Jordan, 1981 oral history interview.

[22]Tompkins, op. cit., p. 35. Shadid and Belden's activities were reported in detail by the *Grange News*, from August 18, 1945, through July 6, 1946.

[23]Ibid., p. 35, and early GHC minutes. Fred Nelson's name is often spelled "Nelsen" in the record, including frequent citations in *Grange News*, however no Fred "Nelsen" appears in the Polk City Directory for Renton in the late 1940s while Fred Nelson does, and a Fred Nelson was later elected State Grange Master. On this basis, I prefer the spelling "Nelson." Also, the "Seattle Hospital Committee" does not appear in GHC records and Shoudy expressed ignorance of the name in his 1981 interview. Tompkins cites the *Grange News*, August 18, 1945, as his source; however, later *Grange News* reports make several references to Seattle and King County committees, which appear to be either informal designations or names of Grange committees.

[24]Shoudy, op. cit. 1981. Bevan: *Cascade Cooperative News*, June 1950.

[25]*Grange News*, November 10, 1945.

[26]Shoudy, op. cit. 1981, and Edward Henry 1981 oral history interview.

[27]Shoudy, op. cit. 1981. GHA founding: William A. MacColl, M.D., *Group Practice and Prepayment of Medical Care* (Washington, D.C.: Public Affairs Press, 1966), p. 25.

[28]Holden, op. cit. pp. 38–40, early Board minutes, and *The Seattle Times*,

April 16, 1945.

²⁹Shoudy, op. cit. 1983.

³⁰Official minutes for dates cited.

³¹Ibid.

Chapter 2

¹Ibid.

²The date of adoption of life memberships is not recorded, but anecdotal testimony establishes that they were being sold by December 1945. Refund terms are stated on printed "Membership Application." Jordan, op. cit., and Shoudy, op. cit. 1981.

³Shoudy, op. cit. 1981.

⁴Ibid. Shoudy and Shadid's 1945/46 conversations are presented as Shoudy reconstructed them in 1981.

⁵1981 "Pioneer Questionnaire" responses and oral history interviews of Eugene Lux, Grace Crecelius, Harry Stockinger, Woodrow and Margaret Dougherty, and Frederick West.

⁶Shoudy, op. cit. 1981.

⁷Board minutes for December 28, 1945, January 11, 15, 18, and April 24, 1946; Holden, op. cit., pp. 42 and 43; and Byron Fish, "The Story of Group Health" (unpublished manuscript, GHC, 1972), p. I-8.

⁸Renton negotiations are detailed in Board minutes from January 11 through June 7, 1946; and described by Holden, op. cit., pp. 39 and 40.

⁹Board minutes, March 14, 1946.

¹⁰Description of the Kirkland forum is based on a notice in the *East Side Journal*, Kirkland, February 28, 1946; Jack Cluck and William MacColl's 1981 oral history interviews; and a letter from Chuck and Etta Marie James to Nan Fawthrop, December 27, 1986.

¹¹History of medical profession in Washington State is condensed from essays in *Saddlebags to Scanners: The First 100 Years of Medicine in Washington State*, edited by Nancy M. Rockafeller and James W. Haviland (Seattle: Washington State Medical Association, 1989).

¹²History of the Medical Security Clinic is based on records in the GHC archives and an unpublished history of GHC by Nancy Rockafeller.

¹³W. MacColl, 1981 oral history interview, and author's conversation with Caroline MacColl, Dr. MacColl's second wife, in 1996.

¹⁴MSC records in GHC archives. The 1945 MSC purchase agreement does not mention the satellite clinics, but later sales documents were executed by Beeler as president/general manager of MSC. The value of these properties was listed as $59,150 in a September 30, 1945, appraisal.

¹⁵W. MacColl, *Group Practice and Prepayment of Medical Care*, p. 12.

¹⁶Ibid., pp. 88-93.

¹⁷J. Kloeck, 1981 oral history interview.

[18]MacColl 1981 interview.

Chapter 3

[1]Kloeck, 1981 oral history interview.

[2]Shoudy, 1981 oral history interview; Board minutes, June 7, 1946.

[3]W. MacColl, 1981 oral history interview. MSC records, GHC archives.

[4]Board minutes, June 7, 1946.

[5]Kloeck, op. cit.; MacColl, op. cit.; Board minutes, June 17, 1946.

[6]Shoudy, op. cit. Beeler: *Pacific Northwest Co-Operator*, November 1946.

[7]Shoudy, op. cit.

[8]Board minutes, August 14, 1946.

[9]Board minutes, July 22 and August 30, 1946.

[10]Shoudy, op. cit.

[11]Board minutes, September 4, 1947. Bylaws quoted as adopted September 4 and amended October 17, 1946, and subsequently published.

[12]Shoudy, op. cit.

[13]MSC medical staff minutes, September 5, 1946, cited in GHC Association of Retired Medical Staff Newsletter, Fall 1995, p. 7. Board minutes, September 13, 1946.

[14]Ibid.

[15]GHC archives for membership meetings in 1946. Charles Baker description is taken from *The Seattle Times*, December 8, 1969, obituary, and Pacific Northwest *Cooperator*.

[16]GHC, ibid. "The Committee" leaders' descriptions taken from October 4, 1946, letter signed by C. Hurley.

[17]October 15, 1946, letter signed by C. Hurley, GHC archives.

[18]Board minutes for October 17, 1946.

[19]Shoudy, Cluck, W. Philipp, B. Pearce, M. Wiberg, and D. & L. Harstein 1981 oral history interviews. Ella Williams' essay, *View*, 1962, p. IV-4.

[20]Board minutes, op. cit. Pearce, op cit.

[21]GHC archives.

[22]PNWCHF: *Pacific Northwest Co-Operator*, November 1946.

[23]Board minutes for October 24, 1946. In her oral history interview, Martha Wiberg states that MSC opponents deliberately dragged out the discussion knowing that Bevan had to attend an IAM meeting later the same evening, and that she took over the chair upon his departure. The official minutes do not reflect this.

Chapter 4

[1]Frank Hart, 1981 oral history interview.

[2]MSC Medical Staff meeting minutes.

[3]Board minutes, November 8, 1946. There is some confusion in the record and historical accounts regarding this price. Some accounts fold the St. Luke's mortgage into the price, but its assumption was a separate obligation. This is confirmed by Bob Scott's financial committee report, published in the November 1947 "Activity Report to Membership."

[4]Bernard Pearce, 1981 oral history interview.

[5]Letter as published in *Pacific Northwest Co-Operator*, November 1946.

[6]MSC stock sale contract, GHC archives; *Cooperative Health*, April 1947. For tax and accounting purposes, Medical Security Clinic survived on paper several more years as a corporation wholly owned by Group Health.

[7]*Cooperative Health*, April 1947. The delay of the formal MSC takeover was approved by the Board on December 13, 1946.

[8]Policies and Organization, adopted December 30, 1946; Board minutes, December 18, 1946.

[9]Ibid. Staff identified from subsequent documents and reports. Contemporary reports give conflicting numbers for Group Health's initial medical staff, ranging from 18 to 15 physicians. The first GHC medical staff bylaws were signed in December 1946 by 14 medical doctors and the lab director, John Kloeck. Adding Dr. Beeler, the count of medical professionals at the time of the MSC/GHC transition stood at 16.

[10]Frank Hart also quotes Dr. Beeler as stating that GHC would take over MSC clinics in Renton and Kirkland, but these properties had been sold months earlier. GHC did not establish its first suburban clinic, in Renton, until July 1948.

[11]F. Hart, op. cit.

[12]Doris Ptolemy and Frank Hart, 1981 oral history interviews.

[13]G. Bansmer, "The Joy of Joining Group Health in 1947," Association of Retired Medical Staff newsletter, GHC, date unknown.

[14]W. MacColl, 1981 oral history interview.

[15]Hart, op. cit.; J. Kloeck, 1993 interview by N. Rockafeller; GHC Medical Staff minutes, January 16, 1947.

[16]B. Pearce, 1991 interview by N. Rockafeller; Board minutes, December 13, 1946. *Group Health News*, January 6, 1947, reported 383 members as of January 1.

[17]Clare Johnson letter of February 10, 1987; W. Jordan, 1981 oral history interview; *Group Health News* and *Cooperative Health*, 1947 editions.

[18]*Cooperative Health*, April 1947. Mitchell's death is noted in the minutes of the May 12 membership meeting and in a report on the annual meeting of the Cooperative Health Federation of America in September 1946.

[19]W. Philipp, 1981 oral history interview.

[20]I. Johnson, E. Lux, and R. Scott, 1981 oral history interviews.

[21]Membership meeting minutes for dates cited. The March 21, 1947, edi-

tion of *Group Health News* reported a membership of 521.

[22]Annual meeting minutes and *Group Health News*, October 20, 1947.

[23]Annual meeting minutes. The precise date of the district sales plan's implementation and its authors are unclear from the record, but it was in place by October 18, 1947. B. Fish credits J. Fortnum with the idea on page III-3 of his unpublished history of GHC.

[24]Beeler's shortcomings and reassignment are discussed by A. Shoudy in his 1981 oral history interview. Staff and Board changes are noted in Board minutes.

[25]*Group Health News*, December 17, 1947, noted bond income and 1,016 family members. Renton election reported in *The Seattle Times*. N. Rockafeller notes 376 GHC members in "Renton and outskirts" on page II-31 of her unpublished history of GHC.

[26]Satellite clinic plans are described in the April 1948 "Activity Report to Membership." Draft papers to purchase the Kitsap Cooperative Hospital Association are filed in the GHC archives. Failure of the Bremerton public hospital district is mentioned in the minutes of the November 17, 1948, annual meeting.

[27]Renton-area membership is given in the April 1946 "Activity Report."

[28]Board minutes; J. Cluck, 1981 oral history interview. KCMS influence on the VMF is documented in GHC vs. KCMS, Brief of Appellants, 1950, p. 236.

[29]The Renton opening and staffing are described in the June 22, 1948, *Group Health News*. Dr. Bunker's assignment is mentioned in the minutes of the November 17, 1948, Annual Meeting.

[30]Board minutes, March 22 and August 23, 1948; Holden, op. cit. p. 49.

[31]Holden, op. cit. p. 50; Tompkins, op. cit, p. 95.

[32]*Group Health News*, May 27, 1948; Fish, op. cit., p. III-4.

[33]Rockafeller, GHC history, p. II-41; Activity Report to Membership, April 1948; Board minutes, July 22, 1948.

[34]*Group Health News*, August 23, 1948; Activity Report to Membership, November 1948.

[35]Activity Reports, April and November 1948.

[36]Ibid.

[37]Activity Report, November 1948; *View*, XXVI-2, February 1984; History of Group Health Credit Union; *Group Health News*, January 1949.

Chapter 5

[1]J. Cluck, 1981 oral history interview; GHC vs. KCMS, Brief of Appellants, 1950, pp. 25 and 241.

[2]Amos Huseland, 1987 "Early Pioneer Questionnaire"; Appellants, p. 234.

[3]Shadid, *Crusading Doctor*, p. 134.

[4]*Grange News*, November 10, 1945.

[5]*Grange News*, February 9 and August 10, 1946; *Bulletin of the KCMS*, March 3, 1947.

[6]MacColl, 1981 oral history interview.

[7]Tompkins, op. cit., p. 95; Dr. McNeel's reports, Activity Reports to Membership, April and November 1948.

[8]Bansmer/Rockafeller, op. cit.; author's conversation with retired insurance agent and State Rep. David Sprague, 1995.

[9]Bansmer, 1992 interview with N. Rockafeller.

[10]Rockafeller, *Scanners to Saddlebags*, p. 85; Bansmer, "Joy of Joining Group Health," p. 7; Austin Ross, *Vision and Vigilance, the First 75 Years of Virginia Mason Medical Center* (Seattle: VMMC, 1995), pp. 15 and 37.

[11]Rockafeller, unpublished GHC history, pp. II-12 and II-13.

[12]E. Conrad, 1981 oral history interview; C. Strother, 1991 interview with N. Rockafeller.

[13]Rockafeller, GHC history, II-43; *Group Practice*, 214.

[14]*Group Health News*, July 26, 1948, and *GHC News & Information*, April 1950; MacColl, op. cit., p. 32.

[15]Shoudy, 1981 oral history interview. Although Shoudy never mentions the AMA manager by name, historian N. Rockafeller deduced that it was Dr. Lull (see her history of GHC, p. 141).

[16]Shadid, op. cit., pp. 305-310; MacColl, op. cit., p. 214.

[17]Ibid.

[18]Rockafeller, GHC history, p. II-44; Bansmer, "Joy of Joining GH," p. 9.

[19]Beeler memorandum to McNeel, June 7, 1949; Bansmer/Rockafeller, 1988; GH *News & Information*, June 1949.

[20]McNeel to Watt, August 10, 1949.

[21]Rockafeller, GHC history, p. III-3.

[22]Appellants, pp. 46, 73, passim.

[23]Rockafeller, GHC history, pp. III-5 and III-6. The formal title of Group Health's suit is "Group Health Cooperative of Puget Sound, a charitable nonprofit corporation, Dr. John McNeel, Dr. William MacColl, Dr. Raymond J. Bunker, Dr. Gustav Bansmer, and Dr. Albert A. Seering and Amos Huseland, plaintiffs, vs. King County Medical Society, a corporation, King County Medical Service Bureau, an unincorporated association, Dr. Charles E. Watts, President of said Society and member of said Bureau; Dr. Ralph H. Loe, President-Elect of said Society and member of said Bureau, Public Hospital District No. 1 of King County, a municipal corporation, and Elmo Wright, Rudolph Seppi and Frank D. Hanley, commissioners thereof, Dr.s D.J. Laviolette, Edward W. Roberts, M.J. Schultz and Lloyd F. Lackie, members of said Bureau, and The Swedish Hospital, a corporation, and King County Medical Service Corporation, a corporation, defendants"; King County trial number 89-90 (1950); Washington State Supreme Court case number 31591.

[24]Ibid.

[25]Ibid., p. III-4.

[26]H. Findley, Memorandum of Opinion, July 14, 1949.

[27]Rockafeller, op. cit., p. III-14.

[28]Ibid., p. III-16.

[29]Shoudy, 1981 oral history interview.

[30]Washington Decisions, 1951, p. 586.

[31]Bansmer, "Joy of Joining GHC," p. 9. Bansmer says that Jack Cluck phoned Group Health with news of the Supreme Court decision, but Board minutes indicate that Cluck was in Europe attending an international conference of cooperatives at the time.

Chapter 6

[1]Holden and Tompkins, op. cit. Early membership data lists "families" rather than individuals served.

[2]Board minutes, July 2, 1951; June 25, 1953; April 20, 1955. Group Health reported a loss of $18,000 on the ILWU contract in 1954.

[3]Rockafeller interview with G. Bansmer, 1991.

[4]Ibid.; staff count cited in minutes of April 23, 1949, annual meeting.

[5]Board minutes, January 17, 1951.

[6]1952 mortality rates cited in Board minutes, January 29, 1953. MacColl, 1954 Annual Report.

[7]Board minutes, July 2, 1948; *News & Information*, April 1950; Annual meeting, 1950.

[8]Board minutes, January 21 to December 28, 1950.

[9]Board minutes, January 21, February 24, and March 24, 1951. Purchase of the drug store was not completed until September 28, 1955, per Board minutes.

[10]Staff and enrollment reported in Board minutes for May 22, 1952.

[11]Board minutes for January 16, 1947; March 23, 1948; and December (undated) 1948.

[12] Board minutes, February 26, 1949.

[13]Board minutes, January 27 and July 2, 1951.

[14]Board and membership meeting minutes for dates cited. New districts were approved at the April 7, 1955, annual meeting.

[15]Pennock account based on general historical sources; minutes for dates cited; B. Jordan, A. Shoudy, and A. Davis 1981 oral history interviews; and author's 1996 interviews with J. Caughlan and L. Mercer.

[16]MacColl, 1981 oral history interview; Quinn quoted by G. Bansmer in 1991 interview with N. Rockafeller.

[17]Membership meeting minutes, November 11, 1950.

[18]Dr. Nieman's plan was presented to the Board on December 28, 1950.

[19]Dr. Nieman to Executive Committee, March 12, 1951.

[20]Dr. McNeel's letter of resignation, March 15, 1951.

[21]Dr. G. Bansmer declared in a 1991 interview with N. Rockafeller that Dr. McNeel took his own life in St. Louis by jumping from a ferry, but the

author has not been able to confirm this.

[22] Jordan: Board minutes, July 27, 1951; membership meeting minutes, November 17, 1951.

Chapter 7

[1] Scott 1981 oral history interview.

[2] Board minutes for January 31 and February 28, 1952; Quinn memo, February 29, 1952.

[3] Board minutes, February 28, 1952; Executive Committee minutes, March 20, 1952.

[4] Board minutes for March 27, April 5, and April 30, 1952; minutes of special staff meeting, March 21, 1952.

[5] 1991 N. Rockafeller interviews with C. Bansmer, A. Davis, J. Kloeck, and B. Sachs.

[6] Minutes and interviews cited above.

[7] 1991 Rockafeller interviews with G. Bansmer and A. Magar.

[8] Board minutes and Magar interview.

[9] Board minutes and additional data in N. Rockafeller ms., Part III. Rockafeller misassigns some 1952 events and documents to 1951 on pp. III-33 and III-34.

[10] D. Northrop to R. Scott, May 25, 1951.

[11] Report as described by N. Rockafeller ms., p. III-33.

[12] Board minutes, July 12, 1952.

[13] Dr. Quinn to P. Goodin, July 15, 1952.

[14] "Nursing and clerical staff" to P. Goodin, July 31, 1952; Report of Special Investigating Committee, February 4, 1953.

[15] Board minutes, July 31, 1952.

[16] Board minutes, September 25, October 30, November 19 and 25, 1952.

[17] Board minutes, November 25, 1952.

[18] Board minutes, December 30, 1952.

[19] W. MacColl, 1981 oral history interview.

[20] 1991 A. Davis interview with Rockafeller.

[21] Ibid.

[22] Ibid.

[23] C. Strother, 1995 memo to History Committee and 1991 Rockafeller interview.

[24] Renton S.I.C. report, February 4, 1953.

[25] C. Bansmer, 1987 oral history interview; : Dr. Lavizzo is not identified in GHC records, and state records of her discrimination complaint have been destroyed. Based on a suggestion from Dr. James Garrison, the author contacted her daughter, Dr. Risa Lavizzo-Mourey, who confirmed that her mother was the applicant in question.

[26]Ibid.; N. Rockafeller ms., pp. III-54, III-55, III-56.

[27]R. Joyner, 1996 interview with the author.

[28]N. Rockafeller, op. cit.; Annual meeting minutes, April 25, 1953.

[29]N. Rockafeller, op. cit.; H. Birnbaum 1991 interview with Rockafeller; *The Seattle Times*, February 9, 1984; Dr. James Garrison, 1996 interview with the author.

[30]Board minutes, September 8 and October 29, 1953.

[31]Board minutes, April 9 and June 25, 1953.

[32]Board minutes, July 30 and November 2, 1953; Keigwin Clinic: March 23, 1955.

[33]Board minutes, May 28, 1953, and July 20, 1955.

[34]*News & Information*, October 1953.

[35]Board minutes, November 30 and December 28, 1953.

[36]Annual meeting minutes, April 24, 1954; Board minutes, June 24, 1954.

[37]Board minutes, January 26, 1955.

[38]Annual meeting minutes, April 7, 1955.

[39]W. MacColl, 1981 oral history interview.

[40]C. Strother and H. Birnbaum, 1991 interview with N. Rockafeller; Board minutes, June 2, 1955.

[41]Board minutes, June 29, 1955.

Chapter 8

[1]A. Davis 1991 interview with N. Rockafeller.

[2]"Chronological History of GHC, 1955-65."

[3]James' request was treated as a resignation by the Board on June 2, 1955. His position was eliminated on October 26, 1955.

[4]"An Evaluation to be used for Planning Group Health Facilities and Services," J. Kahl, October 3, 1955.

[5]Board minutes, November 2, 1953, March 23 and April 11, 1955. Annual meeting minutes, April 11, 1956.

[6]Annual meeting minutes, April 24, 1954; Board minutes, October 27, 1954, April 22, July 20, and September 28, 1955; author's 1996 conversation with Peter Steinbrueck.

[7]"Service and Facility Analysis for Group Health Board," J. Kahl, October 26, 1955.

[8]Board minutes, August 24, September 28, and October 31, 1955; annual meeting minutes, November 29, 1955.

[9]Annual meeting minutes, April 11, 1956.

[10]J. Kahl, "What's In Our Future," April 11, 1956; *News & Information*, May 1956.

[11]Lou Anne purchase, for $135,000 on April 20, 1956, reported in *News & Information*, July 1956. Street vacation issues reported in *News & Information*, September 1956 and January 1957.

[12]*News & Information*, November 1956.

[13]Ibid., December 1956; Board minutes, July 25, 1956, and January 23, 1957.

[14]Annual meeting minutes, April 6, 1957.

[15]Special Board Session minutes, April 10, 1957. Board minutes, January 23 and March 27, 1957. C. Strother, 1991 interview with N. Rockafeller.

[16]*News & Information*, January 1956. C. Strother, op. cit.

[17]Board minutes, January 23, May 8, June 13, and September 4, 1957. *News & Information*, July 1957. Hilde Birnbaum, 1991 interview with N. Rockafeller.

[18]Board minutes, February 27 and June 26, 1957.

[19]Ibid., September 4 and November 11, 1957.

[20]Ibid., January 3, 1958.

[21]*News & Information*, February 28, 1958; Board minutes, December 3, 1958.

[22]A. Davis and H. Birnbaum, 1991 interviews with N. Rockafeller.

[23]"Report and Recommendations of Consultant," Dr. E. Daily, July 18, 1958.

[24]Ibid.; Medical staff bylaws, 1956; W. Miles, 1992 interview with N. Rockafeller; N. Rockafeller ms., pp. IV-10, IV-11, IV-12.

[25]Board minutes, August 27, September 24, and October 22, 1958.

[26]*View*, Fall 1958; Annual meeting minutes, April 11, 1959.

[27]Board minutes, March 24, 1959. GH Dental's proposal for "combination" with GHC was first presented to the Board on September 4, 1957, and the subject would be revived in 1964.

[28]Annual meeting minutes, April 11, 1959; *View*, Summer 1959.

[29]Board minutes, July 22, October 7, and December 10, 1959. Burien Clinic architects approved, January 27, 1960.

[30] Board minutes, December 10, 1959; *View*, Winter 1960.

[31]Medicare discussion based on Board minutes for July 22, 1959, and January 6, 1960, and *View*, Summer 1960. Staff misgivings were expressed in a 1962 *View* article on the King-Anderson Medicare bill.

[32]Annual Report, April 1960.

[33]*View*, Winter 1960/61; H. Birnbaum, 1991 interview with N. Rockafeller.

Chapter 9

[1]Board minutes, April 27, June 29, and July 27, 1960.

[2]Board memorandum to membership, "Proposed Dues Increase for 1961," December 30, 1960; Board minutes and attached "Analysis of Costs," January 23, 1961.

[3]Board minutes, June 1 and September 28, 1960. JDC reform was implemented in 1961.

[4]J. Kahl, "Suggested Answers to Problems," February 27, 1961.

[5]Board minutes, March 1, 1961. This count does not total 6,861, presumably because of defective ballots.

[6]Board minutes, August 6, 1961.

[7]Board minutes, October 26, 1960; H. F. Newman, 1993 interview with N.

Rockafeller.

[8]Ibid. Staff count reported by Dr. Kahl at the April 1961 annual meeting.

[9]Board minutes, September 27, 1961; H. F. Newman, 1993 interview with N. Rockafeller.

[10]Board minutes, July 27, 1960, August 9 and November 29, 1961.

[11]Board minutes, June 28, 1961.

[12]Board minutes, July 26 and September 27, 1961.

[13]Board minutes, March 29, September 27, and November 29, 1961.

[14]Board minutes, December 20, 1961.

[15]Board minutes, December 20, 1961; *View*, November/December 1961.

[16]Board minutes, March 7, 1961, and May 23, 1962.

[17]Board minutes, May 23, 1962.

[18]Select Committee on Public Relations report, September 21, 1962.

[19]Joint Conference Commitee minutes, July 16, 1962; Board minutes, July 25, 1962. The staff voted 21 to 17 in favor of the PSCL.

[20]Board minutes, October 3, 1962.

[21]Ad Hoc Committee on District Problems report, October 15, 1962; Board minutes, October 24, 1962.

[22]Board minutes, August 22, 1962. Dr. Arst recommended eliminating prescription coverage on October 3, 1962.

[23]Board minutes, November 20, 1962.

[24]Board minutes, June 25, 1958; March 30, May 12, and June 29, 1960; November 29, 1961; October 3 and November 20, 1962; December 18, 1963.

[25]Board minutes, November 20, 1962, and January 23, 1963. H. F. Newman 1993 interview with N. Rockafeller. GHC ended 1962 with 65,675 enrollees, an increase of 2,103 over 1961, according to J. Tompkins, op. cit.

[26]Board minutes, January 23, 1963.

[27]Annual meeting minutes, April 20, 1963; Board minutes, April 24, 1963, passim.

[28]J. Kahl, "Discussion of Whether Group Health Should Grow Beyond 80,000 or Not," December 5, 1963.

[29]Board minutes, December 18, 1965; Enrollment figures reported in J. Tompkins, op. cit.

[30]Board minutes, February 18, April 21, and April 29, 1964. *View*, Spring 1964.

[31] *View*, VI-1, 1964; H. F. Newman, 1993 interview with N. Rockafeller.

[32]*View*, VI-1 and VI-2, 1964.

[33]Board minutes, October 28 and December 2, 1964.

[34]K.W. Schaie, "Membership Attitudes and Opinion in the Group Health Cooperative of Puget Sound," October 1964.

[35]Board minutes, December 18, 1963; April 29, and December 2, 1964.

[36]Board minutes, January 27, 1965, and December 9, 1970.

[37]Board minutes, March 31, 1965; *View*, VII-2, 1965; C. Strother to author.

[38]J. Kahl chronology.

Chapter 10

[1]See Paul Starr, *The Social Transformation of American Medicine* (New York: Basic Books, 1982), pp. 368-387 passim for an excellent summary of Medicare's economic consequences.

[2]H. F. Newman described Group Health and allied programs' lobbying efforts in a memo dated September 27, 1965.

[3]Board minutes, January 5 and 26, and February 22, 1966. Nonmember Medicare recipients were charged $7/month for Part B coverage. The age limit was eliminated by the Board on September 24, 1980.

[4]Board minutes, January 5 and February 22, 1966.

[5]H. F. Newman, "Revised Plan for Growth of Group Health," May 26, 1965; Board minutes, March 16 and 30, and July 27, 1966. Launch of the Home Health Agency on June 1, 1966, is noted in the minutes for April 26, 1967.

[6]Board minutes, March 30, 1966. Demographers terminate the baby boom in 1964, when annual U.S. births dropped below 4 million.

[7]*View*, VIII-5, 1966.

[8]Board minutes, June 22 and August 31, 1966. Dr. Quinn's column appeared in the November 1966 edition of *The Cooperator.*

[9]*The Cooperator*, August and November, 1966.

[10]*View*, IX-1, 1967. Board minutes, September 28 and November 30, 1966; May 31 and August 30, 1967.

[11]Annual meeting reports, April 22, 1967; H. F. Newman, "Ten-Year Plan for Future Growth," March 20, 1967; Board minutes, April 26, 1967.

[12]Board minutes, January 3 and April 23, 1968; J. Tompkins, op. cit.

[13]Board minutes, June 24 and October 30, 1968; January 29, 1969. *View*, X-4 and 5, 1968.

[14]Board minutes, September 25, October 30, and December 11, 1968; June 25, 1969. *View*, XI-4, 1969.

[15]Board minutes, April 23 and May 22, 1968; June 25, 1969.

[16]Board minutes, April 29, 1970. J. Tompkins, op. cit., pp. 290 and 302.

[17]H. F. Newman, 1993 interview with N. Rockafeller.

[18]Board minutes, January 29 and February 20, 1969.

[19]*View*, XI-3, 1969.

[20]*View*, XI-5 and 6, 1969; XIII-5, 1970. *View* published only three issues in volume XII in early 1970 and then jumped to volume XIII.

[21]Board minutes, January 29 and February 26, 1969. *View*, XIII-5, 1970; XIV-7, 1971.

[22]Board minutes, September 23, 1970; *View*, XIII-6, 1970.

[23]J. Garrison, 1996 interview with the author.

[24]Board minutes, December 9, 1970.

[25]G. Hartquist, 1992 interview with N. Rockafeller.

[26]J. Tompkins, op. cit., pp. 95 and 109.

[27]H. F. Newman, "Ten-Year Plan for Future Growth," January 1971. Board retreat minutes, March 11, 1971.

[28]Board minutes, February 24, 1971.

[29]*View*, XIV-7 and 8, and XIII-3, 1971. (The last issue is misnumbered and should be XIV-9.)

[30]P. Starr, op. cit, pp. 395-398.

[31]Board minutes, September 23, 1970; March 31, 1971. H. F. Newman, 1993 interview with N. Rockafeller.

[32]Special meeting minutes, May 24, 1971.

[33]H. Birnbaum, 1992 interview with N. Rockafeller.

[34]*View*, XIII-3, 1971 (See note 27 re misnumbering); *The Seattle Times*, February 9, 1984.

[35]G. Hartquist, 1993 interview with N. Rockafeller.

[36]Board minutes, June 30, 1971, and January 31, 1972.

[37]G. Hartquist, 1992 interview with N. Rockafeller.

Chapter 11

[1]H. F. Newman, 1993 interview with N. Rockafeller.

[2]Ibid. Board minutes, May 31, 1972.

[3]Board minutes, October 25, 1972. H. Birnbaum, 1992 interview with N. Rockafeller.

[4]*View*, XIV-7 and 8; XIII-4, 1971 (misnumbered). East Wing opened January 25 and the Family Health Center opened March 1, 1971.

[5]Board minutes, April 29, June 29, and December 8, 1971; January 31, 1972; March 3, 1973.

[6]Board minutes, December 13, 1972, and March 27, 1973.

[7]W. Miles, 1992 interview with N. Rockafeller.

[8]Board minutes, April 28, July 1, and December 17, 1970; March 11, April 29, September 29, and October 27, 1971; May 31 and July 26, 1972. David C. Carson, "Satellite HMO: Development of a Prepaid Group Medical Practice in a Small City (Seattle: GHC, 1972). *Daily Olympian*, January 23, 1972. Bolotin's double duty as trustee and paid GHC architect had long made Hilde Birnbaum nervous as a source of potential conflict of interest. The rules of FHA, which helped finance the Olympia Medical Center, required that trustees of recipient organizations not serve as consultants or employees.

[9]H. Kirz, 1996 interview with the author.

[10]Board minutes, June 30, 1971; May 3 and September 27, 1972. Dr. Hanschin first proposed a foundation in May 1970. GHC earned 501(c)3 status in June 1971. The Board approved the breast cancer study on September 27, 1972.

[11]Board minutes, January 24, 1973.

[12]*View*, XV-6, 1972.

[13]Board minutes, December 8, 1971. L. Mercer, "The Role of the Member in

GHC," paper presented at the HMOS Feedback Session, December 1972.

[14]H. Birnbaum, 1992 interview with N. Rockafeller. Board minutes, March 28, 1973. *View* and other sources report the date of this first meeting as March 28, but Board minutes date it one week earlier.

[15]The special interest group policy was adopted on June 28, 1976.

[16]H. Birnbaum, 1992 interview with N. Rockafeller.

[17]*View*, XVI-6, 1973.

[18]*View*, XVII-3, 1974.

[19]P. Starr, op. cit., pp. 402-405. Board minutes, May 29 and July 31, 1974.

[20]P. Starr, op. cit. p. 405.

[21]Ibid. Board minutes, July 31, 1974. View, XVII-2, 1975 (misnumbered; XVIII-3 in sequence). (The repeat of volume XVII was never corrected in subsequent numbering.)

[22]Board minutes, July 31, 1975. *View*, XVII-1 and XVII-2, 1974, and XVII-2, 1975 (misnumbered).

[23]P. Nudelman, 1996 interview with the author.

[24]Board minutes, April 18 and October 2, 1974. H. F. Newman,1993 interview with N. Rockafeller. View, XX-2, 1978.

[25]*View*, XVII-6, 1974.

[26]Board minutes, January 8 and 29, 1975. An original plan for a 20.5 percent dues increase was reduced to 15 percent, as reported in *View*, XVIII-1, 1975.

[27]*View*, XVII-2, 1975 (misnumbered).

[28]Board minutes, May 7, 1975.

[29]Board minutes, September 10, 1975. "Medicare Program Study Session" minutes, August 1, 1979. H. F. Newman, 1993 interview with N. Rockafeller.

[30]P. Nudleman and C. Strother, 1996 comments to author.

[31]Board minutes, July 30 and December 3, 1975. *View*, XVII-3, 1975 (misnumbered). The significance of Dr. Newman's leave was indicated by H. F. Hartquist and A. Davis in interviews with N. Rockafeller, and D. Brennan and Grant McLaughlin in 1996 interviews with the author.

[32]Ibid.

[33]Board minutes, January 7 and 28, March 31, 1976. *View*, XVII-5, 1975.

[34]R. Thompson, 1992 interview with N. Rockafeller.

[35]G. Hartquist, 1992 interview with N. Rockafeller.

[36]Final Patient's Bill of Rights as adopted December 1, 1976, and Consumer Bill of Rights as printed in *View*, XIX-6, June 1977.

[37]Board minutes, June 28, 1976; *View*, XVIII-3 and 4, 1976; Governance Task Force Final Report, May 10 and June 1, 1978.

[38]Board minutes, April 28, 1976. *View*, XVIII-1, 1976.

[39]*View* XVIII-6, 1976. A. Davis 1992 interview with N. Rockafeller.

[40]*View*, XVIII-6, 1976.

[41]G. Hartquist and A. Davis, 1991 interviews with N. Rockafeller; D.

Brennan, 1996 interview with the author.

[42]Board minutes, July 28, 1976.

[43]*View*, XVIII-6, 1976.

Chapter 12

[1]The Board named Brennan acting executive vice president September 22, 1976. The appointment was made permanent by April 22, 1977.

[2]Special meeting for presentation of "Problems of Appointment Availability for Ambulatory Care" consultant report, September 1, 1976.

[3]Board minutes, January 5, 1977. The elected chief of staff was replaced in 1982 by a medical director appointed by the medical staff executive council.

[4]Board minutes, December 1, 1976. G. McLaughlin, 1996 interview with the author.

[5]Board minutes, April 20 and 27, 1977. A. Davis, 1992 interview with N. Rockafeller. A. Davis and G. McLaughlin, 1996 interviews with the author.

[6]Board minutes, April 28 and October 27, 1976. *View*, XIX-6 and 7, 1977. 1978 Medical Staff Annual Report.

[7]Board minutes, February 23 (Boston study) and June 15, 1977.

[8]1977 Medical Staff Annual Report. Board minutes, September 28, 1977. Midwifery Task Force Final Report, June 30, 1978.

[9]1977 Medical Staff Annual Report.

[10] H. Kirz, 1996 interview with the author; G. Hartquist, 1992 interview with N. Rockafeller.

[11]*View*, XIX-10, 1977, and XX-4, 1978.

[12]Board minutes, January 4, 1978.

[13]*View*, XX-7, 1978; D. Brennan, 1996 interview with the author.

[14]Board minutes, May 31, 1978.

[15]Board minutes, September 29, 1979; April 29, 1970; August 28 and November 14, 1973.

[16]Board minutes, July 16, 1978.

[17]Board minutes, September 27, 1978.

[18]Board minutes, September 27, October 4 and 25, 1978. W. Miles, 1992 interview with N. Rockafeller. G. McLaughlin, 1996 interview with the author.

[19]Governance Task Force reports, May 25 and June 1, 1978. Board minutes, January 25 and February 15, 1978.

[20]*View*, XXI-1, 1979.

[21]Study session minutes, December 19, 1978.

[22]W. Miles, 1992 interview with N. Rockafeller; KCMS records.

[23]W. Miles, 1992 interview with N. Rockafeller.

[24]Board minutes, February 28, 1979.

[25]Task Force on Aging Report, December 27, 1978; Board minutes, January 31, 1979.

[26]Board Minutes, April 25 and September 26, 1979. *View*, XX-10, 1978.

²⁷*View*, XXI-6, 1979; Board minutes, May 2, 1979.

²⁸Interim Report to the Membership: Growth and the Management of Growth, attached to Board minutes, February 28, 1979; *View*, XXI-4, 1979.

²⁹Board minutes, January 2 and March 24, 1980; D. Brennan, "Medicare Risk-Sharing Experience," February 27, 1980

³⁰Board minutes, February 27, March 24, April 30, 1980. *View*, XXIII-3, 1981.

³¹Board minutes, February 18, 1981; *View*, XXII-5, 1980, and XXIII-3 1981.

³²Board minutes, April 30 and May 18, 1980; D. Brennan to R. Bremer, May 28, 1980; D. Brennan, 1996 interview with the author.

³³Board minutes, June 25, 1980.

³⁴Board minutes, June 25 and November 19, 1980; *View*, XIII-3, 1981.

³⁵Consumer Criteria for the Assurance of the Quality of Health Care, Recommendations of the Health Care Committee, February 1980; *View*, XXIII-1, 1981.

³⁶Board minutes, November 19, 1980. H. Kirz, 1996 interview with the author.

³⁷Board minutes, January 7 and April 29, 1981. *View*, XXIII-3, 1981.

Chapter 13

¹G. Warden, 1993 interview with N. Rockafeller. In the same interview, Warden relates how he was awakened one night shortly after arriving in Seattle by a trustee offering to sell him firewood. Contemporaries regard this anecdote as greatly embellished.

²Annual meeting minutes; *View*, XXIII-3, 1981.

³Board minutes, February 18 and June 24, 1981, and September 29, 1982; *View*, XXIV-1, 1982.

⁴Board minutes, June 24, 1981; *View*, XIII-5, 1981.

⁵G. Warden, 1992 interview with N. Rockafeller; Board minutes, July 29, 1981.

⁶Health Care Committee "Current Situation Profile," November 3, 1981.

⁷"Report from the President," *View*, XXIV-3, 1982.

⁸"Report from the C.E.O.," *View*, XXIV-3, 1982.

⁹"Medical Staff Report," *View*, XXIV-3, 1982. Board minutes, June 24, July 29, and October 28, 1981; and May 26, 1982. H. Kirz, 1996 interview with the author.

¹⁰Board minutes, January 12, 1982; *View*, XXIV-2, 1982; G. Warden, 1992 interview with N. Rockafeller.

¹¹A. Davis, 1992 interview with N. Rockafeller.

¹²Board minutes, April 28, 1982.

¹³Board minutes, January 27, 1982; 1979 and 1982 Annual Reports; *View*, XXIV-4, 1982.

¹⁴Board minutes, June 30, 1982; *View*, XXVI-1, 1983; G. Warden, 1992 interview with N. Rockafeller.

[15]*View*, XXV-2, 1983.

[16]Board minutes, January 26, 1983; G. Warden and R. Thompson, 1992 interviews with N. Rockafeller; H. Kirz, 1996 interview with the author.

[17]Ibid.; *View*, XXV-3 and 4, 1983.

[18]Board minutes, April 27, 1983; G. Warden, 1992 interview with N. Rockafeller.

[19]Board minutes, February 23, March 30, and July 29, 1983; G. Warden, 1992 interview with N. Rockafeller.

[20]Board minutes, June 29, 1983.

[21]Ibid.; *View*, XXV-5, 1983.

[22]Board minutes, June 29, 1983; *View*, XXV-7, 1983.

[23]C. Strother, 1996 History Committee comments.

[24]Board minutes, December 2, 1981; *View*, XXV-3, 1983; *The Weekly*, June 1, 1983; *Seattle P-I*, August 3, 1983.

[25]*View*, XXV-7, 1983; Board minutes, May 28, 1986.

[26]Board minutes, July 27 and September 28, 1983.

[27]*View*, XXV-9, 1983, and XXVII-5, 1985; Board minutes, January 28, 1987. The first Chambliss Memorial Health Team was dispatched to Ethiopia in 1986.

[28]Board minutes, December 7, 1983; *Seattle P-I*, November 11, 1983; *View*, XXVI-1 and 5, 1984.

Chapter 14

[1]Board minutes, January 25, April 25, and July 25, 1984; January 30, 1985. H. Kirz, 1996 interview with the author.

[2]Board minutes, February 22, March 28, and November 7,1984; 1984 Annual Report and Medical Director's Report.

[3]Board minutes, March 28, 1984.

[4]"Report from the President," *View*, XXVI-4, 1984.

[5]Annual meeting minutes, April 28, 1984; Board minutes, February 22 and May 23, 1984.

[6]D. Barash, "The Loss of an I," *The Seattle Times*, May 20, 1984. This "letter to a friend" was originally published in *The Village Voice*, April 17, 1984.

[7]Report from the Medical Director, December 1984.

[8]W. Manning et al., "A Controlled Trial…" (pp. 1505-1510) and A. Enthoven, "The Rand Experiment and Economical Health Care" (pp. 1528-1530), *New England Journal of Medicine*, June 7, 1984. Later Rand findings were published in *Lancet*, May 3, 1986; *Health Services Research*, August 1986; and *Annals of Internal Medicine*, January 1987.

[9]*View*, XXVI-10, 1984.

[10]Ibid.

[11]Board minutes, September 26 and November 7, 1984; *View*, XXVI-9 and XXVI-10, 1984.

[12]Board minutes, January 3, 1985.

[13]*View*, XXVII-4, 1985.

[14]Annual meeting minutes, April 27, 1985.

[15]N. Gallo, "Group Health's Bold Move...," *The Weekly*, July 17, 1985.

[16]Board minutes, July 24, 1985; View, XXVII-9, 1985

[17]*View*, XXVII-9, 1985.

[18]Board minutes, July 24, 1985.

[19]Board minutes, January 30 and July 24, 1985.

[20]Board minutes, November 6 and December 4, 1985.

[21]Board minutes, January 29, 1986.

[22]*The Seattle Times*, November 18, 1985; *View*, XXVIII-1, 1986; G. Warden, 1992 interview with N. Rockafeller.

[23]Board minutes, January 8 and February 26, 1986.

[24]Board minutes, January 8, 1986; *View*, XXVIII-1, 1986.

[25]Board minutes, January 29, 1986.

[26]*View*, XXVIII-6, 1986.

[27]*View*, XXVIII-3, 1986; 1986 Annual Report.

[28]Board minutes, July 23, 1986; *View*, XXVIII-7, 1986.

[29]Board minutes, June 25 and October 1, 1986; G. McLaughlin, 1996 interview with the author.

[30]Board minutes, October 1 and December 3, 1986.

[31]1986 Annual Report; *View*, XXIX-1, 1987.

[32]History Committee review comments, 1996.

[33]1986 Medical Director's Report.

[34]Board minutes, April 29, 1987; *View*, XIXX-3; H. Kirz, 1996 interview with the author.

[35]Annual meeting minutes, April 25, 1987; Board minutes, April 29, 1987.

[36]Board minutes, April 29, 1987; *View*, XXIX-3 and XXIX-4, 1987.

[37]Laws of Washington, 1987, Volume 2; *View*, XXVII-3, 1985; Board minutes, March 27, 1985, and April 29, 1987. Gov. Booth Gardner signed the Health Care Access Act on June 2, 1987, and it was implemented in 1989.

[38]Board minutes, May 27 and June 22, 1987; G. Warden, 1992 interview with N. Rockafeller.

[39]Board minutes, September 30, 1987.

[40]Board minutes, October 7, 1987.

[41]H. Kirz, Medical Director's Report, January 6, 1988.

[42]*The Seattle Times*, October 28, 1987; *View*, XXIX-6, 1987, and XXX-1, 1988.

Chapter 15

[1]A. Davis interview with Don Glickstein, *Group Health News*, December 16, 1994, and 1992 interview with N. Rockafeller.

[2]Board minutes, January 13 and March 17, 1988; 1987 Annual Report.

[3]*View*, XXXV-5, 1988.

[4]Board minutes, July 13, 1988; *View*, XXX-5 and 7, 1988; History Commit-

tee comments.

[5]1987 and 1988 Annual Reports.

[6]*View,* XXXI-3, 1989

[7]*View,* XXXI-4 and 5, 1989.

[8]History Committee comments; A. Davis, 1992 interview with N. Rockafeller; P. Nudelman, 1996 interview with the author.

[9]Kristine Moe, "The Nursing Shortage," *View,* XXXI-2, 1989.

[10]"Summary of Issues: The Group Health Nurses Strike of 1989," GHC Public Relations, October 1989.

[11]Ibid.; *View,* XXXI-5, 1989.

[12]Board minutes, July 26, 1989; *View,* XXXI-6, 1989.

[13]Board minutes, November 29, 1989.

[14]*View,* XXXI-5, 1989.

[15]Ibid.

[16]1989 Annual Report

[17]Board minutes, January 3, 1990; *View,* XXXII-2, 3, and 4, 1990.

[18]Board minutes, February 7, 1990; *View,* XXXII-1, 1990.

[19]Board minutes, March 28 and April 25, 1990; *View,* XXXII-5, 1990.

[20]*View,* XXX1-5, 1989, and XXXII-5, 1990.

[21]*View,* XXXII-5, 1990.

[22]*View,* XXXII-7, 1990.

Chapter 16

[1]P. Nudelman, 1996 interview with the author; Board minutes, July 9, 1991.

[2]Ibid.; 1992-1996 Strategic Plan, adopted June 24, 1992; "Primary Care Vision for the 1990s," December 1991.

[3]Board minutes, April 27 and July 24, 1991.

[4]Board minutes, November 28, 1990, and July 22, 1992; *View,* XXXIII-2, 5, and 6, 1991, and XXXIV-2, 1992.

[5]1992 Annual Report; *View,* XXXIII-5 and 6, 1991.

[6]Board minutes, February 13, June 26, and July 24, 1991; *View,* XXXIII-6, 1991.

[7]*View,* XXXIII-6 and 7, 1991; XXXIV-6, 1992.

[8]Board minutes, October 3, 1991; View, XXXIV-1 and 2, 1992. The Board voted to close the Medicare high-option plan on September 22, 1993.

[9]Board minutes, July 22, 1992.

[10]*View,* XXXIV-2, 3, 5 and 6.

[11]Board minutes, December 2, 1992; *View,* XXXIV-7, 1992; *The Seattle Times,* November 23 and December 3, 1992.

[12]Board minutes, December 2, 1992; *The Seattle Times,* November 20, 1992.

[13]Board minutes, October 28, 1992, and January 13, 1993; G. McLaughlin, 1996 interview with the author.

[14]*View,* XXXV-5, 1993.

[15]Board minutes, June 23, 1993.

[16]Board minutes, July 28, 1993.

[17]Board minutes, July 28, 1993; *View*, XXXV-7, 1993.

[18]Board minutes, September 22, 1993; *View*, XXXV-6 and 7, 1993.

[19]*The Seattle Times*, November 10, 1993; *View,* XXXVI-1, 1994.

[20]C. Scott, 1996 interview with the author.

[21]"1993 Update, 1992-1996 Strategic Plan," as adopted, June 23, 1993; "Group Health Cooperative and Partnerships," July 30, 1993; *View*, XXXVI-1, 1994.

[22]C. Scott, op. cit.; P. Nudelman, op. cit.

[23]C. Scott, op. cit.; *The Seattle Times*, November 10, 1993.

[24]P. Nudelman, op. cit.

[25]*Group Health News*, May 17, 1996.

[26]*View*, XXXVI-6, 1994.

[27]Ibid.

[28]*The Seattle Times*, July 7, 1994.

[29]CEO Report to the Board, February 1995.

[30]*Group Health News*, May 17, 1996; *View*, XXXVI-7, 1994.

[31]1994 Annual Report.

[32]*CEO Letter*, May 31, 1995

[33]*Group Health News*, September 22, 1995; R. Thompson, 1992 interview with N. Rockafeller.

[34]*The Seattle Times*, March 9, 1995.

[35]P. Nudleman address to Leadership Conference, May 15, 1995.

[36]*Seattle P-I*, August 31, 1995, et seq.

[37]*The Weekly*, January 10, 1996; *NW Health*, XXXVII-5, 1995. GHC and VM's first joint clinic in West Seattle was union, but their next operation, in Kent, was not. *View* was renamed *NW Health* in January 1995 but retained the original numbering system.

[38]Board minutes, April 12, 1995; CEO Report to the Board, February 1996.

[39]*NW Health*, XXXVII-6, 1995; *Group Health News*, September 8, 1995.

[40]*The Seattle Times*, October 12, 1995.

[41]History Committee comments.

[42]Author's notes of the annual meeting debate, October 14, 1995; *NW Health*, XXXVIII-1 and 2, 1996.

Index

Shamansky, Sherry, RN, 209-210, 219
Shaudies, Sid, 15, 41, 53,
Shaver, Robert, 165-166
Shaw, Rev. Robert, 37, 38, 40-41
Shorter, Rev. Fred, 10, 38
Shoudy, Addison, 10-11, 12-17, 18-20,
    30, 31-33, 38, 41, 42, 49, 53-54, 60-
    61, 69, 72
Siegal, Arthur "Art," 90, 113, 117,
    123, 144, 204
Sinclair, Upton, 10
Sisters of Providence, 167, 205
Silver Glen, cooperative senior
    housing, 205
Skaret, Art, 206
Skratek, Sylvia, 186
Snyder, Gary, MD, 194
Socialist Party, members, and
    influence, 4, 6, 8, 9, 39
Social Security Administration, 21,
    24, 132, 145-146, 166-167
Sosne, Diane, 181, 231
Sound Health Association, 136, 159-
    160, 165
Southwest Oncology Group Project,
    156
Spady, Richard "Dick," 164
Spalding, Wade, 115
Spence, William S., MD, 163
Spiller, John, 90
Sprague, State Rep. David, 123
Spratlen, Lois Price, 186
Standards Review Organizations
    (SROs), 142
Starr, Paul, 143
State Clinic, Seattle, 24-25
Steinbrueck, Victor, 94-95
Stensager, Mark, 205
Stewart, Frank, 50, 60
Stewart, Louis, 140, 142, 150
Stockinger, Harry, 15, 16
Stoneman, Ruth, RN, 73
Strother, Charles "Chuck," PhD, 83,
    85, 90, 91, 99-100, 107, 111, 117,
    118, 119, 131, 164, 180
Stuart, Mike, MD, 177
Student Cooperative Association,

University of Washington, 11, 15
Suffia, David, 189
Sumption, Kathleen, RN, 95
Supreme Court, United States, 62
Supreme Court, Washington State,
    65
Surgical Adjuvant Breast Cancer
    Project, 146
Sweeney, John, 192
Swedish Hospital, 58, 65

T

Tacoma (also see Sound Health
    Association, and GHC, facilities,
    Tacoma Specialty Center), 68
Tacoma Dome (1985 GHC annual
    meeting), 191-193
Talmadge, State Sen. Phil, 218
Target Seattle, 182
Taylor, Lily, 12
Temple, Paul, 143, 183
Thompson, Robert "Tommy," MD,
    147-148, 177-178, 230
Thurston County Medical Bureau,
    138
Tinker, Richard, MD, 138
Tricare, 219
Tri-Cities, 194, 200, 201
Trinity Hospital, Little Rock, Ark., 13
Truax, Harmon, MD, 43, 46, 82, 124
Truess, Jim, 219
Truman, Pres. Harry, 59, 60, 61
Truscott, Al, MD, 163, 201, 214, 222,
    225
Turner, Edwin, MD, 58-59
Turnipseed, Richard, 127
"Twenty Points" (AMA ethical
    standards for prepaid plans), 61,
    62, 64

U

Unemployed Citizens League, 10
University of Washington School of
    Medicine, 58-59, 91, 100, 102, 103,
    106, 127, 131, 168-169, 194-195,